Chow
MAINE

# Chow MAINE

## THE BEST Restaurants, Cafés, Lobster Shacks & Markets on the Coast

Nancy English

The Countryman Press
Woodstock, Vermont

We welcome your comments and suggestions. Please contact Editor, The Countryman Press, P.O. Box 748, Woodstock, Vermont 05091, or e-mail countrymanpress@wwnorton.com.

Library of Congress Cataloging-in-Publication Data has been applied for.

ISBN 0-88150-637-0

Book design and composition by Melanie Jolicoeur
Cover photograph of lobster shack © Michele Stapleton;  lobster courtesy of Comstock
Clip art from Nova Development Corporation
Interior photographs by the author unless otherwise indicated

Published by The Countryman Press, P.O. Box 748, Woodstock, VT 05091

Distributed by W. W. Norton & Company, Inc., 500 Fifth Avenue, New York, NY 10110

Printed in the United States of America

10 9 8 7 6 5 4 3 2 1

To EJDWE,
who knows her crème brûlée
backward and forward

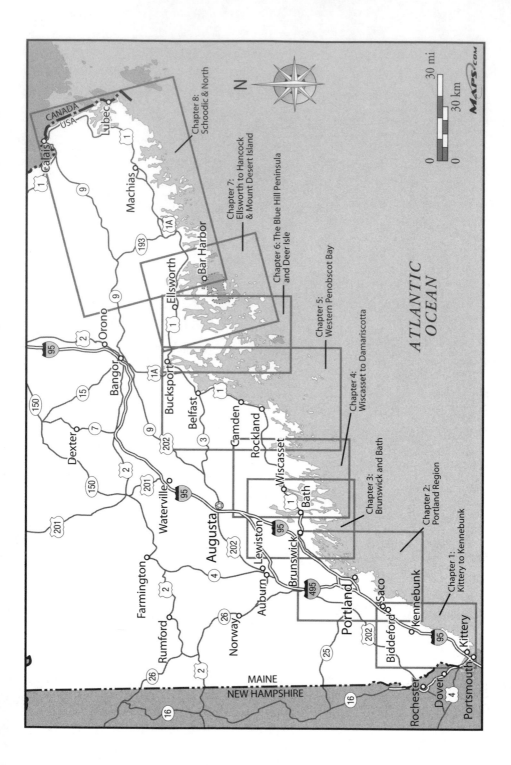

# Contents

# Acknowledgments

**F**OOD NEEDS THE WORK OF MANY HANDS to get to the plates in front of us, and I hope that some of the typing of my own hands gets you in front of some wonderful plates of food. But I first needed the people who had the kindness to tell me about where to find the best food on the Maine coast.

The locals always know what place is cooking fresh, delicious food, and they always know the places to avoid. Ed and Nancy Ludwig of Thomaston, Roy Kasindorf and Helene Harton of Bar Harbor, Jonathan Chase of Blue Hill, Jane Hurd of Boothbay Harbor, Ellen Barnes of Camden, Bob Bartlett of Goulds-boro, Michael and Sarah Coughlin of Portland, and Nancy Swenson at Beach Farm Inn in Wells all guided me to great places along the coast, and they have my gratitude. Many others gave tips along the way, like Miles, who drove the golf cart at Spruce Point Inn in the summer of 2004 and loves the doughnuts at Boothbay Harbor's Baker's Way. Thanks also to Daphne Sprague, who knows where to go with her wheelchair.

Owners of farm stands and bakeries and wine shops who had their own opinions, and gave them generously, earned my appreciation over and over again. I know how busy everyone is, and I remain grateful to every person who took time to speak to me.

Friends, of course, put up with a lot, trying places out and sometimes paying for dinner. Thanks to Lori Eschholz, Nicholas Vasilatos, Bill Curtsinger (who reported back on his own research), John and Simone Reynolds, Elizabeth Edwardsen, Robert Solomon, and Nancy Barba and Cynthia Wheelock for heading out to dinner, sometimes many times. I know it was hard work, but someone has to do it. Thanks for all the nights out.

The person who spent the most nights out was my daughter, who was 11 years old while this book was being written. Thanks to Emma, whose companionship on the road, aside from the rare moments when we were driving each other crazy, gave this project its spirit of adventure.

Thanks to Kermit Hummel, editorial director of The Countryman Press, who took the chance on a new guidebook, and a new author, and made it work for all of us. Jennifer Thompson, assistant production manager at Countryman, dealt with the complications of unreadable files with calm and courtesy. Thanks to you both for the development of this manuscript, and its transformation into a published book.

The project editor, Kristin Sperber, will forever have my gratitude, for keeping my mistakes from the eyes of others, and giving my prose a high polish. Thanks also to David Corey, from The Countryman Press, who was inspired by his love of lobster to write the Lobster Primer on page 166.

This book's range would not have been possible without the assistance of Chris Tree, the travel writer and author of *Maine: An Explorer's Guide,* among many other books. Chris's experience and long familiarity with the state gave me a fighting chance of finding the coast's great places. Many thanks go to Chris for all her help, and for sharing her knowledge.

# Introduction

**T**HIS BOOK IS FILLED with places to eat, from roadside take-out stands to elegant restaurants that won't let you make a shadow in the doorway without a jacket. Some have long descriptions, others just a line or two. But each place in here I can recommend as a place worth eating at, where you can find something fresh and enjoy the fruit of someone's skill in the kitchen.

The last line of the information block for each restaurant will provide a quick read of what the place does; the price of the entrées should convey the cost of dinner. The hospitality line in each restaurant description indicates that I went to the restaurant myself. The staff's ability to make me feel welcome and comfortable ranks high as a qualification for a place I want to dine at.

I've included some places that I criticize but that had good food to offer. Others aren't in here at all because I can't recommend them, or because it just didn't seem necessary. I can't tell you the number of places I visited that were overwhelmed with tourists, where the food was ordinary or substandard, and where the staff was too busy to answer questions. Those places will do just fine without me anyway.

I included many restaurants and lobster shacks on the recommendation of people I trust. Please let me know if your experience mirrors mine. Write to the publisher, The Countryman Press (P.O. Box 748, Woodstock, VT 05091, or email countrymanpress@wwnorton.com), to let me know if you think a place I have included isn't good. I want to hear about it. If I missed a good place, I'd like to know that too. If there is a restaurant that you believe should be in here, please let me know why, and I will follow up with a visit.

I plan to keep visiting the places I have included, as well as take note of new or improved places, with the hope of writing an updated edition in a few years. Restaurants pop up on the horizon, flourish, and flare out as fast as shooting stars. Pagliarulo's, an upscale Italian place in Bar Harbor, came and went in one summer, and I'm sorry not to be able to include it here.

That reminds me—call the places you're heading to first, and make sure they are open. They might have closed for the season, or for good. Also, business hours are always changing, and the ones I listed may have altered.

I did not impose a rating system on the restaurants in this book, but a few meals remain in my memory as some of the most pleasant I have ever had. It is a real privilege to eat in a restaurant that has a great chef, as I have a few times.

*Fall sunshine on York Beach*

But the best meals I ate were wonderful for a variety of reasons. The restaurants don't fit in a narrow category, so they can't be easily compared. You'll encounter my finds in the descriptions of Pentagöet Inn, Pilgrim's Inn, Sue's Seafood, and George's, among many others—places that range from linoleum to linen. I *can* rate crabcakes, however. The best crabcakes I've ever eaten are served at the elegant Back Bay Grill in Portland.

I leave it to someone else to compare all the lobster rolls you can buy on the coast of Maine. But let me share a few details.

A certain fast-food chain restaurant sells lobster rolls for $6.99. That will buy you just 2 ounces of lobster meat, and you can be certain the meat is processed, frozen, and gets to Mc . . . ooops, that chain, on the back of trucks.

But in the spring, when lobsters are still barely awake, nobody has enough lobsters to steam, cool, and shuck their own. According to my expert, even in the summer when lobster is plentiful, most places use lobster meat that has already been taken out of the shell by a shellfish company. There just isn't time to do that work when the line is stretched out the door, and the customers are hungry.

But some places do cook fresh lobsters and pick their meat, and you must wait for it. Harraseeket Lunch and Lobster in South Freeport has a wait every day of the week. Their lobster roll, $13.95 in 2004, is full of big pieces of lobster.

Cheaper rolls have less lobster.

Four ounces of lobster is the premium quantity at the places best known for a good roll, and two of them face off across Route 1 in Wiscasset: Sprague's Lobster and Red's Eats. Red's offers rolls with melted butter or with traditional mayonnaise. Sprague's has the mayonnaise. Their rolls are equally full of lobster. Sprague's is cheaper.

Then there is the lobster meat itself. The stuff packed and frozen in the United States is required by law to be rinsed, which strips it of its salty juices. The kitchen has to add salt to the thawed meat when it goes into a roll. But Canadian frozen lobster retains the creatures' cooking juices and tastes better. Try asking where the lobster meat comes from.

Readers are welcome to inform me which Maine lobster roll they think is best.

Restaurants have changed for the better over the last 20 years.

Now, I want them to take a few steps backward.

The cheapest restaurants would do us all such a big favor if they could go back to making every part of their meals from fresh ingredients, and stop buying frozen boxes off the back of the tractor trailer. A few are out in front, like Tall Barney's in Jonesport, with its sublime pies and good frying oil. There's one off the coast, the Brookside Restaurant in Smyrna Mills, not in here but too good not to mention, with its turnips and new potatoes and peas side dishes. I thank the staffs at these restaurants for going to the trouble of working with good vegetables, fruits, and fresh meat.

Too many others make food that is slovenly, with processed ingredients masquerading as real food. We should all be in revolt.

And taking ourselves off to the places written about in this book that make things right.

Enjoy.

**CHAPTER 1**

# Kittery to Kennebunk

S NUG WITH THE SOUTHERN BORDER OF MAINE and traditional vacation destinations of long standing, the towns on this end of the coast support dozens of good restaurants. Many are a summer's night destination
for people in Boston with a little wanderlust and only a little time.

The towns, starting from the southern border and traveling north, are Kittery, York (Cape Neddick), Ogunquit (Perkins Cove), Wells, Kennebunk, and
Kennebunkport, which includes Goose Rocks Beach.

Kittery has its own "food alley," a collection of great food shops, on Route 1
near the bridge to New Hampshire. From the first interstate exit in Maine, merge
into the Kittery rotary and head south on Route 1 to find Mayan chocolates, freshly
made ravioli, wine from southern Italy, and fish from the water right off the coast.

York has many places to eat, fun to go to as much for the view—especially
at Cliff House—as for the food.

The view is always in competition with what's on the plates in a restaurant
perched over the sea, like Hurricane in Perkins Cove, on the southern end of
Ogunquit.

Downtown Ogunquit, as quiet in winter as a midwestern town, becomes a
place without parking in July and August, when tourists crowd the sidewalks and
take the free trolleys to the beach. That long, beautiful, sandy beach was a source
of inspiration for painters who started this town's career as a summer colony, as
artists have been known to do elsewhere along the Maine coast.

Wells, right alongside Ogunquit, has been the middlebrow neighbor, but new
restaurants opening there are changing that description.

Kennebunkport, the flaunting sister of plainer, inland Kennebunk, lords over
all with its vast array of places to eat. As an innkeeper nearby said, "There are so
many restaurants that are so overpriced down here." I've included many Kennebunkport places that have good reputations, but the criticism "overpriced" could
be applicable. It depends on your preferences. For some of us, the silverware and
the quality of the linens don't really matter; for others, all the expensive accou-
trements of fine dining are what make an evening out worthwhile.

Yankees are stubborn, suspicious people, and anyone who lives in Maine is influ-
enced by the land's long-enduring skepticism. It must come into our systems from
the earth itself, growing fine vegetables in its brief summer, but austere under the
winter sky for so much of the year.

You may be one of those in sympathy with local history, preferring a paper plate
of freshly shucked, fried clams to gussied up lobster.

But there are places for all tastes, here as everywhere, on this friendly, accommodating, and eagerly commercial coast.

# Kennebunk

## Cherie's
**(207) 985-1200**
**7 High Street**
Hospitality—Enthusiastic service that's fast
Open for breakfast Tuesday through Saturday 7–11, Sunday 8–1, lunch until 6,
and dinner Wednesday through Saturday 5:30 to close
Entrées $15 to $17
Reservations advised, good children's menu, handicapped accessible

☛ *An attractive space serving good meals all day long*

Dinner at Cherie's flirts between categories, achieving a successful mingling of popular, slightly unusual ingredients and serving up, for the most part, delicious food.

Our starter wowed us and many others. A shrimp and crabmeat "margarita" ($8.50), it was served in a martini glass. The layers inside started with a good black bean salad and went on to tart guacamole paired with a lot of fresh crabmeat. Three blackened shrimp with sweet flesh, curled on top of it all. There was no need to put pedestrian chips on the black, triangular plate the appetizer was served on.

A small dish of ricotta gnocchi baked with smoked cheddar ($6.25) seemed a little heavy, but it fed one appetite at the table perfectly.

Cherie's dining room is double-height in the front, and the small back of the room more sheltered, with white wainscoting around the whole that formed bench backs. A bowl of focaccia is served with a cup of olive oil—you may have to say "When" to your server; I didn't realize this until we had an awful lot of oil in front of us. It's good oil, too, and sad to waste. My Bulletin Shiraz ($5.50) made good company for the bread.

The cornmeal-encrusted trout came to the table burning hot, but the crust seemed too dark. I enjoyed the fish, not overcooked, with the crust cracked off. Herbed spaghetti squash that accompanied it was buttery and delicious. My companion's Caesar salad held a dressing that carried just the right impact of garlic and cheese.

Strange to say, we didn't order dessert—and this is a place that bakes pies and all kinds of sweets in the bakery next door (see page 6). On the list the night of our visit were cranberry coconut bread pudding, vanilla rum crème brûlée, and chocolate toffee torte, all $4.95.

We did buy a slice of Key lime pie from the bakery to take home. Eaten the next day it proved to be a perfect version of that favorite dessert.

## Grissini Trattoria

(207) 967-2211
27 Western Avenue, Lower Village
www.restaurantgrissini.com
Open for dinner daily from 5:30–9, Saturday until 9:30
Entrées $19 to $29

☛ *Northern Italian cuisine on a generous scale*

Owned by Laurence Bongiorno, a Kennebunkport entrepreneur who also owns Stripers, and the White Barn Inn, this restaurant opened in 1996, serving simple pizzas and grilled fish and pasta from away. The linguini *con vogole,* with minced clams, capers, and garlic, and garnished with whole clams, brings the sea along with the pasta. *Carpaccio,* thin-sliced raw beef served with arugula, Parmesan, and a truffle vinaigrette, is a classic dish, as is the *caprese,* fresh tomatoes and fresh mozzarella, with oil and balsamic vinegar and a piece of flat bread.

A margherita pizza, with tomato sauce and mozzarella, could keep the rest of the meal simple; an entrée such as *carre di agnello,* grilled double lamb chops and a braised lamb shank served over potatoes and green beans, would make it big enough for any appetite. Wines from Italy, like a Borgogno Barolo, are of course featured, but several from Californian vineyards, including Cakebread and Frog's Leap, can also be ordered.

## Kennebunk Inn

(207) 985-3351
45 Main Street
www.thekennebunkinn.com
Hospitality—Affable and knowing, and still swift to take an order and bring it along
The dining room is open Wednesday through Saturday 5–9. The tavern serves lunch Monday through Friday 11:30–2, dinner daily 4–9.
Entrées $19 to $26
Handicapped accessible, reservations recommended for the dining room

☛ *Yes, really good food that is moderately priced*

With new china and silver, and fresh paint in the whole first floor in fall 2004, the inn Shanna Horner O'Hea, chef-owner, operates with her husband, Brian O'Hea, is delivering on their motto "affordable class." But it's the food that makes it work.

With prices in the tavern ranging from $4 to $15, an evening out with a glass of Le Cigare Volent (a Rhône blend with earthy strength that is usually pricier than $11 a glass) and a pizza isn't too much at all. The grilled, thin-crust pizza represents one item of American regional cuisine served here.

The menu changes with the season. A ginger–butternut squash soup steamed from bowls here in late September, and dessert featured caramel apple cheesecake.

A s'more, created with a graham cracker–almond crust filled with a chocolate pâté made with Grand Marnier, topped with a homemade marshmallow browned in the oven before serving, cost $7. This dense creation delivers a powerful chocolate surge to anyone who enjoys it; the homemade marshmallow on top is unctuous and smooth, far better than the store-bought variety. Available in both the dining room and tavern, all the desserts are made by Horner O'Hea, who, like her husband, has a degree from the Culinary Institute of America.

The seven or eight entrée choices include a Cornish game hen with home-made biscuit, apple brandy, duck sausage, and apple stuffing, with a touch of foie gras butter on top, and homemade cranberry relish with mushroom gravy ($24). A popular seafood entrée is the grilled swordfish with ratatouille and roasted garlic cream sauce ($25). On our visit a new ravioli, made with fresh pasta filled with black mission figs and Blue Mountain blue cheese from France, was on the list. Raviolis vary with the season, with pumpkin ravioli likely in the fall. Standard Baking Company bread, from Portland, is served with the meals, another sign that the quality of your food is taken seriously here.

Fifty-five wines, with eight reds and six whites, by the glass fill the wine list, most in the moderate price range. One wine offered by the glass came from California, a BV Dulcet, and cost $8.

# Windows on the Water
**(207) 967-3313**
**Chase Hill**
www.windowsonthewater.com
Open daily for lunch 11:30–2:30, dinner 5:30–9:00
Entrées $16 to $36
Reservations recommended

☞ *Casual elegance is the motto here, with food that visitors praise.*

My uncle and aunt like to eat here, enjoying the casual elegance and the good food. Flank steak with sautéed peppers, onions, and mushrooms ($23) and roasted haddock with asparagus compound butter ($23) are likely items on the changing menu, as is smoked breast of chicken topped with red pepper sauce over linguini ($20).

Over a hundred wines, stored in a special cellar, are served.

# Bakery, Breakfast, and Pizza

### Cherie's (207-985-1200), 7 High Street.

The bakery is open Monday through Saturday 6–6, Sunday 6–1. The bakery has been operating for 10 years, making blueberry pie, strawberry-rhubarb pie, all kinds of pie—and pastries and cakes and tarts and tortes. We recommend the Key lime pie. The house granola is available for purchase, since customers who ordered it for breakfast demanded some to take home.

Cherie's is open for breakfast Tuesday through Saturday 7–11, Sunday 8–1. The menu listed eggs any style with homefries, toast, and a choice of bacon, sausage, or Canadian bacon for $5.95. "Southern Comfort" consists of black bean fritters on salsa-scrambled eggs topped with guacamole and sour cream ($6.95). Three pancakes ($4.75) or one for a child ($1.50) make this the right spot for a family. Lunch and take-out operate throughout the day, and sandwiches and soups are always fresh.

### Trio's (207-967-5347), 149 Port Road, Lower Village (Route 35).

Open daily 11–9. Pizza and calzones were flying out the slamming screen door shortly after this business opened in summer 2004. Inside, chocolate milk–colored walls and a bar with two wide-screen TVs set to sports channels kept customers happy while they waited. The summer fest pizza has tomato, basil, peppers, onion, eggplant, zucchini, cheese, and tomato sauce on it, $10.75 for a 10-inch pie. Salads and sandwiches to eat in or take out.

**The Kennebunk Farmer's Market** runs from May to the end of October on Saturday from 8 to noon in the municipal parking lot off Route 1, Lower Village.

# Kennebunkport

## Alisson's

**(207) 967-4841**
**11 Dock Square, P.O. Box 344**
www.alissons.com
Hospitality—Good experienced service
Open daily for lunch 11–5, dinner 5–9, closing at 10 on Friday and Saturday
Entrées $14 to $23

☛ *A neighborhood tavern serving the standards you're likely to hanker for*

Right in the middle of town, Alisson's is an old hand at taking care of people and keeps the things most popular with visitors at the top of its good menu. Lobster pie, lobster rolls, lobster bisque, and clam chowder are all here, and you can also order grilled salmon, baked haddock, or seafood fettuccini ($18.95), with the Parmesan cream sauce that makes scallops, shrimp, and lobster even better, for some. But the hamburgers here make a good case for dropping the seafood for a night—the Deedee burger has blue cheese dressing, and sautéed mushrooms and onions for $6.95. Or how about a Guinness and a pizza?

## Bartley's Dockside

**(207) 967-5050**
**By the bridge in Kennebunkport**
www.bartleys-dockside.com
Hospitality—Casual and quick
Open daily for lunch and dinner 11–10
Entrées $14 to $20

☛ *Casual and traditional, with fish delivered fresh daily*

A long-standing refuge from the Kennebunkport sidewalks, this casual restaurant makes some fine dishes, like crabcakes with scallions, topped with a little Dijon cream. The baked haddock ($16.95) is promised fresh, never frozen. Bouillabaisse ($19.95) tops the price list, except for the heavier lobsters. The pie is coveted by all who make its acquaintance, and is sold by the slice. Some customers reserve a slice when they sit down to make sure there's a serving left when its time for dessert. Wild blueberry pie, made by Mrs. Bartley herself, goes for $4.75.

# The Belvedere Club at Tides Inn By-The-Sea
252 King's Highway
Goose Cove Beach
www.tidesinnbythesea.com
Hospitality—Casual, with no attitude but friendliness
Open daily mid-May through mid-October for dinner
Entrées $23 to $28
Reservations suggested

☛ *With integrity in the kitchen, this place has earned a reputation for good meals.*

The Belvedere Club had been offering tavern food before Jeff Savage was hired. In summer 2004, his meals began drawing in the discerning summer people, and the locals were quick to join the trend.

The food at the Tides Inn must please many people, and the menu therefore, as at many inns up and down the coast, stays in a certain groove. Still, within that world of meat and fish, crabcakes and mussels, Savage has been making the best kind of difference. He has jacked up the quality.

With three years' experience in Ogunquit and another three at Portland's Fore Street, Savage knows what it takes to cook great food. "Sam Hayward is a genius when it comes to food," Savage said of his former Fore Street boss, a chef with many honors. "Fore Street taught me to bring down the flavors to a real simple level."

In the case of veal stock, for instance, it takes 10 quarts of water simmering veal bones for two and half days to achieve 2 quarts of golden liquid with the magical ability to transform a meal.

Savage also has a mushroom forager in Scarborough who supplies him with black trumpet mushrooms that make his risotto ($9) superb.

He started to get a following after he pulled the 27 pounds of foie gras left by a former chef out of the freezer and sautéed it for specials. But the lobster, sautéed in butter and briefly simmered in milk for the lobster stew ($11 for a bowl) works just as well. You don't need a lot of seasoning, he said, or thickening, or anything that would mask the flavor of something as good on its own as lobster.

Baked camembert with an apricot garnish ($8) is one of the appetizers. There's a roast chicken breast with mild chipotle-ginger cream ($22), along with nightly specials, such as lamb shanks or veal osso buco, and several other entrées. Almost all of the 26 wines are offered by the glass for around $7.

This chef may vanish before the restaurant reopens in 2005, but perhaps the inn has started down a path it won't be able to turn away from. With a menu

*Cape Arundel Inn*

for the kids, and lots of space for them to enjoy themselves, even a young family could enjoy a great dinner here.

## Cape Arundel Inn
**(207) 967-2125**
**208 Ocean Avenue, P.O. Box 530A**
www.capearundelinn.com
Hospitality—Wonderful service, with an emphasis on cordiality
Open March through New Year's Eve at 5:30 for dinner, daily in the summer, closed Monday off-season
Entrées $24 to $34
Reservations recommended

☛ *The dinners here rival the quality of the beautiful view.*

The dining room of the Cape Arundel Inn has incorporated what was once a porch, filling two walls with windows and the blue expanse of ocean just across narrow Shore Road. Walls paneled with cream beaded board warm the room and sustain the inn's traditional atmosphere, where the very good waiter we had served us generous pieces of butter with silver tongs shaped like a chicken's feet. I'd been missing butter, had tired of olive oil, and loved the butter on my bread. That bread was standing in for the inn's own while a baking oven is replaced, so I cannot say what their bread is like.

We had the best table in the house, in the southern corner at the window, and watched the sea and a rising moon with pleasure, noting the lights coming on in the house at Walker's Point where George H. W. Bush and his wife live.

The crabcakes took up our pleased attention a moment later, crisp and sweet with a little sautéed onion and red pepper and a squiggle of creamy rémoulade. The bottle of Pouilly-Fume my companion chose made a pleasant contrast and tasted good throughout the meal, not turning harsh in my mouth as some whites do. The list itself started out in both red and white categories with some high-priced wines, and settled into a good selection priced between $30 and $40.

My friend complained that the pieces of lobster in her lobster stew, served in a little white china tureen, should be smaller but was otherwise entirely pleased by its milky, savory broth and tender lobster.

I ordered the special, broiled swordfish steak with roasted tomato salsa ($32). Evidently the chef had come upon a very fresh fish, because this was the best piece of swordfish I'd had in years. The forkfuls of hot fish filled my mouth with juice, and the smoky tomato salsa, with its concentrated essence of summer, made for an exquisite meal, a surprise of pleasure.

My friend's duck "duo," duck leg confit and a grilled duck breast in a raspberry honey demi-glace, made a delicious dinner, although she didn't care for the rice, and both of us ignored our vegetables, strips of crunchy carrots. But we're both a little out of date and like our carrots cooked.

The sautéed Maine lobster and wild mushrooms in a whiskey and herb beurre blanc looked spectacular at a nearby table, and I now know that a lobster shell can be used as a wonderful dish. Filet mignon with blue cheese, wasabi vinaigrette, and garlic whipped potato was also on the menu ($34).

Dessert was another occasion for the trumpet fanfares that sometimes sound in my head when a triumph enters my mouth. The profiterole with French vanilla gelato (from New York's Ciao Bella), Amaretto chocolate sauce, and whipped cream made me want to proclaim, as I hereby do, "We have a winner!" We should have ordered two.

By this time a woman was playing the piano, running through "Misty" with professional insouciance, and the gibbous moon had spread a silver avenue across the ocean to the horizon. The restaurant deserves to be called romantic, with the meals shedding love, the shaded candles glowing around the room, and the conversation and piano just noisy enough for us all to feel very much alive.

## The Colony Hotel
(207) 967-3331, 1-800-552-2363
140 Ocean Avenue, P.O. Box 511
www.thecolonyhotel.com

Open daily mid-May through late October for breakfast and dinner, lunch at the side of the pool Monday through Saturday in summer
Entrées $14 to $34
Dinner reservations recommended

☞ *Fine hotel dining in an elegant room*

This is the kind of place to expect fine service, enjoy a big, old-fashioned dining room, and anticipate well-prepared food. The Colony Hotel usually does not disappoint its guests. Of course many of the dishes are made with the desires of a visitor in mind, like the twin lobster dinner with the lobster meat already picked from the shell ($34). You can pick your own meal out of a 1½-pound lobster, accompanied by an ear of corn and steamed potatoes ($22).

But why not go the proper fancy food route with a dinner of twin tournedos of beef with béarnaise sauce and lobster cakes ($18.50)? Another beef entrée, sirloin with roasted-garlic-flavored béarnaise and red onion marmalade, was $19. Seafood and vegetarian dishes are also on the menu.

## Federal Jack's Brew Pub
(207) 967-4322
8 Western Avenue (before the bridge in town)
www.federaljacks.com
Hospitality—Brusque and busy in-season
Open daily for lunch, dinner, and late-night food 11:30 AM–1 AM, Sunday brunch 10:30–2
Entrées $7 to $17

☞ *A great place to try new beers and ales*

This is a favorite place for people who love casual dining and good beer. Lemon-pepper scallops mixed with basil cream sauce and linguini ($14.95) could find a good match with one of the ales brewed here, and so could roast salmon, clam chowder, or a boiled lobster. So could a pepper-Jack burger, with jalapeño-Jack cheese and sautéed onions ($6.95). Our good waitress at the Wayfarer (see page 15) makes this her destination on her night off.

## Hurricane Restaurant
See Ogunquit, where the original Hurricane is still in business.

# Mabel's Lobster Claw

(207) 967-2562
124 Ocean Avenue
Hospitality—Take-out, and a restaurant used to a fast pace
Open daily April through October for lunch and dinner
Entrées $13 to $30

☞ *A casual local favorite for fish and lobster*

Along the section of Ocean Avenue that follows the Kennebunk River, this place is within walking distance of the busy shops, and first on the lists of innkeepers' recommended spots for lobster and fish. Lobster stew, clam chowder, and steamed clams are all offered, along with alternatives, including hot dogs and hamburgers. Might as well make a reservation for dinner.

# Nunan's

(207) 967-4362
Route 9, Cape Porpoise
Hospitality—These folks have been doing this for years and handle the crowds like pros.
Open weekends in May, daily from Memorial Day through mid-October for dinner 5–9:30
Entrées $3 to $21
No credit cards

☞ The *classic lobster shack, intact in all its glory*

This place looks tiny from the front but extends deep through four rooms full of small and large picnic benches, all inside a raftered barn hung with generations of lobster buoys. Its charming exterior—black clapboards with yellow and red trim—and the sturdy tables inside have been welcoming nightly crowds for years. Bertha Nunan filled up a coffeepot with water while telling me she has been working here since 1953. She's semiretired, which seemed to mean she could go home early one night out of the six she came in to help. Her sons have taken over running the business.

The paved area in front of the door (two parking lots just around the nearby house provide all the parking) is called the pasture, she said. By 5:15 the place is often full, and the customers waiting for a table stand out there. "We give them numbers."

Two boiled 1⅛-pound lobsters—for one person only—cost $20.95, a large cup of clam chowder is $4.50. The cheapest meal is the peanut butter and jelly sandwich for $2.95; hamburgers, hot dogs, and grilled cheese are also available for the anti-seafood customers, along with an open-faced grilled chicken sandwich ($6.95) and a Delmonico steak dinner ($18.95). A lobster roll was $9.95, and beer and wine is available.

Pie, cheesecake, and brownies were part of the dessert menu. Although Nunan's does not take credit cards, you can use a personal check or traveler's checks.

## Pier 77
**(207) 967-8500**
**Pier Road, Cape Porpoise**
Open daily for lunch 11:30–2:30, dinner at 5 in-season, closed some days off-season; closed January through mid-March
Entrées $16 to $28

☛ *Fresh combinations and recipes, with an array of casual dishes, offer good choices in this well-received new restaurant at an old landmark spot.*

This restaurant came under new ownership in 2004, gaining with its new name a new reputation for fresh fish and inventive dishes that had innkeepers recommending it to grateful guests.

Oysters bingo, with garlic, spinach, Parmesan and cream is served as an appetizer ($14); chicken fettuccini with roasted mushrooms, red onion, spinach, goat cheese, and a dash of cream figured as an entrée ($16). The seafood stew in saffron broth, $28 on the dinner menu, could be had for $14 at lunchtime.

Chef Peter Morency also presides over a lunch item called Pete's Pulled Pig, a North Carolina barbecue sandwich ($7.95), as well as fish tacos($10). With myrtle topiaries on the dark wood tables and a few Victorian pieces in an upstairs lounge, plus an informal bar called the **Ramp** downstairs where you can get a plate of spaghetti with meatballs, this spot at the end of Pier Road, in the midst of the sea, is ready to nourish all its visitors.

## Stripers Waterside Restaurant
**(207) 967-5333**
**131–133 Ocean Avenue**
www.thebreakwaterinn.com/stripers.html

Hospitality—All business, slightly overtaxed
Open daily in-season for lunch and dinner
Entrées $21 to $46

☛ *Overpriced, casual food in a beautiful dining room*

Stripers Waterside Restaurant presents an enigma. The long, pale blue room, with side chairs slipcovered in blue with pale green piping, is as elegant as possible. A long aquarium fills one end with more blue light, while the dark blue fish inside it flash their cobalt scales.

At the tables a little square vase held a piece of sprouting bamboo and a moribund Siamese fighting fish that I do hope got to go back in the tank at the end of the evening. At the center of the table is a little galvanized bucket of hot sauce bottles, and the napkins are heavy but definitely paper. The first glimpse of the menu leads you further out of the room's elegance to a clam shack, listing battered and "lightly" fried haddock, scallops, shrimp, and sole. Grilled or pan-fried fish and steamed or grilled lobsters, along with a grilled chicken breast, steak, and lamb for anti-sea people, just about covers the main courses.

Salads come in an asymmetrical white bowl, as stylish as you can get in lettuce and tomatoes, but we would have been happier to find a tastier tomato. And The plain grilled yellowfin tuna, cooked rare as requested, was set before another diner, with french fries and a little asymmetrical bowl of mushy peas (more on those later), who missed some kind of sauce or accompaniment for the fish.

The Stripers bento box ($26.50), with its little piece of salmon coated in a miso paste that detracted from its flavor; the single, oily fried oyster in a shell brimming with tartar sauce heavy on the mayo; the two good tempura shrimp, and the two downright off scallops on their bed of decent seaweed salad disappointed me.

It could be that the chowders, crabcakes, or other appetizers exceeded these very ordinary ones. The plain grilled chicken was good, and the french fries were universally praised. But the 2-pound lobster with fries simply cannot be worth the $46 charged.

The mushy peas, cooked until soft and blended with cream and mint, tasted delicious, but it's an inadequate foundation for an expensive dinner ($195 for four, before the tip).

And one of us could not get over the fact that the piece of blueberry pie ($8.25) was served ice-cold, its scoop of ice cream disinclined to melt.

We can give complete praise to the sundae with peanut-butter sauce that held bits of HeathBar, and the berries with cream ($6.25) were presentable. We liked the wine, a lot of it from Australia and New Zealand, including the Bulletin Shiraz ($6.50 a glass), and the Chilean cabernet sauvignon from Casa Lapostolle ($8.50) was also satisfying.

## The Wayfarer
**(207) 967-8961**
**Pier Road, Cape Porpoise**
Hospitality—Friendly women take care of you in this casual, pretty place
Open Tuesday through Saturday for breakfast, lunch, and dinner; breakfast on Sunday from 7–noon
No credit cards

☛ *A simple, well-kept restaurant for good chowder, fine lobster rolls, and a relaxed meal*

Our lobster rolls fit the classic mold: lots of sweet fresh lobster on a buttered and grilled hot dog bun, with a little mayonnaise and a lettuce leaf. The mayo was a generic brand from the SYSCO truck, our waitress said. The regular lobster roll went for $10.95, and a large for $13.95.

But maybe, just maybe, you've had enough lobster. This is just the place for a very good chicken salad sandwich. The chicken was fresh, in good-sized chunks, and the toasted wheat bread gave the sandwich a nice crunch. Both the roll and the sandwich were served with potato chips and a good sour dill pickle spear on a big white plate.

The striped wallpaper and white wood booths make this a pretty place, with tables and a counter. When offered blueberry, strawberry-rhubarb, or raspberry-peach pie ($4.25) we chose the last; its crust was a little underdone, but we excavated all the sweet fruit and ate the ice cream without blinking an eye.

## White Barn Inn
**(207) 967-2321**
**37 Beach Avenue**
www.whitebarninn.com
Hospitality—Formal, with a highly trained staff
Open for dinner Monday through Thursday 6–9:30, Friday and Saturday 5:30–9; closed most of January
Prix fixe menu for $88 per person
Dress code: jackets required, ties optional; no jeans or sneakers

Reservations are required, along with 24-hour cancellation notice. If the reservation is canceled with less than 24-hour notice, the full amount is charged to the credit card used to take the reservation.

☛ *The king of the mountain for formal restaurants in Maine*

This is one of the highest ranked restaurants in New England.

The silver is real, the tablecloths are linen, and the barn sure doesn't hold any farm animals anymore, unless they've been roasted and sauced to perfection.

And speaking of roasting, a gentleman who dined here in summer 2004 and removed his jacket because he was too warm was quickly requested to put it back on.

Clearly this immaculate, elaborate restaurant is designed for those of us who love formality and special arrangements. There comes a time in our lives when all this makes sense, when some of us want to really go all out and be floored by the ambience, the flowers, the swift service on silent feet. That's when a splurge can make sense.

The changing menu has included smoked haddock and clam chowder, scallops on pancetta-braised butter beans, or a lobster spring roll to start; a serving of avocado lime sorbet to wake up those taste buds; and then a main course of roast cod and shrimp croquettes with squid, winter squash puree, and applesauce, or chicken on sautéed spinach with truffle-mashed potatoes and chardonnay sauce. You can opt for wines that fit the menu, already picked out for you, for another $50 per person, or buy one of the 7,000 bottles stored in the wine cellar.

Dessert could be coconut rice pudding, sorbets, or a peach tart, among other choices. And obviously there's an army of dessert wines, ports, and liqueurs. A two-ounce "flight" (one of my favorite things) of an older, pricier Grand Marnier, Cordon Rouge 100 and 150, costs $41.

You can also order the tasting menu ($108) that could take you from a "tian" of crab, tomato fondue, and fennel, to smoked lamb with pureed eggplant, to scallops with lobster and corn stew, to duck breast with a puff pastry with wild mushrooms, to cheese, to chocolate soufflé. Wines chosen from the tasting menu are more expensive, at $65 per person.

# Farms, Fish, Wine and Treats

**Cape Porpoise Lobster Company (207-967-4268; www.capeporpoise lobster.com), 15 Pier Road.**

Open year-round. Fresh fish, lobsters, and clams are sold. "Everything that we have is local," the manager said, and comes right off the boat that caught it. In the summer cooked seafood is available for take-out.

## The Clam Shack (207-967-2560 for take-out, 207-967-3321 for the seafood market) is right in the middle of Kennebunkport at the bridge.

Fried fish comes through the take-out window from Mother's Day to Columbus Day, and the seafood market, selling lobsters, clams, and fish, remains open year-round.

## Port Lobster (207-967-2081), 22 Ocean Avenue (before the Colony Hotel on the right).

Live or cooked lobsters packed to travel, and lobster and crab rolls to go.

## Old School House Farm (207-967-8018), 162 Goose Rocks Road. Take Route 9 north from Kennebunkport to Log Cabin Road, then turn left onto Goose Rocks Road)

Buy vegetables and flowers at the farm stand, or pick your own.

# Kittery

## Bob's Clam Hut
### (207) 439-4233
### 315 Route 1
### www.bobsclamhut.com
### Open year-round, Sunday through Thursday 11–8, until 9 on Friday and Saturday
### Entrées start at $9.75 for fried scallops

☛ *The first place to eat Maine seafood, and open in the winter*

An old establishment with a great new attitude, Bob's gives people 60 and older 15 percent off on Tuesday. Order the cream-and-milk-broth clam chowder, unthickened, for a cold winter day. Or the basket of fried oysters ($11.50). In good weather, there are tables outside along Route 1 and around the corner of the restaurant. That's when you could try to snag a picnic table in the back by a little garden, and definitely finish up with Ben & Jerry's ice cream, available at its own window. If you drive up the coast frequently, take one of their five-punch cards; after it's full you get a free small cone. You can eat lobster stew, lobster rolls, and lobster salads here, but plain boiled lobsters are not on the menu.

## Cap'n Simeon's Galley
(207) 439-3655
**Pepperell Cove (on Route 103 between Kittery and York Harbor)**
**Kittery Point**
Open daily in summer 11:30 AM through dinner, closed Tuesdays in the off-season
Entrées $11 to $19

☞ *An old building on the sea, originally a store that opened in 1828, serving seafood and burgers*

Broiled haddock and broiled scallops are the most popular entrées, with fried oysters (often from Prince Edward Island, $11.95), clams from Ipswich, and many other fried dinners served here year-round. Thirty-five tables seat 120 diners in the old, beamed dining room, which overlooks the ocean and two lighthouses—Whaleback Light and the lighthouse at Fort Constitution, a Coast Guard station in Newcastle, New Hampshire. Fort Foster and Fort McLeary are also visible through the big dining room windows; you may have to wait if you want a window seat on a summer weekend.

## Chauncey Creek Lobster Pound
(207) 439-1030
**16 Chauncey Creek Road, Kittery Point**
www.chaunceycreek.com
Hospitality—Counter service, often with a wait in the busy summer months; the meal is brought to you at a sheltered or outdoor table.
Open daily from Mother's Day to Labor Day 11–8, Tuesday through Sunday until Columbus Day
Entrées $1.75 for a hot dog; $17 to $20 for a pound-and-a-half lobster

☞ *An authentic lobster pound, with the basics and more, at outdoor picnic tables*

One of travel writer Chris Tree's favorite lobster shacks in Maine, this place has been serving up boiled lobster, steamers, chowder, and mussels for over 50 years. You find a seat first at one of the more than 40 blue-, pink-, or orange-painted picnic tables, because you need to put down the wine and glasses, salad, or whatever else you brought along to supplement the menu. Order at a window, and the staff brings your meal out to you at the table number you gave them. Some of the tables are under shelter; convenient if you visit on a day with iffy weather. They also have screens to keep out the bugs.

Like Miller's farther Downeast, there is no fried food here. But you can get raw shellfish, like oysters ($7 for a half dozen), and clams on the half shell. Make that bottle of wine a muscadet, and drink in the river view.

There is a chicken dinner ($7.95), and you can also order a hot dog. But the main event is the lobster, in a range of sizes, because it was the lobster that got things going in the 1940s, when this place was a lobster pound only. Now people have such a good time here, you are asked to stay no longer than two hours.

## Warren's Lobster House
**(207) 439-1630**
**11 Water Street (Route 1)**
Open Sunday through Thursday 11:30–8:30, Friday and Saturday 11:30–9
Entrées $13 to $17, more for lobster

☛ *A longtime lobster shack with a giant menu and lots of tables*

Look for the big sign when you cross into Maine from Portsmouth, New Hampshire. This place has a big salad bar with more than 50 choices, just like the sign says, and could be a southerner's first chance to crack open a Maine lobster. Around since the 1940s, when it had six stools and served only clams and lobsters (at 25¢ a pound), the long menu will now please just about anyone, and the staff knows how to take care of crowds. The restaurant can seat 350 and bakes its own breads and cakes. Every party that sits down gets a key to the Captain's Treasure Chest, in the gift shop, where they are encouraged to see what their luck can bring. Kids get a long menu, too, and can eat a dessert called the Cool Dog—ice cream shaped like a hot dog in a cake bun, with hot fudge sauce for ketchup ($3.50).

## Food Markets, Bakeries, and Fish and Wine Stores

It's enough to make anyone wish they lived in Kittery: a whole neighborhood of high-quality places to get dinner, from artisan bread to fresh fish to just ground beef and fresh pasta, with a bottle of the best Chianti and the freshest salad thrown in.

### Beach Pea Bakery (207-439-3555), 53 State Road (Route 1).

Open Tuesday through Saturday 7:30–6. Fougasse—made from rosemary dough, brushed with olive oil and sprinkled with sea salt, and formed like a fat pretzel-shaped leaf—is the bakery's most popular bread. All are hand-formed, European-style breads, according to Mariah Maher, who co-owns the business with Tom Roberts. Open since January 2001, this place is hopping, with cakes, croissants, coffee cakes, and cookies, all made with high quality natural ingredients. Sandwiches are made with meats roasted on the premises, and the owners plan to offer soups in the near future.

### Cacao Chocolates (207-438-9001), 64 Government Street.

Open Tuesday through Friday 12–6, Saturday 10–4, closed Sunday and Monday and the month of August (because it's too hot for chocolate). *Cacao* is the Latin name for the cocoa bean plant, pronounced ka-COW. Homemade chocolates are taking exciting new directions here, with ingredients like chèvre, curry, and juniper. Dense, pure, luscious flavors fill your mouth. The 22 truffle varieties include blueberry-lemon in Belgian white chocolate, creamy curried walnut, and chèvre with cognac. Two tea-flavored truffles, maybe Japanese green tea, are always in the case, along with caramels with French sea salt and a juniper truffle that contains crushed juniper berries macerated in boiled cream used in the ganache. Handmade English toffee and an array of chocolate bars are also available. Hot cocoa mixes ($9.25 for 14 to 16 servings) are sold in a cinnamon and a Mayan flavor, among others.

"The truffle with the cult following is the Mayan truffle; it has spices and red chili," Susan Tuveson, the owner, said. "The chocolate sings all the way through it." It's decorated with a piece of 24-karat gold and costs $32 a pound, around $1 a piece.

### Carl's Meat Market (207-439-1557), 25 State Road (Route 1).

This custom butcher shop is run by a man who grinds his own hamburger. You can order however much you want, from whatever cut you like.

### Enoteca Italiana (207-439-7216), 122 State Road (Route 1).

Open Monday through Saturday 10–7, Sunday 12–4, closed Tuesday. Antipasto platters and lots of Italian wine. A lot of small house wines, from Sicily and other regions, are sold here; 90 percent of the store's offerings are Italian wines. Importers out of New York, including Via, allocate wines to this shop. "The quality of juice for a $10 bottle is amazing," said Chris Souder, who owns the store with his wife. He admires the southern ethic that has kept prices low while boosting quality. The Puglia region, the heel of the boot, makes wine with the primitiva grape, called the original zinfandel grape. Salice Salentino, fast becoming a favorite wine area within Puglia, is starting to appear in wine magazines as a source of good wine. Twenty kinds of olives, 130 cheeses, 20 salamis, and different hams, mortadella, and pancetta are also for sale.

### The Golden Harvest Produce Market (207-439-2113), 47 State Road (Route 1).

A long-standing market that features local produce in-season, and specialty items, like ramps, when they can be found at the wholesaler.

### Sue's Seafood (207-439-5608), 54 State Road (Route 1).

Open year-round 7–7, closing at 9 PM on Friday and Saturday in summer. Much of the fish sold here comes from local fishermen, when they have what Susan Allen accepts. She opened in this location in 1999, after operating another fish store elsewhere. "I have refused so much stuff that they won't send me what's not fresh. Two kinds of tuna (locally caught bluefin and big-eye from

*Owner Tim Roberts making cookies at Beach Pea Bakery (left), and the rack of breads for sale (right).*

Hawaii), fresh haddock, cod, sea scallops, and an array of other shellfish (shucked if you want) were available when we spoke. A selection of cooked and fried fish (the salmon nuggets are recommended) and take-and-bake entrées are also offered. Bait and tackle is for sale for sportsfishermen, and recommendations for charter boats can be had here too.

Lunch at Sue's Seafood in Kittery

**Terra Cotta Pasta Co. (207-475-3025), 52 Route 1.** Open Monday 10–6, Tuesday through Saturday 9–6:30, and Sunday 12–5. A 2-pound bag of fresh egg linguini, made Tuesday and Wednesday, is the most popular item here. Raviolis are made on Friday, and range from roasted garlic with three cheeses, to sweet potato and butternut squash, to wild mushroom with roasted shallots in a lemon thyme pasta. A Mediterranean ravioli has eggplant, feta, and sun-dried tomatoes in a black olive pasta. Lasagnas, other meals to go, and a variety of cheeses are offered. A deli case contains other prepared foods. A lot of samples are available on Saturday; you can always try something from the deli case, or whatever soups are on the menu.

Terra Cotta Pasta

# Ogunquit

## Arrows
**(207) 361-1100**
**Berwick Road, P. O. Box 803**
Hospitality—Oppressive elegance
Open for dinner Tuesday through Sunday in July and August, decreasing off-season
Entrées $40 to $44; $69 for Kobe beef
Reservations urged, credit card numbers taken, and a 24-hour cancellation policy is in place; there is a $50 per-person charge for canceling with less than 24 hours' notice.
Dress code: Jackets and ties are recommended; no one in shorts or blue jeans will be seated.

☛ *A place renowned for its food and feared for its bills*

Doom always seems to haunt my visits to Arrows. The first time, despite a long wait, the evening was salvaged. But not this last visit. My friend, who had driven up from Boston, was turned away for wearing jeans. It got under his skin, and he couldn't stay even to eat elsewhere and drove off in a roar. I sat in the bar contemplating the framed accolades from *Bon Appétit*, *Gourmet*, and *Time*, feeling bad.

The host had attempted to dress my friend in spare pants; they were rejected. Hadn't the person on the phone said the policy was "not strictly enforced"? No, that was the jacket and tie. The jeans and shorts part of the policy was strictly enforced. But I was not to be charged the $50 per person fee for a cancelled reservation if I couldn't stomach eating alone, he said. That is charged to people who cancel less than 24 hours before their dinner. When I made the reservation I was given clear instructions. It was my fault for not telling my friend. All true.

Well, I was there, it was going to be a busy summer, and I was going to have a hard time getting back. I said I would eat after all.

"Just give us a few moments to adjust your table," a woman said. When she came to get me she said, "Someone will be happy to carry your wine for you."

"Can't I do it for myself?"

"We like to do everything we can for our guests," she said. A little late for that, I thought.

Buck up, I told myself. As Calvin Trillin said, everything is potential material for a writer. Everything.

After gourmet butters were offered and declined, regular butter accepted, bottled waters offered and declined, tap water accepted, I ate my nice crunchy bread stick, counted up 21 wines by the glass on the menu, and stared out at the garden at the iris leaves that had been chopped at alternating lengths to create a certain effect.

My square plate of deep-fried soft-shell crab and crab timbale was accompanied by a mound of seedling arugula and Swiss chard. I didn't understand what they were at first, but when I asked I was told they were micro-greens. They are the seedlings you pull when you thin the plants, I thought. I was reminded of my absent companion's crack about vegetable infanticide, and I missed him.

Salty caviar on the timbale seasoned the precious greens. My glass of Italian Terradora Estate Falanghina ($10.95; wine ranged from $10.95 up to $18.95 per glass for Perrier Jouet) had the "mild acidity, good crisp summer flavor" the waiter had described. It was cool and sophisticated.

"May I remove this for you ma'am," asked a server, a minion in black. She thanked me and swept the crumbs up and then apologized for giving me a clean knife and fork.

Here was a lobster threesome: a pudding, a ravioli, and a cannelloni.

"What's with the multiple births?" I asked. The waiter with the unctuous voice said it's the fault of Thomas Keller, who runs the famous restaurant French Laundry, in California—Arrows had once served a plate of eight preparations with eight cheeses. It's a tradition at Arrows.

My lobster ravioli had fresh mozzarella, the cannelloni was full of melting ricotta, the pudding full of bread and butter and tough lobster. I left a lobster claw and the pasta behind, but not the pea shoots, allowed to live two weeks longer than the micro-greens. They had a lot of flavor, took up more room, and took me some time to eat.

Two black-jacketed underlings spritzed a new tablecloth next to me and smoothed out every wrinkle, achieving perfection. I contemplated the desserts: duos, trios, and a quattro. No thanks. But here, a waiter said a moment later, compliments of the chef, are a couple of sorbets and a piece of cornmeal shortbread to console me. I pushed my fork into the shortbread, a piece shot into my lap, and I ate it, unconsoled. The two raspberries sitting on the plate for garnish were good.

I left an extravagant fallout of crumbs from the shortbread on the tablecloth to be swept away, and paid my bill. It came to $93.95, even with a free glass of wine and dessert; $111.95 with tip, because those people are so good, almost like sharks in their surveillance of the dining room. It occurred to me that I'd paid a trio of ones, a matched set, a French Laundry kind of tab, ever so symmetrical.

# Barnacle Billy's and Barnacle Billy's Etc.
(207) 646-5575, 1-800-866-5575
**Perkins Cove**
www.barnbilly.com
Barnacle Billy's Original opens for lunch and dinner at 11 daily; Etc. opens
daily at noon, May through October
Entrées $2.50 to $7

☛ *A classic lobster shack with a view and some ambition in the menu*

You have to get over the fee for parking and enjoy the view after you make it to
this classic lobster shack on the water. The Grande Lobster Shack, perhaps, the
place you get whisked away to from Boston. Pricey, of course, but knowledgeable about lobsters. The shedders were running $20.95 for a pound and a half
in 2004; bigger, hard-shell lobsters came in at $28.95 for a 2-pounder. You get
your steamed clams with butter and broth for $15.95, and cheeseburgers for the
know-nothing kids are $4.35 (but you are grateful they can't stand lobster and
keep the bill from achieving orbit). The onion rings have been known to be soggy,
but sitting on the outside deck over the water makes all things seem right.

Two fireplaces warm things up when the cove is fog-bound.

A bowl of lobster stew ($15.95) and corn on the cob from Chase Farms
($1.95) round out the proper menu for a city slicker out for a Maine meal.

Maple syrup comes with the scallops wrapped in bacon.

# Cliff House
(207) 361-1000
**Shore Road, P.O. Box 2274**
www.cliffhousemaine.com
Hospitality—Competent service
Open daily late March through December for dinner
Entrées $19 to $30
Reservations recommended, handicapped accessible
Dress code: jackets required, no shorts, sneakers, or jeans allowed

☛ *A sea of tables overlooking the sea, with some good dishes and
others that miscalculate*

We came into the dining room from a side door that had led us past the new "van-
ishing edge pool," an impressive sight curved on the top of a terrace overlooking
the sea. The scale of things at the Cliff House matches its exalted location on top

of the cliffs at the edge of the sea, and its new spa looms above when you park in the parking lot.

The big dining room, with corporate carpet and drop ceiling, is furnished with cream swags over the wide windows and reproduction Queen Anne side chairs at the tables.

The theme song from *Chariots of Fire* played on the sound system in a lush orchestration, moving on to "Norwegian Wood," and a sprightly "These Are a Few of My Favorite Things." Many of the diners were old. A long table was set for a sales-conference meal, some 25 seats to a side. We ate too early to encounter these diners except to pass them outside the dining room, in the cavernous lounge area, where the almost entirely male 40-something group enjoyed cocktails and looked somewhat bored.

My first course made playful reference to a sundae, and was made with toasted bread piled with caramelized onion, strips of ham, and a heated round of goat cheese, with a topping of tapenade and a caper berry standing in for the cherry ($9). It was a delicious mess, slithering off the toasted bread with lots of salty olive and sweet onion and creamy cheese. Rockport's State of Maine Cheese Company had a spot among the appetizers with a sampler plate, and at the top was a lobster bisque ($7) and clam chowder ($6). A choice of Caesar or house salad came with the entrées; served on a glass plate on a doily on a white plate, our little Caesar was gobbled up in a minute, light and nicely dressed. It proved the simplest part of the meal, and the only thing made on a modest scale.

Outside, on the water below our windows, a tour boat waddled by.

*The Cliff House stands on the rocks of Cape Neddick.*

We'd gone on an adventure with our choice of entrée, just to see if what the menu described could possibly be good. It was, like the appetizer, a visual diversion. The Cliff House Blueberry Halibut ($25) came with two pieces of fried spaghetti, like antennae, sticking out of the piece of fish, which was set on blueberry compote on a disk of sticky rice that sat on an inner circle of mango puree and rayed outer circle of raspberry puree. The halibut was perfectly cooked, and in and of itself a lovely thing. But it didn't work with the rest of the dish.

Our other entrée was a partially boned half chicken ($24) roasted and set on lush potatoes that had been mixed with too much fat, possibly oil. There was no butter on the table with the mediocre rolls, but a saucer of bland oil with a puddle of red vinegar stood ready for us to dip into.

Piano music took over for the absurd Muzak. My dessert, Indian pudding, was another pastiche, the humble molasses-sweetened cornmeal stodge hidden inside a buttery hive of one large gingersnap under a round of good ice cream and a lot of whipped cream. Our old friends, mango and raspberry coulis, decorated the plate. I smashed through the couture shell of gingersnap and ate the plain pudding with pleasure, missing raisins.

That over-elaborateness must seem de rigueur to the management of this resort dining room, but it didn't make for much pleasure at the table. A few good things cooked with the skill the kitchen was full of would give a lot more pleasure.

## David's Restaurant
**(207) 646-5206**
**21–23 Shore Road**
Open April through October
Entrées $12 to $24
Reservations necessary, handicapped accessible, BYO wine

☛ *One of the hottest places for lunch and dinner in town*

Chef-owner David Giarusso Jr. has been operating this casual, fine-dining restaurant since 1998, and nowadays the place is fully booked for dinner every night of the summer. You need to make a reservation two nights in advance to eat dinner here. Part of the reason may be the reasonable prices, which Giarusso attributes to owning the building and keeping the dining all outdoors.

The heated outdoor café here attracts everyone from the street, and the food has locals happy to recommend it. Five outdoor heaters keep the brick terrace as warm as 85 degrees; in late September diners eat outside in short-sleeved shirts. Sandwiches, 15 different salads, crabcakes, and mussels Provençal figure on the lunch menu. Dinner turns to fresh fish, lobster, and seafood stuffed mushrooms, among its 25 possibilities, and there are always five specials. A Delmonico steak is $18. Fresh pasta is delivered from Massachusetts.

"Unless you want fried clams, there's no reason not to eat here," Giarusso said. There are a lot of vegetarian choices; vegetarian lasagne, seasonal vegetables layered with ricotta topped with a pomodoro sauce, is one of the favorites.

The apple and Vidalia onion roast pork tenderloin ($15.95) over garlic mashed potatoes sells out every night, he said.

Desserts like chocolate raspberry torte, and homemade apple and blueberry pie, are made by his pastry chef.

This is a BYO wine place with nice atmosphere. Giarusso asks that diners bring wine if they want to drink it with dinner, not a six-pack of beer.

## Fisherman's Catch
(207) 646-8780
134 Harbor Road
Hospitality—A casual place with experienced owners, good service
Open May through October
Entrées $6 to $18
Handicapped accessible

☛ *A fish place with some imagination, especially off-season*

This weathered, shingled building stands in a salt marsh; you can eat at outdoor picnic tables or head indoors for casual dining. The lobster knuckle appetizer tops the list of favorite starters in the summer ($4) when the place is focused on its homemade chowders, lobster dinners, fried oysters ($12), fried mussels ($8), and seafood platter with haddock, shrimp, scallops, and clams ($17).

For dessert people get a little wild about the bread pudding with whiskey sauce ($4), a special that gets made more off-season than on, like the Louisiana Crab Soup ($4)—just another reason to visit the area in September and October.

## Five-O Shore Road
(207) 646-5001
50 Shore Road
www.five-oshoreroad.com
Hospitality—Fabulous service and great bartending

Open daily for dinner 5–10 in summer, Thursday through Sunday in winter
Entrées $20 to $29

☞ *A favorite of some locals for martinis and a fine meal*

Wood and terra-cotta-colored walls give the bar a warm glow, and make it a good place to start an evening. One person we know extols the bartending, Rick Dolliver's territory. He prides himself on remembering customers' "regulars," which could be one of the martinis or one of the other drinks, like a cosmo.

Customers who get to like this kind of thing can join the Five-O Club, and receive a $50 gift certificate for food and drink after spending $500. (Only the first 550 applicants can join; as of this writing, the list was still open.)

Black tablecloths cover the four outdoor tables set in front of the building on busy Shore Road; things are quieter in the dining room, where Chef Jonathan MacAlpone jazzes up standards, like clam chowder with a little pancetta.

The always-changing menu may feature seared yellowfin tuna encrusted with coriander, a grilled ruby grapefruit, and salad of gingered edamame ($29). Another possibility is ginger-marinated salmon grilled and served with sweet chili sauce and cold sesame lo mein ($23). Steaks are on the list, one a filet mignon with wild mushroom demi-glace.

The yellowfin makes the starter menu too, seared with black sesame seeds and served in a rice-paper cup ($11.50). Mussels change every day and were served at least once with garlic, Danish blue cheese, and cream ($9).

Lemon *panna cotta* with a little fresh fruit ($8.50) and a fresh fruit *crostate,* with fruit baked in pastry ($8.50), look good on the dessert menu, if you can resist a chocolate tort ($8.50) made with Callebaut chocolate.

## Gypsy Sweethearts
(207) 646-7021
30 Shore Road
www.gypsysweethearts.com
Open June through September for dinner Tuesday through Sunday at 5:30, weekends only in spring and fall
Entrées $17 to $27

☞ *An established business with some Caribbean dishes, good wine, and a happy staff*

"The menu is definitely going a little more Caribbean," said Tony Tarleton, chef-owner Judy Clayton's business partner. The meals served in the pretty old rooms have been pleasing customers for over 20 years. The menu is pretty much set at the beginning of summer, with daily specials like Caesar-glazed sea bass, slightly crisp on top with its Parmesan ($27). Jamaican jerk chicken ($18) comes with sautéed bananas and rum-flavored pineapple. Poblano *rellenos* are roasted and filled with corn, *tetillo* cheese, scallions, and currants, and served with smoky salsa and beans and rice ($17).

The desserts are homemade and have included ice cream, cappuccino cream brûlée, and chocolate mascarpone tart (all $7).

Things are not changing a lot here, and that makes the days run smoothly. Tarleton still employs the restaurant's original hostess, who started in 1982. "We don't have much turnover." He said most people are happy here, and joked that he paid them more than he paid himself. He was funny in a Rodney Dangerfield kind of way about the entrées he gets to eat—like the ones that fall on the floor.

This is one of the first restaurants to receive the *Wine Spectator* Award of Excellence, for a reasonably priced wine list with 80 wines, 21 available by the glass.

# Hurricane Restaurant
**(207) 646-6348, 1-800-649-6348 (from ME and NH)**
**Perkins Cove**
www.hurricanerestaurant.com
Hospitality—Brought all we asked for, after only a brief hesitation
Open for lunch and dinner 11:30 AM–10:30 PM in summer, until 9:30 winter, closed for two weeks in January
Entrées $18 to $45
Reservations advised

☛ *With your feet almost in the water, the view triumphs; the food is uneven, sometimes great.*

Yes—the view, the view, the view. An expanse of rocks at low tide and a promontory of barnacle-crusted bedrock somehow challenged us through the window, and at the bottom edge of the glass, shards of shore grass gleamed lime green in a weird light. We looked out there a lot. The rocks seemed to speak, somewhat disrespectfully.

It helped to fill my mouth with Four Vines Zinfandel ($10 per glass), one of many choices on the long wine list.

Our oysters seemed thin and wan; perhaps, as M. F. K. Fisher suggested, they are depleted at the end of spawning season? But they ought not to have been sink-

*Hurricane's windows overlook Perkins Cove*

ing in the melted ice underneath them. We weren't confident about these Spinney Creek and Washington oysters ($18 for a dozen). The flatbread with *pancetta,* Parmesean, and spinach ($10) was dry.

My friend's apple-pear hash was sweet and right, the sautéed spinach good, and the pork chop fine. I had wondered about the cool plates under our hot entrées, which quickly brought down the temperature of the meat. It's true the place had filled up and grown noisy and very busy. My own beef tenderloin, perfectly rare, sang in my mouth, and the wild mushroom bread pudding outdid itself in the chorus, the best of part of the meal. The thin, crisp, golden fried onion rings crowning my meat disappeared first.

The third member of our party enjoyed the herbed flavor of her roasted chicken, while wondering at the watery consistency of the pesto sauce. And she did not, despite her greed for this dessert, eat any of the Key lime tart with graham cookie crust ($7) after a first bite. Its cheesecake-like, starchy density made appetite pall.

But two of us demolished the Hurricane ($7), with its cream mousse, layer of ganache, and thin crust of cake. Would someone please start serving more crème anglaise than the little dots and squiggles we quickly sopped up?

## Jackie's Too Restaurant

(207) 646-4444
Perkins Cove
Open for lunch and dinner 11–9 in summer, lunch until 3 in winter
Entrées $7 to $30

☛ *Casual meals revolving around seafood, on a deck with a view*

A favorite for dinner at Jackie's Too is the baked stuffed haddock, with lobster, crab, and Ritz cracker stuffing ($17.95). But the biggest sellers at lunch are "stand your spoon up thick" clam chowder ($4.95 a bowl), and lobster rolls ($11.95), with lobster meat mixed with mayo, celery, and a tiny bit of chopped lettuce on grilled hot dog rolls. They fly out the door, and out to the deck, an enclosed space with heaters that operates until October and opens up again in April. In mid-winter, meals are served inside.

## Jonathan's Restaurant

(207) 646-4777
92 Bourne Lane
www.jonathansrestaurant.com
Open daily for dinner at 4:30 in summer; check for hours off-season
Entrées $18 to $24

☛ *A longtime presence on the restaurant scene, with a big menu*

The 600-gallon aquarium is an attraction, and the gardens outside the windows fill the view with greenery and flowers. This restaurant remains some visitors' favorite place in town. Johnathan's serves fresh oysters a variety of ways—Oysters Russian are served with vodka, sour cream, and red and black caviar ($10.95)—the focus is on fish and meat. The entrée considered a "signature" is the caramelized salmon marinated in a Grand Marnier vinaigrette and served with a lemon beurre blanc ($22.50). But you can also find dishes from another era, like Kiev saltimbocca, "boneless breast of chicken wrapped around toasted pro-sciutto, garlic, butter, Parmesan, Romano, and sage baked and served with mushroom supreme sauce" ($18.75).

## Lobster Shack

(207) 646-2941
Lower End of Perkins Cove
Hospitality—Counter service for lobster, with a short menu

**Open daily for lunch and dinner at 11, mid-April through mid-October**
**Entrées $2.25 to $20**

☛ *All that's needed for a fine lobster dinner is here.*

This simple little restaurant is filled by just 12 tables, each made of one solid pine slab. Built in 1963, they are refinished every year and give the small space a golden light.

Steamed clams were $14.50 a quart because of the red tide in 2004. Lobster rolls ($11.95) are made from fresh-cooked lobster meat with a little mayo, on the classic toasted hot dog bun, absolutely no lettuce or celery.

Lobster is the big thing here, and was running $20 for a pound and a half in 2004. A 3-pound creature would cost between $45 and $50. There's a sink in the dining room to wash up at after you crack the shells.

The house chowder, a combination of haddock and clam with potatoes and onions, comes in a milk-and-cream base, without any flour thickening. Jason Evans, the owner, is stepping into his father's shoes (his father bought the place in 1986) and said he'd grown up on the unthickened chowder in Portland.

Desserts, from Bread and Roses Bakery (see page 37), are just apple and blueberry pie, $3.95 a slice, $4.95 with ice cream. "Just plain and simple," Evans said.

*A curve in the road in the tiny peninsula called Perkins Cove*

# 98 Provence

(207) 646-9898

262 Shore Road, P.O. Box 628

www.98provence.com

Hospitality—Great service with minimal fuss

Open for dinner **Wednesday through Monday** in summer, less in the off-season

Entrées $26–$38

Reservations recommended, handicapped accessible

☛ *Classic delicious food from southern France, made with an artist's eye for color*

Late August is a great time to visit Provence—the restaurant—when the nearby farms are finally harvesting food that carries the rich flavors typical of the region of France the restaurant's named for. A yellow-tomato gazpacho, with a mound of avocado mousse in the center, came freckled with paprika and was the richest saffron yellow. It was ready to have its portrait painted but was too delicious to stare at for long.

The wine list is dominated by French labels, and there are a few $26 bottles from both the United States and France. Some, like the Chateau des Annereaux Lalande de Pomeral, are available in a glass. That wine ($10 a glass, $48 a bottle) filled my mouth with its silken heaviness, reminding me of the sophistication of the French palate and its dedication to flavor.

Who else could have bred geese and cultivated them to make the exquisite foie gras, served at 98 Provence on our visit in a little herb-crusted cylinder with small buttered, toasted baguette rounds ($20)? You feel seduced even when you are all alone at the table. Alongside the liver terrine was a lovely arrangement of lightly cooked, thin green beans, thin-sliced radish, and a new carrot, among other things, that made a satisfying vinegary mouthful between bites of the rich foie gras.

I'm betting what they say about red wine is true, and I need not fear for my heart if I drink it with such rich food.

The veal medallion was cooked rare without our asking for a preference—make sure you make yours known. Accompanied by little scoops of yellow squash, red onions, spinach, peas, and morels all drenched in cream sauce, it was another pretty, and pretty rich, plate. The veal and the filet mignon were served with deep-fried small shapes of potatoes dauphine, a revelation—Tater Tots deified.

98 Provence offers diners both a prix fixe and an à la carte menu, and if we could have been content with the $48 prix-fixe selection, we would have saved

money. But the items on the other menu pages tempted us, as they had the crowd that filled the dining room within a half hour of opening early that Thursday night, and will tempt us back. Business had been hopping, our well-trained waiter told us, even though other local businesses hadn't done well that cold summer.

People who vacation in Ogunquit depend on the great food here, including sorbets like mango, coconut, and raspberry, or a glassful of berries in cream, or the banana *clafoutis* we obediently ordered with our entrées, so it could be ready in time, and that came accompanied by coconut ice cream.

## Ogunquit Lobster Pound
**(207) 646-2516**
**504 Main Street**
**Open daily for dinner at 5 in-season, weekends only in winter**
**Entrées $11 to $30**

☞ *A log building that's seen 80 years of lobster cooking*

You can pick your own lobster and watch it cook in the big outdoor cookers, or relax with a beer at an outdoor picnic table with some steamers without worrying about the dripping butter. But people who want other items can find them on the big menu. Although one local called this place "incredibly expensive," it does have the beauty of its history, and a deep understanding of how to take care of the season's hordes of tourists.

The pies come highly recommended.

## Poor Richard's Tavern
**(207) 646-4722**
**125 Shore Road**
**www.poorrichardstavern.com**
**Open Monday through Saturday for dinner 5:30–9:30**
**Entrées $17 to $24**
**Reservations suggested**

☞ *New England comfort food*

This business started nearby in 1958 and keeps its food tied to its roots. Yankee Pot Roast Jardiniere ($16.95) is a standard on a menu that features New England classics. Another is the lobster stew dinner ($19.95) that also holds crabmeat and haddock in its creamy depths. Richard's Lobster Pie ($22.95) is always a favorite with visitors.

You can also find a filet mignon with béarnaise sauce ($23.95). Everything is served with buttermilk biscuits.

# Breakfast, Take-Out, Wine, Bakeries, and Ice Cream

## Amore Breakfast (207-646-6661, 1-866-641-6661; www.amorebreakfast.com), 178 Shore Road.

Open early spring through mid-December 7 AM–1 PM, closed Wednesday and Thursday. The friendly ambience of this favorite breakfast spot, with its knotty-pine paneling and white wooden chairs, is enhanced by the good smells. Maybe they come from the Mama Mia omelet, with sausage, onions, green peppers, basil, and provolone ($7.50), or the Oscar de la Renta Benedict, with asparagus and crab on an English muffin with dill hollandaise ($8.95).

No—it's from the pecan-coated, cream-cheese-stuffed French toast, with a side of sautéed bananas in a rum syrup; $7.50 for a full order but the half order ($5.50) is just fine. Plenty of free parking.

## Beach Plum Lobster Farm (207-646-7277), Route 1, across from Beach Plum Farm.

Open in summer; call for hours. This place sells just lobsters and clams, boiled, steamed, or raw. If you bring your own butter and paper towels, you could eat the creatures outside on a fine day, at one of the picnic tables or by the little pond next door. Two gas-fired cookers sit outside the door, simmering all day long.

## Bread and Roses Bakery (207-646-4227), 28A Main Street.

Open daily at 7 AM (the retail side opens later in January and February). Fabulous cakes, pies, cookies, brownies, and cinnamon-raisin and whole wheat bread. Because it's a vegetarian bakery, the breads are made with high-quality ingredients; some are vegan or kosher. Salads, sandwiches, and paninis, and fresh homemade pizza.

## Congdon's Doughnuts (207-646-4219), 1090 Post Road.

Open daily 6 AM–3 PM in summer, closed Tuesday in the shoulder season, open Friday and Saturday from November to April. Rumor has it that the delectable doughnuts sold here are cooked in lard, but management says "we're not giving all our secrets away." These are the doughnuts to eat, when it is time to eat a doughnut.

Scones, muffins, elephant ears—puff pastries with cinnamon or raspberry—and sticky buns are all also out front. A full-service restaurant in back features a variety of Benedicts and hashes along with the regular eggs and pancakes.

### Cove Café (207-646-2422), Perkins Cove.

This sweet little café, open daily at 7 AM, is set in a white cottage with a blue-and-white-striped awning and serves good variations on the standard breakfast menu, like a tomato, basil, and mozzarella omelet ($8.95), or a crabmeat, cheddar, and asparagus omelet ($9.95).

*Happy customers at Amore Breakfast*

### Fancy That (207-646-4118; www.villagefoodmarket.com/fancythat), Main Street (at the corner of Beach Street and Route 1).

Open daily mid-April through mid-October, 6:30 AM–11 PM in summer, closing earlier in spring and fall. Promising strong coffee, baked goods, and bagels, and sandwiches and chowders for lunch. This place advises you to call in a lunch order before 11 AM so you won't have to stand in the long line that forms at noon in the summer. The Italian Pavilion is an amazing sandwich creation: baked ham, bacon, provolone, Boursin, black olives, and green peppers with more veggies on French bread (large $6.25, small $4.50). Chicken salad is chopped fine, and the lobster rolls are not on hot dog buns and include lettuce, tomato, red onion, and sprouts. Hmmm—sounds like heresy!

### The Village Food Market (207-646-2122; www.villagefoodmarket .com) 230 Main Street.

Open 6:30 AM–11 PM daily in-season, closing earlier later in the year. Sandwiches include Italian, chicken, and cheese grinders, pre-made in the summer. There are 2,500 bottles of wine, a large array of cheeses, and a prepared-food case with pasta dishes and prepared meats for bringing dinner home. In the summer it goes upscale with fresh grilled marinated vegetables, like zucchini and red peppers, paired with grilled sirloin or chicken. Baked lasagne survives year-round, as do other Italian dishes from the Italian chef. Bagels are from Finagle a Bagel in

Boston and are delivered every day. The bakery makes pies, cakes and tortes, cookies, and bars; many are sold to local restaurants.

## Perkins and Perkins (1-877-646-0288; www.perkinsandperkins .com), 478 Main Street.

Open Monday, and Wednesday through Saturday, 10–6; Sunday 12–5; open limited days in January. Ample parking. Wine and more—cheese, mustard, salsa, olives, and pâté. All of it to buy and much of it to try at the adjacent wine bar, **Vine,** open at 4:30 from the end of May to Labor Day, with outside dining on a heated patio. French onion soup and clam chowder (both $7), a blue cheese bruschetta ($7), or a shrimp ceviche ($9 to $12) can precede a charcuterie plate with pâtés and sausages ($10), for a light dinner, but more substantial dishes are on the menu too.

The food store makes its own line of chocolate, jam, and candy, and many of the savory sauces and chutneys it sells. Caribou Crunch, a combination of popcorn, caramel, chocolate, pecans, and spices, is the top seller.

# Wells

## Joshua's Restaurant and Bar
(207) 646-3355
1637 Post Road
www.joshuas.biz
Hospitality—Swift, intelligent service
Open for dinner 5–10 daily in summer, closed Sunday in the off-season
Entrées $17 to $28
No reservations, handicapped accessible

☛ *This newcomer makes ambitious meals with local food.*

Set in an old building just north of the junction of Routes 109 and 1, Joshua's has undergone renovations that have transformed this old private home into a restaurant with modern design and features like handicap accessibility.

One of the owners, Joshua Mather, former executive chef at Five-O, works with meat and produce from local farms (and some from his own farm) and seafood from local boats. He makes his own bread at the restaurant. Busy in 2004, its first season, this place has already earned high recommendations for the haddock served with a caramelized onion crust and wild mushroom risotto ($18), the vegetable lasagne made with their own pasta ($17), and the rack of lamb stuffed with mushrooms and basil ($28). Tourists can find Lobster Pie, baked in a crust with a lovely sauce ($24). Starters have included yellowfin tuna sashimi with a soy-sesame slaw ($12) and Maine crabcakes ($8).

Fudge Pie looks like the way to go for dessert, but there are other pies made with fresh fruit, and cobblers and crisps (all $6).

# Wine, Fish, Farms, and Ice Cream

### Chick Farm (207-985-2787), 779 Chick Crossing Road (two miles from Route 9A).
Organic vegetables and fruit, fresh eggs year-round. Call for hours.

### Moody Cow (207-646-1919), 259 Post Road.
Ice cream, and a deli that makes standard cold-cut and salad sandwiches.

### Pine Tree Place Home & Garden (207-646-7545), 411 Post Road.
A farm stand here sells produce from local Maine farmers in-season. The farm stand opens May 1 and stays open till the end of October. A deli, selling locally made pies and breads, also operates in the summer, making sandwiches with a Maine theme from its own baked meats, as well as salads and soups. Carpe Diem coffee from a Maine entrepreneur is ready to pour, and wine is for sale too. This gift store and farm market is one of the oldest in southern Maine, in business since 1928. An outside café is anticipated for 2005. The tagline "from apples to Zinfandel" fixes their ads in readers' minds.

### Scoop Deck (207-646-5150), 6 Eldridge Road, just off Route 1.
Open daily late May through September; 11–11 in July and August, 11:30–9 or 10 after Labor Day. The ice cream comes from Thibodeau Farms in Saco; you order inside a handsome white-clapboard barn, where Doug Erskine, the owner for 20 years, can scoop up one of over 40 flavors or give you a frozen yogurt or sorbet. "What's Triple Chocolate Ecstasy?" a customer asked when we were there. She sat on the outside benches with her cone and found out.

### Seafare Market (207-646-5460), 231 Post Road (Route 1).
Open daily 10–7:30, closing earlier in the off-season. Fresh seafood and prepared items like crabcakes, lobster cakes, and lobster-stuffed shrimp ($2.99 each).

Everything from haddock to swordfish, sole, and tuna; and shellfish, from oysters to littlenecks to soft-shell clams, from up and down the coast. House-cured gravlax—salmon pressed and cured with sugar, salt, and dill for 48 hours, then sliced paper thin—goes for $5 for a 3-ounce package.

**Spiller Farm (207-985-2575), Route 9A, 4 miles west of Route 1 at 1123 Branch Road.**
The farm store is open year-round, and pick-your-own strawberries, peas, raspberries, beans, apples, and pumpkins are available in-season. The phone number gives a recorded message about picking availability. Tours given.

**The Wells Farmer's Market** runs from the end of May to the end of September on Wednesday from 2–6 at the Wells Town Hall parking lot on Sanford Road (Route 109), a half mile from Route 1.

# York, Cape Neddick, York Beach and York Harbor

## Clay Hill Farm
(207) 361-2272
220 Clay Hill Road, Cape Neddick
www.clayhillfarm.com
Open daily for dinner at 5:30
Entrées $18 to $26
Reservations recommended

☛ *Fine dining with an emphasis on serving meals people like*

This is a professional place, with a highly trained staff and a lot of experience serving good, traditional meals. The gardens are well kept, and the 30 acres that surround the building foster trees and wildlife; the National Wildlife Federation praised the business for making its land a bird sanctuary.

Many customers find their own civilized refuge on arriving here.

Scallops wrapped in bacon with a pineapple dipping sauce ($7.50), shrimp cocktail ($8), crabcakes ($8), and baked artichoke dip ($7) are on the appetizer list. They are followed up with entrées that include a seafood scampi of lobster, shrimp, and scallops sautéed in white wine with lemon butter served on linguine

($25) and pretzel-encrusted halibut steak ($19). The filet mignon is served with a mushroom-Stroganoff sauce and whipped potatoes ($26).

Desserts include white chocolate crème brûlée, chocolate mousse, and lemon sherbet. A fine wine list, with an award from *Wine Spectator,* offers lots of good choices at reasonable prices, along with splurges like Opus One Cabernet Sauvignon ($180).

## Fazio's
**(207) 363-7019**
**38 Woodbridge Road, York Village**
www.fazios.com
Open for dinner Monday through Thursday 4–9, Friday and Saturday 4–9:30, Sunday 3–9
Entrées $15 to $19

☛ *Classic Italian meals, a pizzeria next door, and homemade pasta*

This place has won a lot of praise for its good Italian cooking, great marinara, and homemade pasta. Located just outside of York Village, the yellow dining room makes a fine destination on any night of the year; you can start your meal with *arancini,* a Sicilian rice ball stuffed with ground beef and peas, served with tomato sauce ($6).

The entrées are reasonably priced and wide ranging, with the option of simply enjoying the pasta with a sauce ($6 for a small serving, $9 for a large), a perfect choice for the child tagging along.

Linguini with clam sauce, garlic, and a little hot pepper ($11), meat lasagna ($10), and manicotti with ricotta filling and tomato sauce ($10) are three classics from southern Italy. Seafood Tecchia ($16), scallops and shrimp cooked in a white wine and lemon-garlic sauce on linguini, would go over well with someone who simply cannot eat enough seafood; and the daily ravioli, the veal *piccatta,* or the *bistecca* could take care of anyone else in the family. Or order an eggplant Parmesan sub next door at **La Stalla Pizzeria (207-363-1718),** or an Aegean pizza with pesto, sliced tomatoes, artichoke hearts, and olives with fontina and ricotta ($10.95 for a 10-inch pie).

## Frankie and Johnny's Natural Foods
**(207) 363-1909**
**1594 Route 1, Cape Neddick**
www.frankie-johnnys.com

Open Wednesday through Sunday 5–9 in July and August, Thursday through
Sunday 5–9 April through June, and September through November
Entrées $17 to $27
No credit cards, BYOB

☛ *A healthy food place with vegan options and great meat*

With entrées like blackened pork Delmonico with pear cream sauce ($19.75)
and grilled salmon with mango-pineapple salsa ($19.95), this place can feed the
heart and soul. Brightly painted rooms make it cheerful, and the fresh pasta is a
crowd-pleaser.

## Flo's Hotdogs
No phone
Route 1, Cape Neddick
Open for lunch
Entrées $1

☛ *Hot dogs served with a secret sauce
and mayo in a low building*

A recipe available on the Internet for Flo's special sauce calls for yellow onions, molasses,
white vinegar, brown sugar, crushed red pep-
pers, and hot sauce. Boil it up and slather it on, or stop at Flo's, where they do
it for you. Flo, who ran this eatery for 41 years, died in 2000 at the age of 92;
her daughter-in-law Gail carries on. Schultz hot dogs, soda, milk, chips, long
lines, and discipline.

## J. Ellen's Wine Bar
(207) 363-3751
Meadowbrook Plaza at 647 Route 1, York
Open Tuesday through Saturday for lunch 11:30–2:30, for dinner 5–10
Entrées $15 to $27
Reservations are a good idea on weekends

☛ *A good place to get to know some new wines, and a new friend*

Diners can enjoy entrées like a haddock *de la mer,* with shrimp, scallops, and lobster cream sauce ($21.50); rack of lamb ($23); or a seasonal butternut and sage
ravioli with brandied apple-butter sauce and roasted wild mushrooms ($19.50).

Around 17 red wines and 19 whites are offered by the glass, and 8 to 10 flights of three 2-ounce wine tastings change with the seasons. There is also a full martini menu and bar, with everything from watermelon martinis and Heath Bar martinis to a blood orange cosmo with Grey Goose vodka ($8.50). Try out one of the wine dinners; they start with hors d'oeuvres and champagne, and one in fall 2004 featured Australian wines and cost $65 per person.

## Stonewall Kitchen Café
**(207) 351-2719**
**Stonewall Lane, York**
Open for take-out Monday through Saturday 8–6, Sunday 9–6; café dining
Monday through Saturday 11–3, Sunday brunch 10–3
Entrées $11 to $14

☛ *Popular for its great food, this is the place everyone is talking about.*

Stonewall Kitchen was already famous for wonderful jams and other condiments, made since 1991, as well as an ever-growing list of mixes, desserts, and other foods. It was already a popular tourist stop, because so much of what it sold was offered as free samples in the stores, here in York, in Portland, and in Camden, to name just those few. The café opened in 2004 at its present headquarters in York and serves many dishes made with the mixes and jams, vinegars, mustards, and other delicious things you can now buy, after a meal, next door.

A lobster salad BLT, on toasted brioche with basil aioli and served with coleslaw, was on the fall café menu ($15). Grilled pork loin with lemon smashed potatoes and a tamarind velouté ($14) and a Tuscan sandwich with fresh mozzarella, tomato, cucumber, and basil aioli ($10) were other choices. Chai ice cream with bittersweet chocolate sauce and cranberry crumb torte make fine finishes.

## Wild Willy's Burgers
**(207) 363-9924**
**765 Route 1, York**
Open for lunch and dinner year-round
Entrées around $4
No credit cards

☛ *Beloved for delicious burgers and freshly made french fries*

The menu has focus. Burgers. Fries. Some of the burgers come with sautéed onions, others with barbeque sauce, but every one has withstood the test of customer satisfaction to stay on the menu, and to bring customers back over and over. Order at the counter and wait for your number. Enjoy.

## Cape Neddick Lobster Pound
**(207) 363-5471**
**Shore Road, Cape Neddick**
**Open daily in the summer for lunch and dinner**
**Entrées $15 to $24**

☛ *A local hangout because of its popular seafood and dinner menu*

A sea of SUVs fills the parking lots here on summer nights, when the outside deck is warm enough for an alfresco lobster. The big inside dining room is always ready for customers hungry for seafood. There's plenty of other things to feed kids and lobster haters, but for the rest of us the Shore Dinner, with steamers or mussels and a hot boiled lobster, is all you can ask for.

If fried fish is what you want, ask for the Captain's Platter—fried shrimp, clams, scallops, and haddock ($19.95).

## Breakfast and Lunch, Bakeries, and Nigerian Pygmy Goats

**Carla's Bakery and Café (207-363-4637), 241 York Street, York**
Breakfast from 7 (but sometimes the door is open at 6:30) and lunch until 2,

*Wild Willy's Burgers*

*Cape Neddick Lobster Pound*

open until 3 Monday through Friday, Saturday brunch 7–12, closed Sunday. Carla's is enjoying its eighth successful year, bolstered by an article in *Gourmet* that focused on the owner's flair with baking—try the almond scones—and meals like blue cheese meatloaf wrap or turkey pot pie with salad ($7). Molasses cookies, cappuccino bars, or tiramisu would all taste wonderful at the tables lined up along the wall across from the counter.

### Food and Co. Gourmet Market and Café (207-363-0900), 1 York Street, York

Open Monday through Saturday 8–6, closed Sunday. Cheese, olives, sandwiches, take-out dinners, and wine. The café serves lunch from 11 to 4; join the club and get your tenth sandwich free. Salad plates with hummus, falafel, or Caesar, are also served, or you can order a serving of any of the prepared foods, like roasted chicken, heated up.

### Pie in the Sky Bakery (207-363-2656), 1 River Road (Route 1), Cape Neddick.

Open Thursday through Monday 9–6, closed Thursday October through early May; closed two weeks after Thanksgiving and the first six weeks of the year.

Thanksgiving is the biggest week; when Nancy Stern sells as many as 600 pies. Custom orders from holiday special menus and regular menus are available. Blueberry, apple, and pumpkin are top sellers; variations include pumpkin-pecan pie, sour cream blueberry, jumble berry (blueberry, blackberry, and raspberry), and chocolate pie. Prices range around $22 for a 10-inch pie that serves eight.

### Old Mountain Farm (207-361-2126; www.oldmountainfarm.com), 60 Old Mountain Road, Cape Neddick

Nigerian pygmy dairy goats for custom-ordered milk; call first.

**The York Farmer's Market** runs mid-June through mid-October, Saturday 9 AM–noon, and is located at the Greater York Region Chamber of Commerce near the York exit off I-95, next to the Stonewall Kitchen Factory on Route 1.

**CHAPTER 2**

# The Portland Region

**T**HIS BIG CHAPTER COVERS THE COAST from Biddeford to Freeport, with Maine's largest city, and its varied assortment of places to eat, right in the middle.

One of my predecessors in this line of work, Cynthia Hacinli, who wrote about Maine restaurants in her 1991 book *Down Eats,* reported that the city fathers said Portland had more restaurants per capita than San Francisco. Not true, many others have since argued.

But that conveys the gist of our enthusiasm.

A lot of Portland's residents go out to eat or have something to do with making dinner for others—growing, selling, or preparing the food; serving it up, eating it, and always talking about it. Some restaurants, like Street and Company and Back Bay Grill, have been serving dinner since Hacinli wrote about them. Fore Street, too, is an institution, a revelation to newcomers and a pleasure that the rest of us rely on, especially in the cold winter.

Even the city's best places shun dress codes, having chosen to welcome all their customers, while those diners who like to dress elegantly can outfit themselves to the nines, more for their own pleasure than to conform to demands. Some places don't survive the cold winters, and their empty storefronts are regretted by the faithful, but not frequent enough, customers—Michaela's, for example, where I ate delicious glass eels, and Aubergine, whose chef may be having an influence farther up the coast. But everyone involved in making these places work, from the dreamers who sink their money into a new design to the chefs who insist on high-quality ingredients to the customers who praise and criticize to the servers who can suffer from both the kitchen and the dining room, are trying for the Holy Grail of a night out: the bliss of a perfect meal.

May they get it right, just like Mrs. Dalloway.

# Bar Mills

**Snell Family Farm 207-929-6166, 207-929-5318; www.snellfamily farm.com), P.O. Box 326, Route 112 (or 1000 River Road in Buxton).** Open 9–6 daily in-season. Produce from this big farm comes to Portland's farmer's markets Saturday and Wednesday mornings, but visiting the farm is fun, and you can pick your own apples. The pumpkin selection in the fall is huge. In 2004 you could also pick your own potatoes off the ground after they were dug. Open on Maine Maple Sunday, a Sunday in late March, for a glimpse of sap-boiling operations, too.

# Biddeford

## Bebe's Burritos
**(207) 283-4222**
**140 Main Street**
Hospitality—Friendly counter service; customizing the order is okay; and the meals are brought out to you
Open for lunch and dinner Tuesday through Thursday 11–7, Friday and Saturday 11–9
Entrées $4 to $7

☛ *Good burritos and other basics with fresh ingredients*

This café across from the discount store Reny's is the most colorful spot in downtown Biddeford. The wall on the left as you enter is decorated with a desert scene; the order counter lies in the back, past red walls with blue green trim and exposed brick. I ordered a guacamole tostada ($5.25), two corn tortillas topped with guacamole, mango salsa, lots of lettuce, and a hot chili sauce, which all worked together to make a heap of good stuff. My friend had the chicken burrito ($6.45), filled with the soft stewed chicken we'd encountered at the Mexican Restaurant in Harrington (see page 266), a touchstone of authenticity. The rest of it—beans, cheese, lettuce, tomatoes, scallions, and sour cream—made it taste good. Aluminum foil and tins with plastic cutlery sit by the cash register for take-out. A full bar, and occasional weekend entertainment, round out the scene.

## Buffleheads
(207) 284-6000
122 Hills Beach Road
www.buffleheadsrestaurant.com
Open daily in summer for lunch 11:30–2, dinner 5:30–9;call for hours
off-season
Entrées $9 to $23

☛ *A family-run restaurant with quality food and a place in locals' hearts*

Watch the sea through almost every window, and in the summer enjoy the outside patio; but rest assured the ingredients here are fresh, and the brownie dessert is homemade. A restaurant garden grows some of the vegetables, there's a lot of seafood, and the rack of lamb and baked manicotti keep the rest of the folks happy.

Crabcakes with Cajun mayonnaise ($8.95) make a good starter, and farfalle with scallops and shrimp mixed with black olives, plum tomatoes, and basil ($16.95) would follow that nicely. Hazelnut-encrusted rack of lamb could be great on a cold night. Spaghetti with marinara will take care of the children.

Directions are provided on the restaurant's good Web site, and signs are up on the road to guide you down to Hill's Beach, a little off the beaten track, but not at a place you'll regret seeking.

# Cape Elizabeth

## The Audubon Room, Inn by the Sea
(207) 767-0888
40 Bowery Beach Road
www.innbythesea.com
Hospitality—Welcoming and attentive to every wish
Open daily for breakfast, lunch, and dinner in summer, dinner only in winter
Entrées $24 to $29
Reservations recommended

☛ *A special-occasion place with good food*

We arrived half an hour before our reservation and sipped gin and tonics as we sat in deep cushions on a couch in a wide landing on the stairs, overlooking this big inn's pool and lawn. Then we carried our drinks outside and strolled past the gardens, with their dark purple lettuces tucked in amid the more conventional bedding plants, to a boardwalk that takes you down to the sea, still bitter cold in June.

With our hands chilled a half hour later, it felt good to retreat to the dining room with its Audubon prints and surrounding porch. The peach walls and a carpet patterned with small scrolls of leaves cocooned us while we looked at the lawn and its tidy parterres, and the ocean filling the horizon, from a more comfortable distance.

Our sharpened appetites made a wide bowl of Atlantic surf clam and parsnip soup, a smooth buttery puree with a zigzag of sorrel cream across the top ($8), perfect. Another appetizer on the always-changing menu was the Maine Crab Tower, more like a dense hillock of crabmeat as befits our old and eroded coastal landscape, with a citrus, cucumber, and avocado salsa ($12). The richness of the avocado did its classic dance with the crab, and both sparkled with the lemon and orange juice.

A lobster bisque with tarragon and dry sherry ($10) and a spinach, mushroom, sweet onion, and quail egg salad with poppy seed vinaigrette ($8) were other choices.

A server with obsequious ways—that word originally meant a good thing, and I mean it that way too—set crusty rolls that proved to be made with dried tomatoes and cheese on our plates with silver tongs. The rolls vanished quickly with the dill-sprinkled butter.

The recorded piano music didn't distract, but at the same time, when a moment's silence brought it to our attention, I found it impressive—and that was also the key to the atmosphere, with its unobtrusive elegance.

The sesame seared deep sea scallops on squid ink linguini with mango salsa ($29) was more of a show-off than the Black Angus tenderloin, served in a merlot bordelaise sauce ($29), but not more delicious. A first impression of disappointment on the sight of the rice served alongside the tender, perfectly rare meat gave way as its flavors won me over. The pilaf contained dark grains like wheat berries that were toothsome, and the broth that made it all tender was clearly flavored and freshly made.

The food at the Inn by the Sea gave substantial pleasure.

## The Good Table
**(207) 799-4663**
**527 Oceanhouse Road (Route 77)**
Hospitality—Informal and friendly

Open for three meals Tuesday through Saturday 8 AM–9 PM in summer,
11 AM–9 PM in winter, Sunday 8–3 year-round
Entrées $10 to $12 (twin lobsters $24), lunch up to $11

☛ *A local institution, for families and visitors, with Greek specialties*

A fire that burned the old Good Table down in the summer of 2001 brought such love and encouragement from the community that the restaurant owners needed only seconds to decide to rebuild.

Their new, larger building, just south of the left turn to Two Lights Road, is a place families depend on for good food that pleases kids and grown-ups. It's a great place for lunch, with specials like hot pastrami and Swiss on rye or hummus with fresh vegetables on a tomato tortilla, as well as standard temptations, like the gyros sandwich of spiced beef and lamb, onions, tomato, and *tzatziki* sauce in a pita ($5.75). There's spanakopita, of course, and fish-and-chips. The last item, big succulent pieces of fried haddock with french fries and coleslaw ($10), always reliably well made, is a favorite, and we also like to get the Greek salad, with a ton of crunchy lettuce topped with feta and olives ($6.50). A breakfast menu lists the expectable, along with a few foreign takes, like Greek soul food, incorporating feta, onions, tomatoes, and peppers with the scrambled eggs ($7 if you add Greek sausage).

Dinner offers up lots of fried fish and clams, baked haddock, grilled meat, and salads, all low key and delicious. The screened back porch comes into its glory on summer nights, hung with strings of lights and ceiling fans, and would be a good spot to enjoy a dessert like the too-good bread pudding with caramel sauce, or ginger pound cake with peaches.

Winter nights inside the main dining room, with its old pictures, collection of women's hats, and light wood wainscoting, are almost as nice. And if you're Greek, there are parking spots reserved just for you to the right of the front door.

## The Lobster Shack at Two Lights
(207) 799-1677
225 Two Lights Road
www.lobstershack-twolights.com
Hospitality—Line up at the door for counter service; eat inside or out
Open from the end of March to October daily for lunch and dinner 11–8
Entrées $4 to $22

☛ *One of the best sites for outdoor lobster dinners, with fried seafood and hamburgers too*

A winner for most spectacular setting, the Lobster Shack has been around since 1968 and is now run by members of the Porch family, grandsons of the first owner. The site, at the end of Two Lights Road, next to a lighthouse, is beautiful, overlooking rocks that tumble down to the surf from the edge of the picnic table area, but there isn't a lot of room for cars. Crowds at lunch and dinner can jam the parking lot. Try to arrive early or late to avoid the problem—and drive slowly through the little neighborhood as you wind toward the point so the year-round residents can relax.

You order and pay for your food through a door on the right of the small building, using the time you wait in line to decide between the bowl of lobster stew ($10.95), the lobster salad, the lobster roll, the lobster dinner, or the lobster dinner with an extra lobster ($28 on our visit and changing with market prices).

Of course you can also eat the good fried clams, fixed with crumbs and cooked in soybean oil, as is all the fried food, according to the sign outside. A cheeseburger goes for $2.60, hot dogs are $1.75, but everyone adds in the french fries or onion rings for a couple of dollars more. A veggie burger is available. A glass case by the cashier shows off whoopee pies and other desserts. Once you have your receipt with your order number, it's time to explore; a loudspeaker can reach your ears within a fair distance of the building.

*A picnic at The Lobster Shack at Two Lights*

A leading cause of tension for families here are the same rocks that make such a beautiful foreground to the sea stretching out to the horizon. Figure on anyone under the age of 35 taking off on those rocks and decide beforehand if you can handle it. The cries of parents in full-throated panic attacks— "Don't go any farther! Come back right now!"—are common.

Of course, once your kids are grown up enough, you don't need to watch them so closely. Or do you? Storms that bring huge waves to this shore also attract spectators of all ages who like to creep as close as possible, and people have mistaken the safety range. Although it happens rarely, people have died here. So watch out for your parents, and your friends too, and don't let yourself tempt the sea either, when it has such an unimaginable strength in its stormy moods.

*Bakery*

## The Cookie Jar (207-799-0671), 554 Shore Road.

Open 6–6 Monday through Saturday, 7–5 on Sunday. Just across the South Portland line, this little place does a big business providing local residents' sweet teeth with everything they could desire. Among the many cookies the raspberry-filled and the macaroons stand out. The little tables in the shop's windows are a perfect place to enjoy a cream horn, or another favorite, the Bismarck, a raspberry-and-cream-filled sugar doughnut. Cakes are made to order, and cupcakes are ready at hand.

*Farm Markets*

## Alewives' Brook Farm (207-799-7743), 83 Old Ocean House Road.

Open daily 9–6. Lobsters are sold here, as well as corn on the cob. The lobster season is longer, as is the season for soft-shell clams and the whelks or "snails" that the owner sells to the local Asian market. The whelks come up in the lobster traps along with the lobsters. Strawberries, beets, radishes, lettuce, and other vegetables are available in-season.

## Maxwell's Farm Market (207-799-2940; strawberry hotline: 207-799-3383; www.maxwellsfarm.com), 185 Spurwink Road.

Open Monday through Saturday 9–6:30 May through November. Big pick-your-own strawberry fields are a short drive away on Two Lights Road. The season can run somewhere between mid-June and mid-July—call first to see if the market is open, because a cold spring can make the season late and a hot June can end it fast. The last day of the 2004 season was July 26, when the berries were selling at $1.35 a pound (no credit cards in the strawberry fields). The market itself offers loads of sweet corn, great lettuces, and all the pumpkins you can imagine. Next to the store is a field of flowers where you can cut your own bouquet, after checking in at the store.

# Take-Out and Counter Service

**Kettle Cove Take-out and Dairy Bar** (207-799-3533), Route 77
(south of the Two Lights Road turnoff).
Everyone relies on this place in the summer for homemade ice cream, especially
after going to Kettle Cove or Crescent Beach. The fried haddock sandwich and
other take-out standards are good too.

**Two Lights General Store** (207-347-7165), 517 Ocean House Road
(Route 77).
Pizza and sandwiches for lunch, and coffee and breakfast dishes, can be enjoyed
at tables inside or at picnic tables outside, or taken to the beach.

# Cumberland

## Chebeague Island Inn
**(207) 846-5155**
**61 South Road**
www.chebeagueislandinn.com
Hospitality—Congenial and unpretentious, in a comfortable seaside inn
Open daily in summer for breakfast 8–9:30, lunch 12–2 (brunch 10–12 on Sunday), and dinner 6–9 Sunday through Thursday, until 10 Friday and Saturday;
call for off-season hours.
Entrées $18 to $36
Reservations recommended, especially on weekends

☛ *Great meals in a beautiful classic island inn that's relaxed and refined*

New owners have transformed the Chebeague Island Inn, and it feels as if its best
days are just getting underway. The wide porch looking over Casco Bay toward
Yarmouth has a timeless quality—so we forgot the time. Under its pastel, robin's
egg blue ceiling, we sat on a wicker couch and drank a glass of Cellar No. 8 merlot—"Not your average merlot," our wry server advised, and our mouths agreed
when they tasted the dense depth of fruit in that dry wine. On a rapidly cool-
ing Monday evening in July, with the insistent wind turning the corner of the
porch a few feet away, we decided against eating on the screened porch and
walked into the dining room a while past our reservation time, after relaxing
indeed.

The room's dark, beaded-board paneling placed the atmosphere in the eternal summer of Maine summer cottages.

I liked the quiet tranquility, accentuated by the gray water stretching out and the distant stack of the Wyman power plant with its flashing warning light. It's the perfect place to get to know someone new. But the executive chef, Allan Fisher, said later that over a hundred brunches had been served the previous Sunday, and innkeeper Martha Dumont said all eight of the inn's moorings had been used by guests tying up, and a ninth had been borrowed from the harbormaster. The word is getting out that this is one of the boating crowd's favorite destinations.

Getting there without your own boat is possible by ferry, either in 15 minutes from Cousins Island or an hour and a half from Portland. Parking at a lot on Route 1 for the Cousins Island Ferry cost $10, and round-trip tickets were $11 in 2004; so this might work best as a day trip, with a visit to the island golf course or a bike route thrown in.

The food is worth it. We started with a peekytoe crab napoleon, a squat tower of crabmeat mixed with crème fraîche layered on disks of beefsteak tomato and embellished with swirls of balsamic "molasses" and olive oil. Fisher has a source in Maine for most of his ingredients, with his own private ferry to ship them across

*A corner of the porch at the Chebeague Island Inn*

the channel. The crab was perfectly fresh and the tomatoes delicious, even early in the season. My new friend had a salad of Colson Farm organic baby greens that was simple and good.

Dinner was Pacific coast wild salmon with Thai red curry sauce, and a special, roasted sea bass on broccoli with sautéed lobster and portobello mushrooms, all in a spicy glaze.

The Thai sauce held a choir of harmonizing spices in its sweet-hot hands, a balance that Thailanders create with a mortar and pestle. Indeed, when Fisher came by our table at the end of our meal to say hello, he said he had ground the coriander seeds in a mortar before mixing them with other spices, ginger, garlic, and coconut milk and heating them all gently to make the flavors bloom.

A peach crisp with custardy vanilla ice cream, not too sweet, with the peach peels left on the slivers of still al dente fruit, gave us another reason to return, soon.

## Farmer's Market

**Cumberland Farmer's Markets** happen in two locations. The one in Cumberland is in Cumberland Center at Greely High School on Route 9, every Saturday from 8:30 to noon. The same farmers go to Falmouth's Shops at Falmouth Village on Route 1 every Wednesday 3–6. The season is from late May until mid-September. My favorite farmer is Sally Merrill, whose Sunrise Acres Farm grows beets, lettuce, heirloom tomatoes, and all the greens you can eat along with the meat from its farm-raised chickens, lambs, and beef cattle.

## Falmouth

**Ricetta's Brick Oven Pizzaria (207-781-3100) 240 Route 1.**
This is a good spot for lunch, because they serve a pizza *and* a Caesar salad buffet. Among the many combinations, apple pie pizza stands out for dessert. (They also have a location in **South Portland at 29 Western Avenue; 207-775-7400.**)

**The Falmouth Farmer's Market** is held on Wednesday 3–6 late May through mid-October at the Shops at Falmouth Village at Route 1 and Depot Road.

## Conundrum

**(207) 865-0303**
**117 Route 1, Freeport**
Hospitality—Welcoming and outgoing
Open for dinner and late-night eats Tuesday 4:30–10, Wednesday
and Thursday 4:30–11, and Friday and Saturday 4:30–midnight
Entrées $9 to $15

☛ *With more than 500 wines, and modest prices, this is a place to try
something new.*

Our server offered us a free splash of any wine we wanted to try, so we tried both
a Cline Ancient Vines Zinfandel from California and the Shooting Star Blue
Franc, made from Lemberger grapes in Washington State. Since the Blue Franc
seemed to shrivel the inside of my mouth and I adored the darkness of the Cline,
that is what I drank half a glass of, 2.5 ounces, for the accommodating price of
$4.25. The Blue Franc might have simply needed to breathe. My friend enjoyed
a half glass of Tommasi Pinot Grigio for $3.25. We decided against eating in the
dining room, surrounded by blue walls and dark chairs, and instead sat outside
on a deck at a big wooden table; inside, guests were in full roar by 7 that
Wednesday, and more SUVs trolled the rear lot for parking spaces as we ate.

*Vincent Migliaccio, owner of Conundrum, in front of his extensive wine
collection*

The food is not—or wasn't that Wednesday—the reason to come here, although one of us announced that her Wolfe's Neck Farm burger ($8.50) was "divine." It came with spears of tender sweet potato too liberally sprinkled with dried thyme and a few hot pepper flakes.

Get the burger, or the cheese and pâté offerings, and concentrate on the wine. Owner Vincent Migliaccio said his place has the longest wine list in the state of Maine. What's more, you can go to the store next door and buy bottles of many of his selections. He said he charges less so people can try things out— as they certainly did when we visited. He said he pays the wholesale price for a bottle with the sale of two full glasses, unlike most restaurants, which pay for a bottle with the sale of one glass.

A bottle of Punter's Corner Shiraz from Coonawarra, Australia, for instance, sells for $26.10 on the shelf in neighboring Old World Gourmet (see page 62), a deli and wine store owned by Migliaccio's parents. In Conundrum, a glass of that wine costs $9.50, a half glass $5.25, and a bottle $38.

I can say from experience that the Portuguese Barros 20-year-old port that Conundrum sells for $8 a glass sells for $11 at Hugo's and $12 at Fore Street in Portland.

They aren't all cheap; Conundrum also lists a few 2000 Bordeaux, like a Haut Brion for $900 a bottle.

## Harraseeket Inn—Maine Dining Room and Broad Arrow Tavern

(207) 865-9377, 1-800-342-6423
162 Main Street
www.harraseeketInn.com
Hospitality—Well trained and on top of things
Open Monday through Saturday for breakfast 7–10:30 and lunch buffet
11:30–2 in the Broad Arrow Tavern; daily for dinner in the Maine Dining Room
5:30–9 (until 9:30 Friday and Saturday); Sunday brunch served from a buffet
in the drawing room 11:45–2; dinner is also available in the tavern.
Entrées $26 to $38

🍂 *A big, expansive place with large buffet-style dining and more formal dinners*

The Harraseeket Inn is big, and does business on a large scale. Its staff does an admirable job taking care of many people, from tourists staying at the inn for a "Serious Shopper" two-day visit to people passing through. It's what one lover of fine food I know calls a solid restaurant—both its more formal dining room and the dark green Broad Arrow Tavern.

We admire their posted philosophy, which advocates the use of local ingredients, from farm vegetables to oysters and mussels. On busy Sundays, when the drawing room turns into the setting of an elaborate brunch buffet, you can enjoy poached wild salmon and know you'll be avoiding the farmed variety. The Wolfe's Neck Farm meat a carver is slicing according to your preference is also raised without hormones or antibiotics.

This is a good place to bring a large group, since large groups do not faze the staff. But I wonder if the attention to detail is quite what it would be in a place more focused on individual dining.

The Sunday brunch, and the evening meals, are more gourmet in the old-fashioned sense of the word, complete with a taste of caviar and elaborate cheeses—you can get a chateaubriand for two with bordelaise sauce for $75. The pale dining room with antiques and fireplaces is handsome, and the view of the perfectly groomed gardens pleasant.

## Harraseeket Lunch and Lobster
**(207) 865-4888**
**36 Main Street, South Freeport**
Hospitality—Counter service with clear directions and clean picnic tables
Open daily 11–8:45 from the last weekend in April through Columbus Day
Entrées $9 to 19; lobster rolls $13.95. No credit cards accepted, but there's an ATM inside

☛ *Pretty waterside spot for well-made lobster rolls, lobster dinners, and seafood*

*Harraseeket Lunch and Lobster gets its deliveries from boats that tie up alongside it*

When things are hopping at Harraseeket Lunch, as they almost always are, the attendant in the parking lot will give you fair warning—"there is a 40-minute wait on all orders," she told us one sunny Wednesday in July. Even for a lobster roll? Even for a lobster roll. That's because they steam and shuck and mix the lobster meat right before they put it in

*A young girl makes her first acquaintance with a lobster at Harraseeket Lunch and Lobster*

the roll and send it out for you to eat.

But with everyone around you waiting for his or her order, this can be a convivial scene. A seat at one of the clean red picnic tables under the blue-and-white-striped awning has the shade you need, and the drink orders can be filled right away. As you wait you can get to know other travelers, like a couple from Dixfield, Maine, who come here once a year for a treat and who remembered the place before there was any awning and any deck. The husband, a retired trucker, went over to say hello to some people from Tennessee who had posed for a picture, wondering if they lived near one of his old routes.

"Is number 133 almost ready?" a 12-year-old boy who couldn't take the wait asked plaintively at the order window.

When the lobster roll came, in exactly 40 minutes, it was in a white paper bag and wrapped in a white napkin—a buttered and toasted roll that still felt warm, full of big pieces of fresh lobster in a light mayonnaise dressing. It tasted great, even though the others at the table are grousing about the small size. Although this one cost $13.95, it certainly had everything else going for it.

The location on the water allows you to watch the latest crate of lobsters being unloaded, and at another order window steamed lobster dinners are available. A friendly worker inside volunteered to show off a lobster for a woman with a camera, and a child reached out to touch the mysterious creatures that attract visitors from around the country and the world. It's summer in Maine.

## Breakfast, Lunch, and Informal Dinners

### Isabella's Sticky Buns Café and Bakery (207-865-6635) 2 School Street, Freeport.

Open daily at 7 AM, closing at 5 PM in summer, 3 PM in winter. Isabella's makes the good-for-you and so-delicious food you need to save your soul along

Freeport's outlet-lined Main Street. Just around a corner a block north of L.L. Bean, you can order a wrap made with a chicken salad that includes chicken, grapes, and Gorgonzola, or the popular You Ham, a panini warmed on a panini grill with roasted red peppers, sliced ham, cheddar, and cilantro pesto ($6.99).

Breakfast includes signature sticky buns, of course, and croissants, cinnamon swirls, muffins, and scones, or the eggs Benedict with portobello mushrooms and roasted red pepper substituted for the ham ($6.95) or with lobster ($11.95).

Many of his customers are local people, but according to owner Alex Caisse, "It's hard to not get the tourists in this town. You close your eyes and they appear." The tourists who come here are the lucky ones. Napkin art covers a huge bulletin board on one wall, and you're welcome to add to it. Messages tacked up come from all over the country, and the best artwork is saved in napkin art books you can look at during a visit.

### Old World Gourmet, Deli and Wine Shop (207-865-4477) 117 Route 1, Freeport.

Open Tuesday through Saturday 10–5, Mondays in July and August 10–3. The big selection at this deli means you can come here for a fancy sandwich assortment to throw a party for $5.50 a person, for chicken salad, Mediterranean and Greek salad roll-ups, and Genoa salami; it would be the perfect stop for a house guest who offered to provide lunch. I recommend the Mediterranean roll-up (half, $3.15; whole, $5.25), with its fresh tortilla and spicy contents, from the hummus to the roasted red peppers and havarti cheese. Grilled panini come hot from the grill and can be enjoyed here at one of the tables in the front of the store or wrapped to go. Soups, chowders, salads, and baked goods from pizzas to macaroons and choco-late chip cookies complete anyone's dream picnic, along with a bottle of great wine. This place is located by the tall statue known locally as the Big Indian, north of I-95's Exit 17.

### The Village Store (207-865-4230), 97 South Freeport Road, South Freeport.

A great sandwich place that also makes picnic lunches to order.

# Portland

## Back Bay Grill

(207) 772-8833
65 Portland Street
www.backbaygrill.com
Hospitality—Warm, inviting, swift, and competent
Open at 5 PM for bar service, seating at 5:30, Monday through Saturday
Entrées $19 to $35
Reservations recommended

☛ *A premier place to treat clients and friends*

The big mural on the wall, painted in the summer of 1993 when this restaurant opened in its down-at-the-heel neighborhood, sets a tone of pleasure and animation. The people depicted in the mural are eating steak and quiche, talking up a storm, hitching up a skirt, and grabbing hold of friends. In the real dining room, taupe walls and amber sconces share the scene with an ornate gold mirror and carpeting patterned with swirls of leaves.

Back Bay Grill has been feeding its appreciative customers for 12 years now, enduring flush times and the dot.com bust, and all the while charging prices that vie with Hugo's for the most expensive in town.

Their customers think the great food is worth it, a terrific recommendation in itself.

A newly expanded bar has made room for people looking for a cocktail, and one of the delights there is the blue gin martini with blue-cheese-stuffed olives. We were offered truffle or curry popcorn to accompany our drinks, and enjoyed the curry version, but relished the olives most of all.

On another night, an appetizer made like everything else here, with sophistication and skill, introduced me to the best crabcake I've ever had. Sitting high and wide, a dark golden brown, in a liquid coaster of lemon-pepper crème fraîche, the marvel elucidated crab to the exclusion of almost all else. A bite of the cucumber salad in between mouthfuls of the hot crab fixed me up for bite after wonderful bite.

Even though few places have started going in for fruity accompaniments to seafood, my glass of Domaine Zind-Humbrecht Gewürztraminer, from Alsace ($13.50), a golden wine that smelled like honeysuckle, worked with the crab and pleased with its sweetness.

A different wine, Toad Hollow Chardonnay ($7.50) sent up a far simpler aroma and was refreshing and plain between mouthfuls of fried sweetbreads. The big wine list, 20 kinds by the glass, will fascinate any snob and regale the rest of us with a lot of new possibilities.

The veal sweetbreads revealed their dense smooth white texture, so toothsome under a thin crust. The red grapes had been thoughtfully, if maniacally, peeled, removing any chance of an acid interruption to all the rich pleasure of the sweetbreads and parsnip puree enriched with a dark meat jus and bits of bacon.

Chowder, and salads, and mussels, also figured on the appetizer list, and a romaine salad was served with the leaves layered on top of each other like a pagoda.

The Scottish salmon entrée paired with a lobster citrus salad ($24) gave one of us an appropriate reward for reaching her tenth wedding anniversary (her fresh berries with crème fraîche had "Congratulations" written in chocolate on her plate rim, a friendly touch on the restaurant's own initiative). She called the thick piece of tender fish fabulous, and extolled the crabmeat salad, adding that her husband loved the Vidalia onion soup.

Filet mignon, rack of lamb, double pork chops, and a chicken stuffed with chorizo and rice all beckoned that night, from a menu that changes frequently. Later we remembered another friend's contention that the crème brûlée was fantastic. But there is no resisting something like roasted banana rum ice-cream swans in pooled chocolate, if only to toast the imagination of the chefs whose creations take flight.

# Bibo's Madd Apple Café
**(207) 774-9698**
**23 Forest Avenue**
Hospitality—Informal and responsive
Open for lunch Wednesday through Friday 11:30–2, for Sunday brunch 11–2, and for dinner Wednesday through Saturday 5:30–9, on Sunday 4–8
Entrées $15 to $19
Reservations best during the theater season

☞ *Inventive, good entrées in an arty environment*

Bibo's Madd Apple Café sits next door to the Portland Stage Company and gets most of its business during the weeks shows are being performed there. That makes it a good place to go off-season to escape the summer crowds farther downtown, and its food will delight anyone with an appetite.

Bibo's wine list features domestic bottles and offers a reserve list in the back for pricier bottles like a 1998 T-Vines Syrah ($60). Thirteen wines can be ordered by the glass.

I started off with a glass of Four Vines Zinfandel ($6.95), a smooth wine with a wallop that worked ideally with the hot goat cheese "medallion," a disk of smooth cheese inside a thin crisp crust that brought goat cheese's raison d'être to the fore the way pizza has been doing with mozzarella for generations. A heap of sliced, cooked portobello mushrooms and a circle of red pepper puree completed the dish. My companion chose the black bean and rice cakes with a pineapple tomato salsa and coconut sour cream, a generous serving that unfortunately overwhelmed her appetite for any more dinner.

The entrées were big, including a half chicken on lo mein noodles with vegetables, a meal that came home with us, mostly uneaten, in a plastic container, and my two thick slices of crusted pork loin on a mound of Gorgonzola polenta that carried off the marriage of pungent and bland to create a whole new, delicious entity. A glass of Ercavio Tempralli Cabernet Sauvignon ($4.95), mild on the palette and less aggressive than the zinfandel, washed down the avocado-lime beurre blanc and pork until that sated my appetite. When a nearby couple ordered three appetizers for their dinner, I realized they had a better idea.

But how then to explain the desserts, which both of us ate up without difficulty? Truly, appetite is irrational.

The lemon tart ($6) was a rectangle of gelled lemon curd surmounted by a cumulus of whipped cream and lots of blueberries. On the plate red raspberry and orange-mango purees were used to create a design of four striped crowns on each side and gave the dish elegance. The crème brûlée ($6) met with approval by an expert, who called it the best in the state of Maine, and her plate also held zigzags of fruit puree, all wiped up by her aggressive spoon. The dessert list looked like a destination in itself, including chocolate banana bread pudding cake, very chocolaty, our server said; apple pie egg rolls; and a chocolate espresso buzzicle with whipped cream and macadamia nuts. That might work before a show without any sugar letdown.

With its cantaloupe walls, fuchsia trim, and blue-and-green tablecloths, Bibo's is an exuberant setting for its well-made food—and the quantities may be more welcome in the winter when appetites grow sharp.

# Blue Spoon

(207) 773-1116
89 Congress Street
Hospitality: Businesslike and competent
Open for lunch and dinner 12–9 Tuesday through Saturday, for brunch 9:30–2
on Sunday
Entrées $10 to $14
Reservations for parties of 6 or more only

☞ *Elegant meals for modest prices*

This popular restaurant's eight-table dining room runs along its storefront at the top of Munjoy Hill, along with a short marble bar. A C-bolt, with a nut twirled up both ends, swinging in the ear of the woman who seated us didn't distract from the happy mood fizzing in the room, with its ochre walls and oversized charcoal drawings of women with smooth hairdos.

Owner and chef David Iovino opened the place with the idea of making high quality food without charging a ton of money. He told us he was taking morels off the menu, for instance, because they were getting too expensive, but they'd worked well earlier in the year.

With a background at Savoy in New York, a restaurant that emphasizes green market, seasonal produce, Iovino is intent on finding local sources for his good food.

Artisan bread from One Fifty Ate, a bakery and café in South Portland (see page 98), came with black-peppered olive oil and a dish of chopped eggplant and red peppers, accompanied by a smooth inky Rioja from Logrona ($8) I'd ordered from the modest list of wines.

A little while later, as my companion, a pasta hound from the age of six months, forked rigatoni, cheese, and marinara into her entranced mouth, she was bitterly regretting the four fat slices of oil-soaked country white she'd already eaten. The pasta dish, *timballo,* arrived molded into a dome covered by thin slices of eggplant, with a sauce enriched by ricotta ($10).

A seafood stew with a few mussels, a few clams, shrimp, and chunks of salmon and potato sat in a salty, translucent broth with parsley and a few spinach leaves, a perfect portion, at a perfect $14, that wafted an aroma like incense of the sea.

A party of four skinny women beside us, two in their 50s and two in their 20s, relished the big hamburgers and large bowls of mussels with lemon and garlic ($7) on the simple, satisfying menu.

Vegan and vegetarian dishes are offered, including a vegetarian goat cheese gratin and a vegan balsamic asparagus salad. With a constantly changing menu reflecting what looked good at Harbor Fish Market and nearby farms, the restaurant motto—"Food from friends, family, and travels"—sums it up.

# Cinque Terre
**(207) 347-6154**
**36 Wharf Street**
www.cinqueterremaine.com
Hospitality—Good natured and enthusiastic
Open daily for dinner at 5:30 PM
Entrées $17 to $25, but multicourse Italian meals are encouraged
Reservations recommended

☛ *A place to experience the soul food of northern Italy*

Cinque Terre has undertaken a difficult challenge—to draw Mainers, and their visitors, into another culture. Northern Italian meals with many courses, pasta or risotto or gnocchi always preceding the meat or fish and the antipasti before that, are distinctly foreign and a hard sell when your customers want one or at most two courses. Cinque Terre tried to make it happen with half portions, but then, our server told us, that brought ordering a meal to a slow crawl.

Now a new menu provides portions in between full and half, with the wait staff still gently encouraging guests to try a few dishes, while giving wise insight into the long, entirely Italian wine list.

Putting together a great meal takes a little skill. Marcella Hazan's cookbooks make it easier by giving suggestions. A few Italian *secondi*, or meat and fish courses, include rice or pasta; you'd skip a *primi*, or pasta course, then.

But otherwise, how about a plate of olives, peppers, grilled eggplant, and prosciutto ($9), followed by a homemade ravioli stuffed with veal, summer ham, and ricotta with a balsamic brown butter sauce ($15), and then a nice veal scaloppini with radicchio, pancetta, Gorgonzola *picante,* and *vin cotto* ($18)? The tender veal lightly coated with flour and sautéed made a savory match for the hot Gorgonzola and the bitter radicchio. Eating several courses can allow the flavors to ascend steadily in intensity, and dining to extend steadily into the night, bringing on that Italian pleasure even harder to export than the foods—enjoying the way you eat a meal, stretching it out, savoring it.

Or perhaps you should contrast the ravioli (which, by the way, changes every day) with a sautéed Gulf of Maine sole with parsley, leeks, and tomato ($17).

Or instead of ravioli try the risotto with shrimp, tomato, and fennel pollen ($15).

On our last of several visits, the $8 fungi appetizer, sautéed summer mushrooms on crostini, made us happy, and the $7 crispy Montasio cheese with potato, onions, and white truffle oil caused a sensation.

The woman who ordered it, a new Portland resident, said, "I'm beginning to believe Portland is the undiscovered gastronomic center of the East Coast." *Ecco la.*

# Dogfish Café
**(207) 253-5400**
**953 Congress Street**
Hospitality—Overly casual
Open for lunch at 11:30 Monday through Saturday, with dinner specials
Wednesday through Saturday
Entrées $9 to $17

☛ *A café with appealing cooking*

The Dogfish Café is on the verge of being a restaurant. Sitting at a busy intersection in the midst of parking lots and truck traffic, the back outdoor space is not appealing.

Inside the place is hip, like its name, with brown paper covering the tables and sage green wooden booths under an indigo ceiling. But the wine list is limited to old standbys, the salmon is overcooked, and the bread is too white.

However, the real bar food came out of the kitchen looking great. A big white plate with two crabcakes ($8.95) on a puddle of rosy aioli (that seemed more like a capery tartar sauce) had a side of sweet-sour shaved fennel and dill that worked well with the crunchy exterior, tender crab and bread-crumb interior of the crabcakes. An order of fried mozzarella was another crisp object, this time a round lump of fresh mozzarella cheese in a moat of marinara that got loaded on to pieces of the bread. Toasted, the bread's whiteness was less of a drag.

We weren't finished with these appetizers when the next course was put on the table without apology.

A 7-ounce hamburger on another large plate took on a kind of overwhelming presence next to the remnants of the mozzarella. Maybe the reason you have separate courses is to keep from consciousness the quantity of food you've agreed to eat. But we persevered, discovering the freshly made potato chips were delicious, especially those white areas not fried to a crisp.

A salad of greens, grape tomatoes, and cucumbers in tomato-dill vinaigrette, with grilled Atlantic salmon, lost our interest early when the fish proved dry.

Dinner specials that night included grilled escolar ($12.95), a white-fleshed fish weighing 60 to 80 pounds that is caught in deep water. With a high oil content, it's hard to overcook when grilled. Grilled rib eye with a wild mushroom demi-glace ($17.25) and four-cheese and spinach-ricotta raviolis (both $13.25) were also offered.

Desserts (all $5.50) ranged from peanut butter pie to New York cheesecake to tres leches (three milks). Canned whipped cream came alongside the Chocolate Lava Cake, a cylinder of moist, bitter chocolate, absolutely delicious, that deserved real cream.

## Five Fifty-five
**(207) 761-0555**
**555 Congress Street**
Hospitality—Perfect service
Open for dinner 5–9:30, closed Tuesday, Sunday brunch 10:30–2:30
Entrées $20 to $27
Reservations recommended

☛ *A chef that other chefs are talking about, serving great food*

Serving brunch to the St. Luke's Cathedral Choir can be an exacting task, but this restaurant stood the test, pleasing everyone at the long table, garnering only a few criticisms, and enabling the choir to sing evensong an hour later with credit to all.

A glass of Chilean Veramonte Merlot ($6) was a splendid partner to a shared salad of beets and Maytag blue cheese on greens with spiced hazelnuts. The creamy dressing included bits of salty, pickled lemon peel and impressed the choir director and one of the altos. Judd, a tenor, had declined it because shallots were incorporated in the dressing, a sample of which was brought to the table for him to taste without his asking. When others tasted his sample the salad was ordered anyway.

One of the sopranos lauded the cherry-mascarpone griddle cakes, with nutmeg butter, California spring strawberries, and breakfast link sausages, though there was a general sense that the sausage was too lean. Lean sausage seems to be one of the risks of raising the quality, as if removing the fat were an improvement. Preposterous.

Another soprano sang the praises of her omelet, with a triple-cream cheese and a wedge of Pommes Anna, a cake of thin-sliced Perham Farms potatoes cooked in butter and deep golden brown on the bottom and top. The Traitor's

Eggs ($9.95), where fat was also far from banished, featured pickled shallots, which added a sweet-sour accent to the spinach mired in pure, classic hollandaise and the poached eggs on their crisp round of focaccia.

"The hamburger is a fabulous thing," the director declared; it was offered on the day of this visit with Gruyère, and on another with melted Shelburne Farms cheddar ($10.95).

It's no wonder other chefs in town are talking about this place, where chef-owner Steve Corry took over the defunct Aubergine and started pulling in so many customers that reservations can be hard to come by. His dinners have included *chimichurri*-spiked hanger steak with Hass avocado and cilantro aioli ($21.95) and a vegetarian entrée, Two Peppers Two Ways ($16.95), that featured roasted bell peppers with cheesy corn grits stuffing, turtle bean sauce, and chipotle cream.

I don't know why the coffee was too watery, but given the high standards of everything else, it must have been an aberration anyone else is unlikely to encounter. Next time I'll try some of the fabulous cheeses, like the Willow Hill Farm brebis from Vermont, a pungent sheep's milk cheese, or that sublime Humboldt Fog from McKinley, California, a tangy goat's milk cheese, $4 each with crostini, whole cherries, and spiced hazelnuts.

## Fore Street
**(207) 775-2717**
**288 Fore Street**
Hospitality—Great service without a rush, despite the crowd
Open daily for dinner weekdays 5:30–10, weekends until 10:30
Entrées $18 to $30
Reservations almost always a necessity, or eat in the bar

☛ *Go here for the best evening out, with an exciting dining room and wonderful meat and fish*

"It's been crazy," the Fore Street server said while having a drink on her night off at sister restaurant Street and Company. It's always been crazy at Fore Street, famous and packed on summer nights.

Chef and part-owner Sam Hayward won the James Beard award for Best Chef of the Northeast in 2004. His great recipes are written up in the *New York Times,* and his fans flock here from all over.

But locals fill the place too. It's the best destination on a night of a just bad enough winter storm. Few reservations are canceled, since Fore Street customers slither down the highways like people obsessed rather than miss a meal here.

The great big dining room in an old warehouse centers on the open kitchen and its fires. Servers leap to pick up meals when they're called, and cooks shove roasting pans deep into the wood-burning oven and cut apart great turnspit-roasted loins of pork with triumphant exuberance. It's a feast, a revel, a rout. So much of the pleasure at Fore Street is the spectacle and the action.

When the food shows up you find it's no sham. The greatest problem here is the challenge of self-restraint.

The changing menu keeps up with the available oysters and the season's best fruits and vegetables. Hayward has been buying the best local produce for years, and some of it sits on display like art in the restaurant's glass-windowed produce closet. Richard Penfold gets menu credit for his smoked seafood from Stonington. Wolfe's Neck Farm beef is another favorite.

I eat just an appetizer, sometimes, and it's almost always something full of bird livers, ranging from foie gras (from Carignan, Quebec, one summer night) to plain old chicken. Roasted peach puree and pecan and raisin toast made a fabulous accompaniment to the unctuous foie gras.

The restaurant serves pizza, a spectacular bowl of mussels with garlic almond butter, and a pasta dish that could suit any reasonable child while her parents are rooting in their big bowls of fish and shellfish stew, or platters of wood-oven-roasted wild king salmon or whole lobster. Some children have become roast pork fanatics after a taste of the pork loin ($18), even though they might skip the braised Savoy cabbage and the mustard and cider reduction.

Dessert—that's the real astonishment. You look at it and think, I'll just have a bite, and then you blink and the plate is empty.

A mascarpone cheesecake with lemon curd in its golden-cupped top; and strawberries from Wayne, Maine ($8), performed that sinister magic on me, and the peach tarte tatin with caramel sauce and ginger ice cream ($7.50), its peaches soft as preserves, seduced my friend. It isn't fair, really, to put that much pleasure on a plate.

## Hugo's
**(207) 774-8538**
**88 Middle Street**
Hospitality—Unobtrusive and flawless
Open for dinner Tuesday through Saturday from 5:30
Prix fixe four-course dinner, $52

☞ *Startling and delicious food made by one of the best chefs in New England*

A meal at Hugo's has the fast editing of the best suspense thrillers with the same excitement and only a smidgen of the dread. Each dish forms a beautiful still life and achieves a bravura performance of combined tastes. Having an adventuresome mouth will make eating here more fun.

There is no pretension, at least in the server we encountered, who talked responsively but no more than that. To give you a quick idea of the place, while she poured a glass of San Pelligrino, I said as I read the menu, "Foie gras ice cream float—that's disgusting."

She said, "I thought so too, but now I'm a believer."

None of us would try it.

We chose four courses each and settled into conversation, only to be interrupted by the food. This isn't the kind of food you can gobble up without comment. It's likely to astonish you. It's likely to be more interesting than what you have to say.

My conservative companions ordered the same first course of chilled melon consommé and peekytoe crab panini. They extolled the exquisite clear soup, enjoyed the three melon balls—cantaloupe, honeydew, and watermelon—in the small bowl, and ate up their tiny panini, with toasted bread that tasted like a potato chip.

My own first course, a Japanese work of art, came with a half-dozen small cubes of pickled peach in a row, next to a little rivulet of sabayon dotted with popped rice, next to a cluster of three or four tiny slices of rare duck breast under a round of "melted" foie gras. The duck had been briefly cooked *sous vide*—under pressure, the server said. The meat made my mouth water. The foie gras performed a joyous aria as I ate it.

During our second course, everyone sent her rectangle of barely cooked *toro* to me to complacently eat up like the family dog. They all had chosen the gently cooked (not much) bluefin tuna. But I was the object of envy with my paper cone of french fries and truffle ketchup. I gave some up, and they were pronounced perfect. But what my companions didn't know, because they didn't dare find out, was how perfect my molded cylinder of raw, herbed, chopped beef was, with its raw egg yolk in a rim of cooked egg white, as sensuous a mouthful as exists in the known world.

Next up was an assortment, from a round of "Shake and Bake" rib eye to a seared Scottish salmon that even under the increased cooking my friend requested still tasted as tender as pudding to a teeny-weeny and splendid chicken liver potpie.

We had the wine our server recommended, a 2002 Gruner Veltliner Federspiel from Austria's Dom Wachau ($26). Dry and light with a slight effervescence, it was a fine choice for the orchestrated food. Her suggestion for a dessert wine, a 20-year-old Barros Almeida tawny port ($11) was delicious, and even our 24-year-old companion, who reeled after her first sip, quickly succumbed to its mellow and pungent character.

But I think that the blue-cheese cake tasted a little sickening.

Rob Evans, named one of *Food and Wine*'s best new chefs in 2004, may be feeling extra inventive, and when you're taking such long shots surely some are bound to run foul. My friends scarfed up prescription-strength bitter chocolate cake in a mutual swoon.

We had all had a taste of a chef's brilliance, lighthearted and yet sublime.

## Katahdin
**(207) 774-1740**
**106 High Street**
www.katahdinrestaurant.com
Hospitality—A little haphazard when it's packed
Open for dinner Tuesday through Thursday 5–9:30, Friday and Saturday
5–10:30
Entrées $18 to $22

☛ *A popular neighborhood restaurant and hangout*

This corner building has been a popular place for dinner for years. In its latest incarnation, Katahdin had only the challenge of popular former owners, and their signature biscuits and martinis and fried oysters, to overcome. The martinis and Manhattans still come with a dividend in a little jug in a bowl of ice, so there's no problem there. Sweeping the schlock from the windowsills and replacing it with lush geraniums did a favor to the decor, and a new paint job makes the place bright and attractive.

First, however, we wondered why the wine list did not feature a single bottle under $28, and there was only one of those. The lowest typical price was $34. We loved the Sonoma Cutrer, judged 2002 a lovely vintage for that chardonnay, and $34 seemed a typical restaurant price for a bottle—but why not offer more cheapies, especially during this time of great, inexpensive wine? Of the 13 wines offered by the glass, most were $8, only two were $7.50.

Another drink possibility is any of the seven beers on tap ($4), like Czech Pilsner Urquel or local Bar Harbor Blueberry.

Although there were tempting salads from native greens, we opted for the underwater lovelies, Winterpoint Oysters from West Bath. They were all we know and love, with only a slight scree of shell flecking their perfection.

Then we waited, but Katahdin is a fun place to hang out, and a bar along one wall always has a convivial group earning interest on those dividends and snacking on the appetizers, like the crabcakes with Pasilla chili-lime aioli ($9), or lobster ricotta tart with arugula and pecorino ($12).

Then the ahi, yellowtail tuna, arrived with its avocado, cooked as my friend likes, all the way through. The halibut I ordered was overcooked, and a sugary vinaigrette around the rim of the plate didn't work, but we all loved the sides of oily sautéed greens, cooked just enough. The vanilla-brined roast pork tenderloin danced with its bing cherry demi-glace, and the hanger steak, dense with cumin, was a pleasurable mouthful in its house steak sauce. We were very hungry and glad to eat it all.

We were still so hungry we ordered desserts—and waited another long while. But there was no criticism of the bittersweet chocolate cake with a lava of ganache oozing off the top, and both the blackberry and the bing cherry crème caramels were pleasant and light. A dish of strawberry ice cream completed the dessert list (all $6).

The waiting, which four thin slices of focaccia, requested four times, did not much alleviate, was magically forgotten after the hectic, pleasant excitement of the busy atmosphere. The place is friendly, the customers are all talking and laughing, and the meal seemed slightly beside the point by the end of the evening when all we could recall was what a fun time we had.

## Local 188
**(207) 761-7909**
**188 State Street**
Hospitality—Congenial and ready to elaborate on the choices
Open for dinner Tuesday through Saturday, Sunday brunch
Entrées $15 to $18, tapas under $10

☛ *A hip place with phenomenal food*

There is funky, meaning disheveled, cool, and a little disorganized, and there is funky, meaning sly, hip, and amusing—Local 188 comes in under the latter. On one trip the art on display startled us and set the tone. From a short distance the drawings resembled illustrations from a children's book; but close up we found the bush the goat was munching on was not planted in the ground.

Red Japanese lanterns hang from thick black cords from the olive green ceiling, between an exposed brick wall and a wall painted the color of unsalted butter, in a long room with three rows of tables.

Hungry as always, I opted for tapas, starting with a little dish of shrimp and garlic ($5.75). The small oval bowl of Maine shrimp, served with a tiny bit of red pepper and a lot of garlic, did stimulate appetite without sating it, and worked with the Mad Fish Shiraz ($6). There really isn't enough to share without sorrow, so get a serving for everyone. Ripped up chunks of salted, chewy bread from One Fifty Ate (see page 98) are served with a dish of olive oil, tempting a hungry customer to overindulge, they taste so good.

My second course consisted of five perfectly browned scallops on a pink-rimmed plate, sitting resplendent amid a smoky Canary Island red pepper mojo sauce with capers and thyme ($9.75), which made an even better condiment for the bread. I preferred to eat the sweet subtle scallops without much sauce, to savor their flavor and the texture that the cook had left just on the right edge of done.

My companion chose the seared chicken with Romesco sauce—roasted peppers pureed with almonds, garlic, and bread crumbs—over spinach and rigatoni ($15). Red seemed to be working on us that night, stimulating appetite and gratifying it—the rigatoni, al dente, made lovely missiles of the sauce, and the chicken added browned meat savor.

With the server's advice my second glass of wine was a 1998 Tonio Ribero del Duero from Spain ($6), leaping with raspberry and wood and getting my mouth in the mood for stinky cheese. The last course, a salad of spinach with toasted walnuts, red onions, and Gorgonzola ($7.75), stays on the menu through changing seasons, a constant favorite.

I've heard that when new art is hung in the restaurant, the menu is prepared for the opening and can be sampled for free. But you wouldn't need that information to propel you inside, when just a couple of these modestly priced dishes achieve that sublime thing, a great, inexpensive meal.

## Mim's Brasserie
**(207) 347-7478**
**205 Commercial Street**
Hospitality—Efficient and friendly, fast-paced
Open daily for breakfast and lunch 7–3, for dinner 5–9:30
$7 to $15 for à la carte dishes, sides extra

☛ *Classic, simple French food, with regional innovations*

Mim's took over a curved-front brick building on Commercial Street in spring 2004 and has been filling its small upstairs and downstairs dining rooms since. There's no chance the two terraces, also up and down, will go begging on a sunny day, since the address is tourist central.

Initial grumbling about prices has been overcome by consistent quality and the straightforward good food. Mim's uses ingredients as local as possible, featuring meat and eggs from Sunset Acres Farm in Brooksville, and seafood from markets on Commercial Street. Brunch dishes, like their classic eggs Benedict ($9.50), cannot be improved on, with fresh eggs and tender Maine ham on a thick fresh slice of toasted sourdough bread. On one visit the gnocchi ($9.50), little logs of homemade potato soufflé, needed a little more cooking, but with the bacon lardons, spinach, cherry tomatoes, poached egg, and hollandaise, the dish was inspired. Plain eggs and bacon will be the best of their kind, and the orange juice is as close to fresh squeezed as you can get in a bottle. The iced coffee was superb, the darkest of dark roasts undefeated by its ice.

Lunch salads might be too plain, as my friend said, regretting ordering the romaine salad with slivered almonds, grapes, and *grana padano*. The upstairs dining room, a curved wall lined by a taupe bench with a few white shag pillows and a line of little tables, is a cool environment, with its tables of pale green lacquer, for such substantial things as onion soup with melted Gruyère and a ham on baguette with pickled red cabbage and sharp mustard ($8.50 for soup with half a sandwich). Frisée salad with a poached egg, bacon, chèvre, and croutons ($9), or Maine crab on brioche with tomato and parsley salad ($11), competed with a burger on focaccia with cheddar ($8) on the inviting lunch menu.

I am still not persuaded by the addition of vinaigrette in the raspberry sauce on the chocolate torte, which tasted like a wedge of ganache straight from the cooler, strangely accompanied by salad dressing.

Dinner can be a tender pork chop cured in brine ($13), or a partially boned quail ($12) with a side of spinach in cream ($5) shared by two. With a couple of glasses of wine from a good selection, that tab rolled in at $47.

# 100 Congress

(207) 775-7772
**100 Congress Street (on Munjoy Hill)**
www.100congress.com
Hospitality—Almost perfect, if it wasn't a little patronizing
Open daily for dinner 5–10
Entrées $14 to $20, with half portions available

☛ *A good dinner at a neighborhood place*

This neighborhood restaurant with cantaloupe walls and red-glass votives is an inviting space on a cold night. A fall menu entrée, pepper-pressed duck breast with roasted winter squash and kale in a port wine reduction, tasted like bliss in that weather, full of crisp duck and delicate butternut and acorn squash. We also loved Munjoy Hill Fra Diablo—shrimp, onions, peppers, mushrooms, and spinach in a bright red sauce full of spice and sweet tomatoes.

But the appetizer list was lackluster and short, and the two we tried disappointing. The antipasto leaned heavily on cheese, and could have used a lot more of the kitchen's great vegetables. The wine menu is also short, with only 8 reds and 8 whites, but the Seghesio Zinfandel from Sonoma Valley did its best to stand in for all other zinfandels, and pleased with its strong deep flavor.

Desserts included crème brûlée and a chocolate mousse parfait. The Key lime pie was full of grated lime rind and dense with flavor; the cheesecake with blueberries in its delicate batter made a faint, sweet presence. Both came with the highest quality whipped cream.

# Uffa
**(207) 775-3380**
**190 State Street**
www.uffarestaurant.com
Hospitality—Impeccable service and attention to young and old
Open for dinner Wednesday through Sunday from 5:30
Entrées $23 to $30
Reservations recommended

☛ *Elegant meals in a small restaurant with a good reputation and a lot of charm*

Our first sight of a young couple on their senior prom date on a May evening, two white roses in the girl's wrist corsage, confirmed that the more formal and elegant Uffa is well established. But warm, attentive service ensured no chill emanated from the white tablecloths and long-stemmed glasses. Instead, munching slices of just-baked wheat bread, buttered from a tiny blue-rimmed white tub, and drinking a glass of rich Mission Hills Shiraz, we felt right at home.

The rough wooden booths hark back to an earlier incarnation, candles burn in bottles on the top edge of the white beaded-board wainscoting, and the artwork changes frequently.

Chef James Tranchemontagne, previously a sous chef at Back Bay Grill, jacked up the ambience and is putting splendors on the plates. My pork chop in demi-glace and crème fraîche mashed potatoes ($23) were married in heaven. Filet mignon au poivre with a melting lump of Roquefort and butter on it ($29) aroused all possible carnivorous greed. The fried new potatoes were the best example of themselves, and more evidence that spending years learning to cook can transform the most ordinary dishes, which made the hard carrots, shaped like little missiles, inexplicable, except as a subject on which we can agree to disagree.

The chef is visible from the dining room through a curtained doorway up a half flight of stairs, under a haze from the stove. While he pours sauce on a plate from a skillet and keeps the dinner guests full of anticipation, his performance goes on off-stage, without the brash display in restaurants that feature entirely open, central kitchens.

The server will bring a honey bear for your tea and chocolates with the coffee. Or you can indulge in more. A lemon crêpe with raspberry jam and cinnamon ice cream ($7), two to four bite-size chocolate confections ($3), and a chocolate gâteau filled with praline Bavarian crème topped with chocolate ganache and crème brûlée stood on the spring menu.

We chose the homemade vanilla ice cream topped with chocolate. The ice cream startled our tongues with its fullness, so different from even the most expensive store-bought, and found itself room in our bellies despite the great dinners. The chocolate solidified around it, and a funnel of thin sugar cookie, a *feuille,* offered its contrast of crisp to cream. A small wooden treasure chest bore the "dommage" of a meal we were happy to pay for.

## Street and Company
**(207) 775-0887**
**33 Wharf Street**
**Hospitality—Brisk and capable in a busy atmosphere**
**Open daily at 5, seating for dinner at 5:30**
**Entrées $22 to $29**
**Reservations recommended**

☞ *The best place in Portland for great fish*

This restaurant fits snugly into three brick-lined rooms off cobblestoned Wharf Street. Before you go inside you can stand a moment and watch the cooks through a middle window; they always seem to be working frenetically. That's why you might need to call first for a reservation, although the bar is pleasant and you

*Cracking open an oyster at the bar (left) and cooking a fish dinner (right) at Street and Company*

can order some food there. Street and Company has been in business for a long time and fills its seats with people who have eaten there over and over, confident they can get great grilled fish, or spicy lobster *diavolo* for two ($38.75), or classics like scallops in Pernod and cream sauce, or shrimp and garlic on linguini.

The restaurant offers regular appetizers, including mussels, and oysters on the half shell that can come from the coast of Maine or Washington. A long list of other appetizers is always changing, and included a caramelized onion and fennel tart with Bleu de Basques and fresh figs ($6.95) on one night we ate there. Its buttery pastry shattered under our forks, and the onions and fennel worked well with the hot, strong cheese.

But we had both chosen specials, because, according to my friend's friend, a local chef, that's where those Street chefs show off their chops. My friend's whole sea bass, stuffed with herbs and surrounded by a raft of mussels in saffron cream sauce, tasted best when she got to the part cooked alongside a shaft of rosemary. The tender fish tasted sweet and buttery—if you watched from Wharf Street, you'd know why. The small mussels, including one the size of a fingernail, drank in the saffron cream and danced.

My own halibut ($23.95), dark with Cajun spice on one side, in a honey lavender bacon butter, with beet greens and sweet, pale chiota beets, was set off by a richly browned square of corn pudding. The pudding was like a bread pudding made with lots of cheese, kernels of corn that were slightly toasted and nutty, and, of course, butter. The white-fleshed fish stood up to that Cajun heat with its assertive pure flavor and was perfectly cooked.

We brooded over chocolate soufflé cake, raspberries and blueberries with whipped cream, bourbon pecan pie, or a peach and raspberry crisp for dessert, but opted to share a frozen nectarine tart on an almond crust ($6), a sweet nothing that we ate every scrap of.

The copper-covered tables at Street and Company are small, the rooms full, and the noise level high. That jacks up the excitement, and yet none of the busy staff loses their cool. The bartenders are funny and the oyster shuckers pretty. This establishment has experienced every kind of customer and handles us all with aplomb.

This is the best place in Maine for a perfectly grilled or broiled piece of fish.

# Two Thai Places

Two of Portland's many Thai restaurants have my loyalty. One has been here for a while and resumed operations after a hiatus that followed a tragic fire (one of the restaurant's employees died when she was trapped in the basement).

But now the owner, Suwanna Truong, has returned from soul searching in Thailand and reopened **Sengchai Thai (207-773-1001; www.sengchaithaiport landmaine.com; 803 Forest Avenue).** She's serving the freshest dinners; the most refreshing Tom Yum Koong ($2.50), a savory soup with lemongrass, lime juice, and fresh mushrooms, and the most delicious curries, full of clear flavor and only the freshest shrimp, chicken, or pork. Open daily 11–10, this is a friendly place. Truong came to the United States from northeast Thailand when she was 34, in the mid-1990s, learned English as she worked in a restaurant, and got herself out front once she could handle a few English phrases. She has been carried back into business by her ambition, her tight community, and the ongoing popularity of Thai cooking. Her customers now have to drive a little farther to find her, but it's worth the trip to taste the herbs and spices that Truong oversees and mixes herself. There is plenty of room here for a lot of customers.

## Bangkok Thai (207-879-4089; 671 Congress Street, across from the statue of the poet Longfellow).

Open Monday through Saturday for lunch 11–2:30 and dinner 5–9:30, has the better location, but it suffers from being too small. People cram in anyway, the brightly painted walls jazz up the atmosphere, and nearby Joe's Smoke Shop serves for a bar—because you have to get your beer over there to drink with the meal. We liked the Pik Khing scallops, mixed with green beans, carrots, and sliced lime leaf. The coconut rice pudding is addictive.

# Breakfast, Lunch, and Informal Dinners

## Artemisia (207-761-0135), 61 Pleasant Street.

Open Monday through Friday 11–3, Saturday and Sunday 9 AM–2 PM. This place excels at great grilled sandwiches and inventive combinations. One man I know, a Portland firefighter, orders off the chalkboard because the specials are always delicious. I saw roast beef with Gorgonzola mayonnaise, tomato, and red onion on grilled French peasant bread; that could be perfection.

But the menu's Tuscan Grill, with grilled portobello mushrooms, pesto, goat cheese, and roasted red peppers on grilled Tuscan bread ($6.50), made my day. It's also offered with bacon(I'll try it that way when winter comes). The grilled bread saturated with melting pesto and oozing goat cheese was heaven. The coleslaw beside it was made in the 1950s style, creamy with mayonnaise and a pleasure as well.

The iced coffee was, as the server announced, "The Real Stuff—I wouldn't still be here working otherwise." It vied with Mim's French roast for darkness honors. The blond wood tables and the brilliant colors on the walls make this room attractive. Now, if they would just add a little more oil to the salad offered with the vegetarian dumplings, and not run out of those ginger chocolate-chip cookies next time, I'll be happy.

## The Bayou Kitchen (207-774-4935), 543 Deering Avenue.

Open 7 AM–2 PM Monday, and Wednesday through Saturday, 8 AM–2 PM Sunday, closed Tuesday. With blues on the stereo, red chili lights around the windows, and the heat from the Cajun food off the grill keeping the atmosphere at a simmer, it's just possible to feel elsewhere. As the pierced delivery guy hoisted a box of potatoes on the cook's shoulder, and a trio of 20-somethings played poker while awaiting their 1 PM Monday breakfast, the smoky scent of my red beans and rice ($5.95) kept me focused. Four of the other customers were over 75—this is a place for anyone with a taste for crawfish, gumbo, and andouille. The corn bread comes browned from the grill and buttery, ready to accompany the jambalaya, $6.50, or $8.95 with chicken and crawfish added to the andouille sausage, onions, peppers, garlic rice and "our Jamba juice."

Among the many possibilities, breakfast could be scrambled eggs with crawfish, andouille, jalapeños, and cheddar ($7.95) or raisin French toast ($4.95). Weekends can be jammed. And be warned—they do not accept credit cards.

## Becky's Diner (207-773-7070; www.beckysdiner.com), 390 Commercial Street.

Open daily 4 AM–9 PM. The world-famous Becky's Breakfast is served from 4 AM to 4 PM, without homefries until closing. Breakfast is the focus here, drawing in so many tourists on a rainy morning that the line is out the door even in the middle of the week. The center of this universe grew from a little business started by a woman looking for a way to support her kids. She's come up with a way to buy their sneakers, pay for college, and keep them employed, too.

When we were talking about Becky's in a local law firm's waiting area, the receptionist praised the oatmeal—"cooked to order" according to the menu. Okay, but the rest of us go for the fluffy eggs, the big bowl of fresh fruit salad, always different, or whatever is on the white board for that day's special. The long row of coveted red booths is always full, and a $2.75 slice of pie—apple, blueberry, coconut cream, and peanut butter covered half the list one day—is the best way to end a meal, even breakfast. Customers vary from thick-necked fellows with tattooed heads to older Mainers on Social Security treating themselves. Dinners like meat loaf ($8.95), roast turkey ($8.95), or fried clams ($11.95) were introduced to feed fishermen who were hungry and not in the mood (or the wardrobe) for an Old Port restaurant, but now everyone is going.

You can rely on fast, good, cheap food out of this bustling kitchen on Hobson's Wharf, at the very bottom of High Street, where the biggest challenge is finding a place to park.

## Bintliff's American Café (207-774-0005), 98 Portland Street.

Open daily year-round for breakfast, brunch, and lunch 7–2, dinner Wednesday through Saturday 5–9. Since there is inevitably a line here on weekend mornings, why not have a more pleasant (because less crowded) breakfast during the week? The eggs Benedict ($7.95) comes with heroic portions of homefries, cut in big chunks and darkly browned, and a slice of homemade bread along with the English muffin under the poached eggs, Canadian bacon, and light hollandaise. A sesame buckwheat waffle ($6.95) comes up the stairs to your table, set on its edge in a high fan shape, which might account for its being slightly cold. But that is no deterrence to enjoying it, unmelted butter, maple syrup, and all.     Customers love the miniature jars of jams and preserves—a mini-flask of real maple syrup costs $1.50, but probably won't spill in your purse with its metal clasp shut. Wraps, Cristos, burgers, big salads, and chowder join the unique pancakes—raspberry-almond or banana-pecan (both $6.95)—on the brunch menu. Dinner, with entrées $15 to $23, sticks to classics like steak, pork tenderloin, and grilled fish, with just a couple of vegetarian possibilities and nothing vegan. Among the feather-trimmed lampshades, a framed menu will remind you that once upon a time you could order, somewhere, shortcake with berries for 35 cents.

## The Brea-Lu Café (207-772-9202), 428 Forest Avenue. Open 7 AM–1 PM daily.

With its shelves and shelves of books and an old creaky screen door that slams, Brea-Lu combines short-order cooking with a friendly, relaxing atmosphere. Now that it has air-conditioning the summer weekend breakfast crowds will be more comfortable. When the tables are packed a side room holds the people waiting; they've all signed in on a chalkboard in the passageway between the two rooms. That keeps the cranky hungry customers alert to how long their own wait is— meanwhile they can read the papers.

Breakfast standards are just fine, with crunchy homefries, fried eggs, and toast coming in at $3.35. Specials on the board often include eggs Benedict ($6.95). Enormous pancakes engulf the plates; kids are hard-pressed to finish just one ($2.75). Breakfast burritos and omelets (peanut butter, mushroom and cheddar cheese—both $6) are also served, and lunch is available Monday through Friday— burgers and sandwiches and a couple of salads. One of Portland's best waitresses, Debbie Thibodeau, who makes a meal swift and friendly, also sells her pretty jewelry here when she's on her shift; you can score a friend's birthday present when you're at the register paying for your eggs and toast.

## Gilbert's Chowder House (207-871-5636), 92 Commercial Street.

Open every day 11–11. Cheap, fine fried seafood is served in a plain room and on a wood deck on the wharf in warm weather. There are old ship models and a few old catches mounted on the walls, plain linoleum on the floor, and Formica tables. It's a perfect place for kids, because most of them go for the style of flour-thickened chowder served here in Styrofoam bowls ($4 for a small). Adults can enjoy a pint of local Geary's or something from the full bar, and the fried whole-belly Maine clams or oysters, or broiled or a fried haddock filet ($11.25 for lunch), or a Maine crabmeat roll ($12.95). There's news on the TV over the bar if you need a fix after the long whale-watch delivers you back on shore just down the street.

## Granny's Burritos (207-761-0751), 420 Fore Street.

Open Sunday through Thursday 11–10 PM, Friday and Saturday 11–midnight. This business started around the corner in a small shop, with a few stools and chairs, for take-out only. Pretty soon everyone knew this was where to go when on a strict budget and in need of always fresh ingredients in your large and satisfying burrito. All the burritos are plump handfuls of folded, fresh tortillas—six kinds offered—filled with a choice of black beans or pinto beans or both, and cheese, rice, salsa, tomatoes, lettuce, sour cream, and guacamole ($6), or sweet potato ($6), or chicken with mango salsa ($6.50), or chorizo sausage ($6), among many others. Nachos ($5.25) or just chips with salsa ($1.75) or guacamole ($2.75) are all on the appetizer list, and could go along with a beer upstairs where there is table service every night and all day Friday through Sunday. The menu offers many vegan and vegetarian choices.

## Federal Spice (207-774-6404), 225 Federal Street.

Open Monday through Saturday 11–9; in winter, Saturday closing is at 6. For a fusion of Mexican, Asian, Southwest, and Caribbean, this small lunch place (with lots of outside tables) concocts the best. Locals stream here during the business lunch hour for the ginger lemongrass rice and Asian slaw with curry coconut chicken and peanut sauce wrap—and many other choices. Daily specials might include a pumpkin rice wrap with Asian slaw and Asian barbeque sauce ($5.50). The bright yellow walls and blue bench enliven the dreary location under a parking garage. You can have a local beer to go along with the sweet potato jalapeño corn bread (80¢) and chili ($2.50 for a large) when winter blows into town.

## Flatbread Company (207-772-8777), 72 Commercial Street.

Open Monday through Thursday 11:30–10, until 11 PM Friday through Sunday. Ever since it opened its doors, Flatbread has drawn in big, enthusiastic crowds that enjoy its wood-oven-baked pizzas. A long bar has a lot of stools for people waiting for a table, but even they are often all taken on weekend nights. The big room full of light thrown in off the water through the windows is festooned with banners proclaiming, simply, GARDEN HERBS, or MAINE LOBSTER, or WHOLE-MILK MOZZERELLA. A hobbit-hole-shaped beehive oven with a fire inside attracts everyone's attention, and the children like to gather close while the young man with the long paddle slides the pizzas around to keep them baking evenly. This is a children's restaurant, and for the most part that does not mean it's a place to avoid if you don't have any toddlers of your own. Grown-ups seem just as mesmerized by the fire, or maybe it's the people at work, splitting wood just to the left of the big oven or making pies to the right, spinning the dough and layering the ingredients

The flatbreads, as the restaurant calls them, are offered in several versions, and there is a vegetable and a meat special every night, like a Sunset Acres Farm pork loin with Marsala onion-garlic jam, roasted tomato, mushrooms, Parmesan, and herbs ($17.25).

Regular versions include a personal favorite that is topped with homemade maple fennel sausage and sun-dried tomatoes, caramelized onions, organic mushrooms, cheeses, and herbs, ($16, or a half for $8.75). Or compose your own from the free-form list. We have brought many slices home over the years and found that unlike other leftover pizza, this pizza was always eaten up with appreciation the next day. The Punctuated Equilibrium flatbread is made with kalamata olives, rosemary, red onions, red peppers, goat cheese, mozzarella, garlic, and herbs ($15.25).

The regular dessert, a brownie sundae ($5.50), consists of a rich brownie that gets heated up in the oven a moment before the ice cream and chocolate sauce are piled on. The hot dense cake makes the cold ice cream delicious, or is it the other way around? Often a fruit crisp on the specials board demonstrates the same magic with cooked fruit.

**Norm's East End Grill (207-253-1700), 47 Middle Street,** open daily 11:30–10, Sunday 4–9; and **Norm's Bar and Grill (207-828-9944), 617 Congress Street,** open daily 11:30–10. Friends of mine go to Norm's East End for take-out every Friday night; their barbeque ribs are famous, and the corn bread and fixings rate high. Another friend calls this one of his favorite restaurants. Casual atmosphere and attractive decor are a part of it, but the fact is all the food is well made and delicious. There is only the slightest invention going on, but since most meals transcend their conventional path and achieve greatness, there's nothing to criticize. Meat makes almost everyone's mouth water, and the meat at both Norm's excels. At an earlier location you could sit at the bar and watch it spatter close-up, but now you'll have to wait to feast your eyes until the server brings it to the table. Salads at the Bar and Grill, like a steak salad special ($9.95), with spinach, blue cheese, corn, and a sweet balsamic vinaigrette, had a chorus singing in my head as I debated ordering it or, say, the fish-and-chips or Greek salad with fried calamari ($7.95). Deciding on the steak, I was delighted when it came in a big-rim soup bowl with six slices of rosy rare steak; it quieted down the inner ogre within a minute or two. A slice of pecan pie ($3.50), with its gelled liquefaction of sugar and big pecans, didn't need any of that chocolate sauce; it was superb on its own. Many items can be found at both Norm's, but the famous ribs are all over on the east end, which is always crowded on weekend nights.

### Portland Street Diner (207-761-1811), 40 Portland Street.

Open 6 AM–2 PM, with dinner hours planned, handicapped accessible. This may be the only diner anywhere that has a marble-tile-lined bathroom, a leftover from an earlier incarnation.

The diner got a giant makeover in spring 2004, gaining blue vinyl booths, chrome-rimmed stools at the counters, and a reproduction jukebox along a far wall. Once an eclectic American restaurant, then a good Thai place, Portland Street Diner is a welcome feature in a changing area called Bayside, serving good diner food, like fried eggs, "hash fries" that are browned and crisp, a variety of eggs Benedict, three-egg omelets, and burgers for lunch. Dinner hours are planned; the menu will include the burgers, clam rolls, and sandwiches.

### Scales (207-228-2010), the Portland Public Market, 25 Preble Street.

Open daily 11–8, Sunday 11–5. This place took over seafood sales in the public market, and added its own fried seafood restaurant, a counter-ordering place with high quality ingredients. The fried fish meals come in a wide aluminum cake pan lined with bakery paper, and you carry them to the paper-covered tables, perfect for kids who love to draw. My fried oysters and fried clams ($6.95) with good, freshly made french fries, were great. The delicious onion rings ($2.95) resembled tempura, and the folded cone of blank newsprint that held the fried fish made a perfect disposable bowl. The Shore Dinner consists of a 1¼-pound lobster, count-neck clams, chowder, and corn on the cob ($23.95). A blue-plate special—broiled swordfish, zucchini, and roasted Red Bliss potatoes, with tiny chanterelles added in—cost $10.95.

## Take-Out, Bakeries, and Markets

Portland is blessed with wonderful bread.

In the early 1980s, the now-gone Port Bakehouse was a lone bakery on Fore Street. Bars and clubs have taken over that address, but not far away in the Old Port are several wonderful bakeries, each with its own ambitious excellence, and more do business in the Portland Public Market. New bread-baking businesses are growing, and the old ones continue to surpass themselves—so it seems that more and more of us must be their customers. Maybe someday all the cotton-wool bread factories will shut down.

### Standard Baking Company (207-773-2112), 75 Commercial Street.

Open Monday through Friday 7 AM–6 PM, Saturday and Sunday 7 AM–5 PM.

This is the grand dame of them all, opening over 25 years ago on Wharf Street and selling the best baguettes Mainers had ever seen. They are still the best. The signature morning buns, a sticky bun made with rich, flaky pastry and densely coated with walnuts or plain, has stood the test of time, remaining a popular item. In its present large quarters under Fore Street Restaurant there is a large assortment of breads painstakingly crafted according to the company's high standards, with long, slow rising times and premium flours and spices. I've moved on from the superior baguette to the fabulous rustica, a chewy loaf in various shapes; the dense whole rye and seeded whole wheat; and the amazing fig anise.

Pastries are delectable, from a bittersweet, rich brownie to apricot walnut scones to the excellent gingerbread.

### Sophia's (207-879-1869), 81 Market Street.

Open Tuesday through Friday 9–4. A smaller selection than the Standard Baking Company offers, but a friend who considers himself a critic of the highest order says Sophia's bread is the best around. The Campagnolo, a dense, pungent bread made from several grains, comes already sliced and basted with olive oil, with a thick slice of aged, tawny Asiago, for a baker's lunch offered in the summer ($2.50, $3.50 with anchovies). Stirato, a free-form baguette, and Lunas, soft, floured half-moons of chewy white bread, are also sold, along with pastries like *torta di limone* and pistachio bars. Large pizzas include one with fresh tomatoes, basil, and fresh mozzarella, sold by the slice for lunch on summer Fridays and throughout the week in the winter. Another menu of sandwiches and soup is available the rest of the week.

### The Green Grocer (207-761-9232), 211 Commercial Street.

Open Monday through Saturday 9–6 PM. Look for the sign with three radishes.

The Green Grocer is the best spot to find great cheap and otherwise wine. The owners write mini-speeches on cards and hang them by the cases of wine; every word rings true. There is always something here for $6.99 that tastes great—and bottles to splurge on for your holiday dinner party, after you move to Maine because you love it here so much. Cheese, condiments, and other items are in good supply here, but the store got out of the produce business in early 2005.

**Big Sky Bakery** has two locations in Portland: one at **536 Deering Avenue (207-761-5623),** open Monday through Friday 7–6, Saturday 7–5, and Sunday 8–2; and one in the **Portland Public Market, 25 Preble Street (207-**

**228-2040),** open Monday through Saturday 8–7. I consider Big Sky granola to be the best on planet Earth. Deeply toasted and stuck together in crunchy clumps (if all granola eaters ate stuff this crunchy, they'd deserve their epithet), a mass of almonds, sesame seeds, and oats, this stuff solved the mystery of why anyone would ever consume granola in the first place.

The bakery is a little on the crunchy side, culture-wise. Its big quarters out on Deering Avenue, with tables and newspapers and coffee, are child friendly, with a wad of dough usually available for rolling out and messing around with on a little table. Not for eating, of course. Both locations sell big loaves of honey whole-wheat, oatmeal, pumpernickel, and English muffin bread, and scones and cookies. Both now also sells sandwiches, like roast turkey and mozzarella ($5.35), herbed chicken salad ($5.75), and peanut butter and preserves on white ($3.25).

**Borealis Breads** brought its delicious breads right into the **Hannaford at 295 Forest Avenue,** where it has installed a wood-burning oven. You can buy absolutely fresh *ciabatta,* chewy little loaves that make delicious hamburger buns and were getting snatched up for cookouts one July 4th weekend. Their rye, multigrain, and cinnamon-raisin breads are dense and full of character.

### Foley's Bakery (207-772-5837), 431 Congress Square.

Open Monday through Friday 7–5:30, Saturday 8:30–2:30 (and at the **Portland Public Market,** see page 90). Foley's is going into the bread business from a new bakery branch at Pinelands, in New Gloucester. Since fall 2004 they make loaves that are sold at the Congress Street Bakery, at a new Foley's Bakery (207-883-7800, 241 Route 1, Scarborough), and also at the Maine Roasters Coffee branches (207-846-0995, 82 Portland Road, Yarmouth and 207-781-4837, 244C Route 1, Falmouth) that already sell the cakes and pastries that gave this business its start in the world.

This is where everyone goes to buy a special cake for a dinner party, and almost everyone buys the chocolate mousse cake. Some children have been grateful to see the delicious carrot cake at their birthday parties, and the fresh strawberry layer cake is also a hit. You can order cakes for large parties and tiny tarts for a tiny party, or you can get a slice of coffee cake, an individual fruit tart, or a honey pecan square to eat at a table while you watch the pedestrians pass by on Congress Street. Things inside that shop are particularly delicious during a winter storm when the snow and sleet are flying down between the buildings, and you need to recoup for the rest of the walk home.

### West End Grocery (207-874-6426), 133 Spring Street.

Open Monday through Friday 7 AM–9 PM, Saturday and Sunday 7 AM–8 PM. The best sandwiches, wraps, and salads in town are all made in the small back kitchen of this modest grocery store on the corner of Spring and Park. Daily specials are listed on a piece of paper posted to the right of the ordering counter in the back, and always include a vegetarian choice. Classics include the smoked salmon with capers, cucumbers, and red onion on a baguette; Caesar salad roll-up with chicken (crammed with savory romaine); and a hummus, cucumber, and sprout roll-up. The grilled chicken wrap makes one member of this family's day. On any lunch hour you'll find the back of the store full of locals waiting with patient anticipation for their delicious lunch to go. Fruit, wine, brownies, and prepared meals (in the cooler) are also available.

### The Full Belly Deli (207-772-1227, fax 207-773-3067), Pine Tree Shopping Center, Brighton Avenue.

Open Monday through Friday 7–7, Saturday 7– 4. "All corned beef is not created equal," the ads announce. Corned beef sandwiches with a choice of light, dark, or marble rye bread or a bulky roll, with half a sour pickle spear, are $5.95. But why not become fully initiated—try the George Bress sandwich, filled with corned beef, chopped liver, tongue, and Swiss cheese ($6.95).

### Oh No Café (207-774-0773), 87 Brackett Street (corner of Gray and Brackett).

Open Tuesday through Friday 6:30 AM–9 PM, Saturday 8–8, Sunday 8–6, closed Monday. This small neighborhood café and store opened up in summer 2004. Breakfast sandwiches are made with bagels, croissants, and English muffins; you can mix and match eggs with bacon, sausage, ham, smoked turkey, prosciutto, cheddar, and Gouda. Specials, like a hummus sandwich with red onion, tomato, and lettuce with a side salad of baby spinach with balsamic vinaigrette, are delicious. The menu could feature two great salads, one made with grilled shrimp and the other with spinach and flank steak. The Baja Chicken taco with guacamole, *pico de gallo* (a tangy sauce of tomato, jalapeño, onion, and lime), and plantains is $6.95. You can get some food ready to heat up from a take-out cooler, along with wine, beer, chips, and a small selection of groceries.

### Rosemont Market and Bakery (207-774-8129), 559 Brighton Avenue.

Open Monday through Saturday 8–6. This market, run by one of the former owners of the Green Grocer, opened in January 2005. The bakery is stocked with high-quality breads, sandwiches, pastries, vegetables, fruit, wine, cheese, high-quality meats, and other meal essentials fill the shelves.

# Farmer's Markets

Portland has two chances for lucky consumers to buy the best from local harvests. Saturday from 7 AM–noon farmers line up along a street in **Deering Oaks Park,** off Deering Avenue, selling seedlings from late April and everything that ripens through the summer and fall until the end of October.

Wednesday from 7–2 some of the same farmers park on **Monument Square** around the Civil War statue, **Our Lady of Victories,** in the middle of the city on Congress Street, to sell bouquets, jars of honey, and masses of produce.

**The Portland Public Market,** just a few steps from Monument Square on Cumberland Avenue, sells local produce and many local products from its vendors. It's open Monday through Saturday 7–7 and Sunday 10–5.

# Coffeehouses

My favorite coffeehouse is **Arabica (207-879-0792), 16 Free Street.** Open 7 AM–5 PM weekdays, 7 AM–1 PM weekends. The cappuccino is delicious and comes to your table, after you order at the counter, with beautiful patterns drawn in the milky foam on top. Or is it the chocolate cake with espresso icing, or the dense, unctuous pecan pie, or the great cinnamon toast that I like most?

## Coffee By Design (207-772-5533), 620 Congress Street, and on India Street.

Open 6:30 AM–8 PM Monday through Saturday, 7 AM–8 PM Sunday. Very good coffee, and the changing art exhibits are usually startling, beautiful, or both.

## The Acoustic Guitar (207-774-0404), 32 Danforth Street.

Open 8 AM–10 PM Monday through Wednesday, until 11 Thursday and Friday, 9 AM–11 PM Saturday, closed Sunday. Just up from the statue of Henry Ford that directs traffic, a few slouchy upholstered chairs, a lot of wooden ones, and occasional music from local talent are all offered. Poets read their work here too. Good chai, and fine coffee, of course.

### Java Net Café (207-773-2469), 39 Exchange Street.

Open 7–10 Monday through Thursday, Friday 7–11, Saturday 8–11, Sunday 8–9. A few computers are available to use while you drink a huge cup of tea, or reasonably sized cappuccino. Java Net serves a banana cream pie in a little glass dish that is one of life's good things.

### Breaking New Grounds (207-761-5637), 13 Exchange Street.

Open 7:30 AM–10 PM daily except Sunday, when it opens at 8. A busy place on a summer night, or a winter one, and a good place to get homework done, or brood, or get a good cookie to do homework and brood while drinking tea or good coffee. Also in the **Public Market** (see page 90), providing the coffee you need to enjoy the pastry you just bought at Foley's across the way and want to eat in front of the big gas fireplace while watching the people go by.

### The Udder Place (207-780-6666), 428 Brighton Avenue.

Open 6 AM–5 PM Monday through Saturday, 7 AM–2 PM Sunday. Smiling Hill Farm milk is in the lattes, making them rich and delicious, and a friend considers their cappuccino the best around.

And there is of course the ever reliable **Starbucks, 176 Middle Street in the Old Port (207-761-2797)** and **594 Congress Street, next to the Portland Art Museum (207-761-0334).** Open 5:30 AM–9 PM Monday through Thursday, 6:30 AM–10 PM Friday and Saturday, 6:30 AM–8 PM Sunday.

## Fish Markets

### Harbor Fish Market (207-775-0251, 207-772-6557, 1-800-370-1790; www.harborfish.com), 9 Custom House Wharf (across from the Custom House).

Open Monday through Saturday 8:30–5:30. More than 30 years in the business of selling fish and shellfish, this place is the picturesque storefront photographed in a favorite Portland postcard, and the destination of many, many holiday shoppers. An employee directs traffic as Christmas approaches to keep the customers from arguing in the limited area off Commercial Street where you can park. Visitors can usually get a lobster displayed, and always buy as many as they want. In winter the eel tank draws in the curious. The crabmeat is fresh, the fish is fabulous, and the employees are courteous even at the height of busy days.

**Portland Lobster Pound and Fish Market** (207-699-2400) Hobson's Wharf (behind Becky's Diner).

Open Monday through Saturday 9–6, Sunday 10–4. Lobster, clams, fish, and more.

**Browne Trading Company** (207-775-7560, 1-800-944-7848, www.browne-trading.com), 262 Commercial Street at Merrill's Wharf.

Open Monday through Saturday 10–6:30. This place provides fish to the stars of the restaurant world. New York restaurateur Daniel Boulud is quoted on the Web site, saying he relies on owner "Rod Mitchell's consistently superior products," and you can see Boulud giving a spoonful of caviar the once over. And if you visit the store on Commercial Street, you can get a freshly filleted piece of their extremely fresh fish for yourself, or some of the salmon smoked and packed here, another product sold in high-end markets in New York. Or you can order fish, oysters, and other things for overnight delivery from the Web site. The retail store sells great cheese and wine too (see below) and has the advantage of being open a little later than some of the other places on Commercial Street.

# Wine

My favorite wine store is the **Green Grocer** (see page 87), with its reliable inexpensive bottles of French, Spanish, Argentinean, and Australian red wines. There's lots more at higher prices—all right, it's true, $25 and up seems high to me—and you can ask Nick for a recommendation when it comes time to buy the best bottles for a great dinner.

**Browne Trading Company** (see above) stocks extraordinary wines from around the world. I found a wonderful bottle of 20-year-old port here, and a couple of glasses to go with it, for a Christmas present one year.

**The Clown** (207-756-7399; www.the-clown.com), 123 Middle Street, with branches in Belfast and Stonington.

Open Monday through Wednesday 10–6, Thursday through Saturday 10–7. The Clown has a cellarful of good wine, with an emphasis on Italy, where the owners have a villa. Upstairs is a gallery and collection of European ceramics and kitchenware.

**Miranda's Vineyard (207-228-2016), 25 Preble Street in the Portland Public Market (see page 90).**

A good selection situated close to several good places to buy dinner ingredients. The people who work here are delighted to recommend a wine for a meal, and might be able to order something you want to buy. Good sherry and Manzanilla here, too.

**Market Wines (207-828-0900; www.marketwines.com), 24 Preble Street, across from the Portland Public Market.**

Open Monday through Saturday 11–6. A wide variety of wines are sold during the day. In the evening the wine bar next door, Meritage, offers a great place to try things out. More than 50 wines are offered in the glass, with flights of varietals a fun way to spend an hour, and small plates of cheese, and other dishes, to pair with the wine. And, as their Web site suggests, a glass of port is a great dessert all by itself.

# $\mathcal{S}$aco

## Lily Moon Café
**(207) 284-2233**
**17 Pepperell Square, just off Main Street (Route 1)**
Hospitality—Very helpful, attentive, and eager to please
Open for breakfast and lunch Tuesday through Sunday, dinner Wednesday through Saturday
Entrées $17 to $20
BYO wine

 *A quiet little place with charm and good meals*

The friendly space here is filled with white-painted wooden chairs at wood tables set on black and white squares of linoleum, with a few upholstered booths. Spanish guitar music pleases the ears; bring a bottle of wine brought from the outside (the café will provide you with glasses). This charming place was built with the help of a whole community after the first Lily Moon burned down on Mother's Day, 2003. Despite more trouble from an absconding accountant, Roger and Cathi Cyr are adding a coffee shop across the square, and it looks like their community, in the form of repeat customers, won't let them down.

We chose a couple of dishes served on angelhair pasta on the cold night of our visit. Shrimp scampi ($16.95), with a light sauce of cream, tomato, and red peppers, came in a large bowl with a side of sautéed vegetables and a small slice of cantaloupe. The sauce was indeed light, as described on the menu, and the snow of thinly grated Parmesan made a salty, flavorful crust on the fresh shrimp. We could complain only that the little carrots were dried out and the beans tired; otherwise, the dish was delicious.

The chicken primavera, with marinara and Parmesan, had the same vegetable drawback, but was otherwise delicious, with tender slices of chicken breast made savory with the cheese and the tomato sauce.

Other entrées included a caramelized salmon filet ($16.25), a blackened Jack Daniels rib eye ($17.95), and Tournedos McCallum ($19.25), filet mignon served on baguette croutons with cabernet demi-glace and grilled shrimp.

The Key lime pie ($4.95), festooned with whipped cream, tasted creamy with a quiet lime flavor.

## Coffeehouses and Desserts

### Milliken House (207-283-9691; www.millikenhouse.com), 65 North Street.

Open Tuesday through Friday 5 PM–9 PM in summer, Friday through Saturday 2–10 from Labor Day to mid-December. The couple who bought this house in 1998, Lisa and David Norburg, has restored its interiors from "1960s revival" to the Victorian splendor of its 1877 birthright. And 1877 is the year they want you to think you have returned to when you step inside for a dessert and a cup of tea or coffee. The servers are dressed like parlor maids and curtsy when they greet you. When I was last at Milliken House, Lisa Norburg was at work on a gown based on a design by Charles Worth of Paris, haute couture of the period, that she planned to wear for Christmas teas.

The menu features pear port-wine pie with a creamy filling ($3.95), a Berry Lovely Charlotte ($4.50), a vanilla pastry cream and berries wrapped in a crust of ladyfingers, and many other cakes and pastries, along with ice cream, coffee, and tea. The house silverware is ornate and heavy, the tables in the front parlors are set with linen, and the whole feeling here is formal but with a sense of humor. The fellow in the foyer, Elias, will shake if he's plugged in, but apparently that freaked out too many people—he looks awfully real. A gift shop in the house contributes any profits to missions around the world.

**Lily's Coffee and Tea (207-284-2235), 12 Pepperell Square.**
Open 6:30 AM–9 PM except Sunday. Serving lattes, espresso, and cappuccino, along with tea and other drinks, this is Saco's latest coffeehouse. It's intended to be on a European model, according to owner Roger Cyr, who with his wife, Cathi, owns Lily Moon Café across the street (see page 93). Gingerbread men, whoopee pies, scones, and cake, all homemade, are served; and biscotti and Rinaldi's Gelatto, from high-quality suppliers, fill out the offerings.

## Farmer's Market

You can buy glass-bottled milk, maple syrup, and of course, corn, apples, and tomatoes in-season Wednesday and Saturday 7 AM–noon, mid-May until the end of October, at the **Saco Valley Shopping Center** (www.sacofarmersmarket.com).

# Scarborough

## Black Point Inn
**(207) 883-2500, 1-800-258-0003**
**510 Black Point Road**
Hospitality—Comfortable and formal
Open daily for dinner 6:30–9
Entrées $15 to $28

☛ *An old hotel with new amenities*

A cocktail on the long, wide porch overlooking one of Scarborough's best clam flats would be appropriate before dinner—if it's dark or raining, the small bar is fine; better yet are the upholstered couches of the lobby, in front of the big fireplace. In any event, along with the gin and tonic in its heavy glass you can drink in the Old World surroundings, and catch up with your fellow guests.

Inside the large, carpeted dining room, tables are swathed in smooth white linen and covered with porcelain place settings. The capable staff has gratified every inclination for food and drink on our visits over the years, and the food served hasn't disappointed.

One night, After a salad of plain mesclun in a fruity vinaigrette accompanied by egg-glazed rolls, I savored a rare piece of tuna with a groundnut and ginger crust served in a small pool of gingered sauce. The rosette of mashed potatoes did a better job of looking pretty than pleasing the taste buds, and likewise the green beans and wedges of summer squash, which were undercooked. But the fish tasted so good I didn't much care.

Tortellini with Asiago cheese provided the creamy richness that one of my companions always goes for, with the nutty flavor of that salty Italian cheese. Halibut and lobster salad also fed us well, and our request for additional mayonnaise was quickly accommodated.

We ate raspberry chocolate tart, Key lime pie, and crème caramel for dessert.

Maybe the porch would do even better for an after-dinner brandy. The inn's summertime atmosphereis unhurried, and sometimes uncrowded, making a good setting for remedial work on feeling civilized, especially if frantic days have left you failing in that subject for too long.

## Ken's Place
**(207) 883-6611**
**207 Pine Point Road (Route 9)**
Hospitality—Fast counter service in an immaculate, simple dining room
Open daily for lunch and dinner April through October at 11 AM
Inexpensive

☛ *Squeaky clean, from the floors to the oil that the fish is fried in, with high-quality seafood classics*

Ken's Place, around since 1927 and owned by David Wilcox since 2000, gets plenty crowded in the height of summer, but you can count on Wilcox's crazy energy to keep the freshest, best-quality seafood coming, and to keep the place in order.

This is a classic seafood place, with windowed counters to order from and big menus up on the wall to contemplate during the wait in line. The fried clams, with either crumbs or batter, were $16.99 when we visited—dug from nearby clam flats, they were the best we'd had in years. Fried onion rings ranked above the french fries, the chowder is a past prizewinner, and boiled lobsters, fried scallops, fried shrimp, and fish vie with the clams for first choice. Some people like to come in and buy clam cakes by the dozen.

They put them in the toaster for breakfast, according to Wilcox.

Wilcox said he makes the things people expect from a summer seafood place. His lobster rolls come on the classic buttered hot dog rolls. And he insists on the freshest seafood, and said one supplier called to say he wouldn't bother to bring what was available, because it wasn't going to meet Wilcox's standards.

"I've thrown out hundreds of dollars of seafood," Wilcox said.

Wilcox added that he rotates, filters, and recycles the oil in his six fry kettles daily, and that was clear from the taste of the food, which had no overtones of anything but the fresh clams it was made of.

A raw bar and beer and wine are available in a front corner of the dining room.

Wilcox has some rules—you can't come in without a shirt on, and we saw him usher a visitor out during our dinner. But tables are spread out the front and side lawns for warm nights and summer days, and customers who don't want to put on their shirts are welcome there.

Customers pump their own ketchup out of a container into individual paper cups, and other condiments are available by request at the order counter, to cut down on the mess at the tables, perhaps. The neatness in that dining room made the casual dining more pleasant than usual.

But the high standards for the food itself will get us to come back, just as they do the regulars and summer repeats who make a line out the front door in July and August.

## The Downs Club Restaurant

(207) 883-4331
State Road, off Route 1, Scarborough
www.scarboroughdowns.com
Hospitality—Up or down, depending on your luck
Open for dinner at 6 PM, April through September on race days; call about race times.
Entrées $14 to $20; Wednesday and Friday might still be two-for-one nights

☞ *A meal served while you gamble on you favorites and watch the races*

All right, this is not the best food in the world. In fact, some of it is downright awful. But most of it is reasonably edible, and anyway you won't be paying much attention because your focus is on the race. Order your pasta *olio e olio*—Isn't that *aglio e olio?* But never mind—($13.95) or the grilled pork chops with a caramelized apple ( $15.95), but don't go for the seafood casserole ($18.95) unless your need for cream sauce renders you irrational. And then order another drink, because you've already swallowed the first too quickly in order to hop up the stairs—the tables are set along ascending rows, so everyone can see out the huge windows to the racetrack—to get your bet in on the first race. The daily double will be coming up, so you have another chance in a few minutes, and beginners have a strange knack of picking winners, even when they have no clue about how to read the arcane racing bill. You watch the odds changing on the sign across the track as the bets are placed and the system recalculates. It's so much fun to win an exotic wager, like the exacta for two horses winning first and second in the order you tell the bet taker at the top of those stairs, or the perfecta for first, second, and third, or the four finishers in the superfecta—fun because the odds are astronomical. Sometimes as high as 100 to 1, and more, and less, and almost never achieved. The minimum bet is $2. Seasoned bettors do not try to win the superfecta, but you are not a seasoned bettor, so what the hell. Dinner slowly cools on the plate you're ignoring as the horses round the far turn. Is that your horse in the lead? The restaurant is spellbound, the groans rise from the tables, the tension flares, people shout out—and it's over, and you can't believe it; you won the daily double.

It happens all the time.

# Fish Markets

### Bayley's Lobster Pound (207-883-4571), corner of Jones Creek Drive before the lobster co-op, Pine Point.
Open Monday through Saturday 9–7 in summer, until 5 in the off-season. Also a take-out, this place sells lobsters and cooks them free of charge. Selling both wholesale and retail, they also sell haddock, clams, and other fish. Lobster, shrimp, and crab rolls are sold inside.

### Pine Point Fishermen's Co-op (207-883-3588), 96 King Street, Pine Point.
Open Monday through Sunday 10–7 for retail sales. This is the place the local clam diggers bring their clams, and the boats deliver their loads of lobsters. This is the place to get fresh seafood.

# South Portland

## One Fifty Ate
(207) 799-8998
158 Benjamin W. Pickett Street
Hospitality—Friendly counter service in an informal room and backyard
Open for breakfast and lunch Tuesday through Sunday 7–2, dinner Thursday through Saturday 5:30–9:30
Lunch items $4.50 to $6.50, dinner entrées $10 to $12

*☞ My absolute favorite lunch place, with great soup and fine sandwiches, and now also the place to go for dinner*

This place was my refuge from everything harsh and demanding one year when I ate lunch here two or three times every week. Although I might have started going because the soup's price was right, I ended up staying because the cooks were showing my palette all kinds of things it needed to know, like the splendor of big chunks of salty bacon in a thick black bean soup, or the taste of the best tomatoes when they first come off the vines this far north, sometime in August.

The bagels are renowned. Misshapen, big, and chewy, they wear poppy seeds, sesame seeds, and "everything," including fennel and sunflower seeds. People who want to buy a dozen or more are sent down the road to the branch bakery and deli in Willard Square (see page 100), because the café needs a selection to make the bagel and egg, bagel and egg and cheese, and bagel and egg and ham and cheese ($4.50) sandwiches that light up the breakfast hours. There's also Lefty's Granola Funk Express ($3.50). Come lunch, 11:30 to 2, soups are served with a big chunk of bread according to the lights in the kitchen, always right on. The bakery makes and sells country white and wheat levain everyday, anadama on Tuesday, organic potato on Wednesday, honey wheat on Thursday, and a baker's choice on Friday.

Sandwiches include turkey with green goddess dressing, local greens, and sunflower seeds ($6.50), or a salami, provolone, and tapenade ($6.25). I still hunger for the smoked turkey with pear chutney that showed up on the chalkboard one fall. A cold rice-noodle salad was on the seasonal menu in summer, with carrots, cabbage, and onions in a peanut dressing ($5.50). And the plain egg salad with a touch of mustard was great on that levain.

Dinner entrées, just underway when this book went to press, like seared trout or pasta with chard and blue cheese, were excellent.

The coffee reigns supreme, even under the assault of ice, and could suck you into a slice of the cake sitting on the counter, or one of the other great pastries everyone else has been snatching up as you watched anxiously during lunch. Cream puffs and cheesecake show up at night.

# Bakeries and Take-Out

## One Fifty Ate's Willard Square Bakery and Deli (207-799-0688), 416 Preble Street.

Open Tuesday through Saturday 6–6, Sunday 6–2. An offshoot of the bagel and bread establishment on page 98, the bakery and deli is open more hours and sells a variety of delectable cheeses and sausages. Its Molinari and Sons sopressata, air-cured and "so damn good," sells for $8.49 a pound. The cooler also had some Humboldt Fog, a fabulous California aged goat cheese covered with a layer of vegetable ash, and Vermont Butter & Cheese Company's cultured butter. On the counter stood lavender shortbread and individual lemon pound cakes with blueberries, along with the breads and bagels.

## The Buttered Biscuit (207-799-5005), 347 Cottage Road.

Open Monday through Saturday 10–7:30. Strictly take-out, the Buttered Biscuit can provide you with every course of a great meal. Sesame noodle salad and other dishes show off in the cooler, and boxed chicken potpies ($7.49) sit in the refrigerator case every Wednesday. Other dishes vary; Hungarian mushroom soup ($7.99 a quart) gives way to tomato soup in late summer. The freezer holds artichoke dip, lasagna, and meat loaf, and the baked goods include date bars, brownies, and delectable almond crescents.

**The South Portland Farmer's Market** is held on Friday noon–4 from early May to late October in the Maine Mall parking lot off Philbrook Road, across from Romano's Macaroni Grill.

# Yarmouth

## Royal River Grill House
(207) 846-1226
106 Lafayette Street
www.royalrivergrillhouse.com
Hospitality—Well-trained and adept
Open for lunch Monday through Saturday 11:30–2:30, Sunday brunch
11–2:30, dinner daily 5–9
Entrées $19 to $33

☛ *A local favorite for an upscale lunch, and for making a dinner out of a couple of appetizers*

With a pretty setting on the Royal River along the waterfront in Yarmouth, this spacious restaurant keeps the meals inventive and fresh. A married couple I know likes to come here and make dinner out of a couple of appetizers, choosing from a changing list of items such as duck confit and apple and walnut salad ($10), and fresh mozzarella and heirloom tomato salad ($9), or sautéed Prince Edward Island mussels with garlic herb butter, tomatoes, and Vidalia onions ($12). The crabcakes are good with the roasted red pepper aioli, too ($12). If you want to eat a whole meal, there are entrées like maple and peach brined pork chops with caramelized cranberry and apple chutney ($19), swordfish steak ($24), and fish and shellfish gumbo with andouille, okra, and wild rice ($19). The wine list stretches the envelope with unusual bottles, many in the $20 range, and several up over $100. Either warmed fruit crêpes ($6) or Smiling Hill Farm ice cream ($2.25 a scoop) would make a great dessert.

## Uncle Billy's Village Bar-B-Que
**(207) 846-3770**
**365 Main Street**
Hospitality—Warm and accommodating, even without the grass skirts and coconut bras of yesteryear
Open for dinner 5–9 Tuesday through Sunday
Entrées $10 to $13

☛ *Phenomenal barbeque in a friendly place devoted to the absurd*

*Forecaster* reporter Lori Eschholz says it best: "The velvet Elvis is back up, the jukebox is in place, and the freezer flaps are hanging over the front door. Everything is ready for you to doodle a pig on a napkin to hang on the wall, roll up your sleeves, and get down to some serious bone sucking."

Devotees of Jonathan St. Laurent's various barbeque restaurants, Eschholz among them, have a certain passion for their peculiar spirit. For one thing, the chef is friendly, welcoming, and funny. For another, he cooks fabulous barbeque. The giant meals of brisket, ribs, chicken, and sausage are delicious. A slab of ribs for two ($24.45) comes with a choice of two sides—vegetable of the day, mac and cheese, corn bread, German coleslaw (made with mustard), beans, or mashed potatoes.

Catfish, tilapia, and beef brisket are typical specials. Thursday nights there's music; bluegrass played by a local band—by the end of the night the tables are shoved to the side and the last customers are dancing.

Desserts are homemade and star Death by Chocolate sundaes (with St. Laurent's signature sauce), and a Medina, semisweet chocolate mousse cooked with red wine, served in a coffee cup with raspberry sauce and whipped cream ($3.95).

## Lunch and Take-Out

### Clayton's (207-846-1117), 189 Main Street.

Market and bakery open Monday through Friday 8–6, Saturday 9–5; café open Monday through Friday 11– 6, Saturday 11–3. The "Famous chicken salad" is chicken mixed with Danish blue cheese, mayonnaise, and red grapes; it makes a delicious sandwich ($5.75) on Borealis sourdough bread or in a wrap. Cold weather might develop a customer's appetite for the grilled andouille sausage sandwiches with mustard, and sautéed peppers and onions ($5.95). The good hummus wrap employs cumin for a little something extra; the wrap is tightly packed and stuffed with grated carrot, tomatoes, and lettuce. Special soups are made daily, and while you enjoy your meal at a table in this big, attractive space you can be strategizing about dinner. Wine bottles fill galvanized tubs set inside the Bargain Canoe, and more expensive bottles fill shelves on the wall. Sofrito made by Jenny's Chickens, a one-woman kitchen in Cape Elizabeth, can be bought here, and occasionally the same talented woman's lemon curd is also available. Clayton's bakes brownies, peanut butter bars, and mini lemon meringue pies, among many other things.

### Day's Crabmeat and Lobster (207-846-3436, 207-846-5871) 1269 Route 1.

Take-out window open Monday through Saturday 11–8, Sunday 11–7. This is the place for fresh crabmeat, steamed lobster, and crab and lobster rolls for a picnic behind the business or on your sailboat, ordered from the take-out window. The crabmeat is picked by hand on-site, and one person I know who is a stickler for fresh won't buy it anywhere else. Crabmeat rolls were $7.49 in summer 2004, crabcake sandwiches $6.75, and a full menu of fried fish (and the inevitable hot dog for that unbeliever) filled the rest of a big board by the window. Ten picnic tables sit behind the building along a marsh and its tidal river, and a few more are under an awning on the side.

You can also buy fresh lobsters to take home and cook or ship out.

**CHAPTER 3**

# Brunswick and Bath

**W**ITH THESE TWO LARGER TOWNS along Route 1, the Maine coast begins its unique, glacial topography of long peninsulas stretched south like fingers reaching into the sea. The persistent, unchanging, and unchangeable rural character of the coast develops from this geography, where it really is awkward to "get there from here."

If you miss a turn, for instance—and some of the turnoffs are so discreet they are very hard to see—or if you turn south on the wrong road, you can find yourself a long drive away from a destination that you can see close by, lying across a stretch of water.

But the roads to the Harpswells, and to Georgetown and Robinhood and Cundy's Harbor and Phippsburg, all scenic, all with fine Maine seafood places tucked into their harbors, are all well marked. Be sure to study the map before driving through Bath, however.

If you can afford the greatest luxury of aimlessness on your vacation or your Sunday drive, going down any of the roads that lead to water south of Route 1 can be a pleasure. The landscape and the water are lovely. You will likely find one or more of Maine's charming seafood places; all seem like classics to the people with the good luck to be able to get to them. They vary in atmosphere from as plain as the deck of a wharf to full-service casual, but the best ones are still making their own desserts, picking their own lobster meat, and buying clams from somebody who digs them nearby.

For dinner at a more elegant destination, like the Robinhood Free Meetinghouse (see under Georgetown), you will probably need a reservation, but it's worth a chance if you're nearby to stop and see if there's a table. The chefs who succeed at drawing their customers off the main highway are proven talents, and Robinhood's Michael Gagne has been drawing us in for years. Down winding Route 144 you'll find an elegant old inn, the Squire Tarbox, serving good meals under ships' beams.

But several of the talents in Brunswick and Bath also have our allegiance. In Brunswick, graced with Bowdoin College's elegant campus and its art and arctic museums, Henry and Marty's and the Star Fish Grill both make such good dinners that they are worth a long drive.

In Bath, standing under the tall cranes of its largest employer, Bath Iron Works, the latest company to make this city one of the East Coast's important shipbuilding ports, Mary Ellenz has its ardent fans, and Mae's Café, under new ownership, is collecting them.

# Bailey Island

## Cook's Lobster House
**(207) 833-2818**
**Route 24**
www.cookslobster.com
Open daily for lunch and dinner 11:30–9, closed between
New Year's and Valentine's Day
Entrées $8 to $46

☛ *A giant seafood restaurant with water all around*

This place doesn't do only one shore dinner—it does four. The first and traditional shore dinner includes steamed clams or mussels, a boiled lobster, salad, and potato. From there you could opt for fried Maine shrimp or fried clams instead of steamed clams or mussels, or exchange the boiled lobster for a baked stuffed lobster, or choose both, fried clams or shrimp and the baked stuffed lobster, for $45.95.

Each shore dinner includes a bowl of clam or fish chowder or a cup of lobster stew.

From late June until Labor Day, Casco Bay Lines schedules a ferry from Portland that arrives here at noon, delivering people to eat lunch and taking other people away for an hour-long nature tour among the islands. If you are worried about arriving just as three busloads of tourists dock, call ahead and ask how lunch looks.

Clams are bought from local diggers who visit Look Out Cove, Merrymeeting Bay, and other nearby areas to dig the flats. The fried clam dinner is $19.95 (no à la carte, but you can order a clam appetizer for $9.95), and a fried seafood platter, with Maine shrimp, scallops, clams, and haddock, costs $21.95.

With 40 tables, each of which can handle six people, this place can absorb several busloads. A wharf next door, where lobstermen deliver during the day, sells live lobsters; they can be shipped. Desserts are made in-house, with blueberry pie the most popular, and strawberry shortcake, cheesecake, apple crisp, carrot cake, and ice cream all on the list.

# Bath

## Beale Street Barbeque and Grill
(207) 442-9514
215 Water Street
www.mainebbq.com
Open daily for lunch and dinner 11–9 or 10
Entrées $6 to $18

☛ *Casual barbeque in a laid-back atmosphere*

Mark, Michael, and Patrick Quigg started things here 1996, and now Michael and Patrick run this long-standing barbeque place that serves pulled pork, pulled chicken, shredded beef, and slabs of hickory-smoked ribs. You can choose a couple of sides, including coleslaw, barbecue beans, french fries, and rice, along with a bun or jalapeño corn bread. There is also a sampler platter that heaps up a choice of pulled pork, chicken, or beef brisket with a half slab of ribs, a quarter of a chicken, and smoked sausage. Jambalaya, fish of the day, shrimp Louisianne, and penne al pesto offer some respite from the barbeque. This 50-seat restaurant in an old building in downtown Bath has checkerboard floors, and booths and tables.

Desserts feature Key lime pie and a chocolate special called The Terminator ($4.95) that people like for its cakelike, dense chocolate terrine.

## Mae's Café
(207) 442-8577
160 Centre Street
Open for breakfast, lunch, and dinner Tuesday through Saturday 8 AM–9 PM, Sunday 9–3, closed for one week after January 1
Dinner entrées $14 to $21

☛ *All three meals with a wide choice from a larger menu and excellent baked goods*

Mae's Café is the new name of what was for 27 years Kristina's. The former owner has happily moved on, and since July 2004 Katie and Andy Winglass have been running things. The same bakery staff operates the ovens that bake the "World's best sticky buns," as Katie Winglass called them, along with the pies, scones, dinner rolls, and biscuits that come with every dinner entrée.

The restaurant still serves an enormous breakfast, with big omelets, Belgian waffles, and cinnamon twist bread made especially for French toast, or just plain eggs and bacon. Wireless Internet access works well with the espresso, in this big place that seats up to 120, made of two old farmhouses joined together.

The menu is now slightly more casual, with pizza, large salads, and lunch offered throughout dinner.

Grilled rack of lamb served with homemade mint and herb jelly, and chicken *piccata* with lemon and caper sauce ($16), are both accompanied by salad and rolls. Chicken pie and daily quiches are on a list of light fare.

A full bar upstairs is the site of entertainment, live music that can be found here usually on Thursday night.

*Cookies from Mae's Café honor the 2004 World Series champions, the Boston Red Sox*

# Mary Ellenz Caffe
(207) 442-0960
99 Commercial Street
Open for dinner Tuesday through Saturday at 5
Entrées $8 to $25
Reservations recommended, especially on weekends

☛ *A casually elegant dinner place with an Italian bent*

Portobello Parmesan ($12), grilled mushrooms over pasta with marinara, and *zuppa di pesce* ($25), with shrimp, lobster, haddock, calamari, and clams in a tomato broth and served with grilled bread, are a few of the Italian possibilities here. The balsamic chicken ($17), a sautéed breast with Gorgonzola and a balsamic reduction served with either pasta or grilled polenta, is one of the more popular entrées.

Lobster and artichoke dip, served with bruschetta, makes an elegant appetizer ($12).

Two Mary Ellens own this place, Mary Ellen Hunt and Mary-Ellen Pecci. They opened in 2000 with an emphasis on Italian from Hunt's close acquaintance with an Italian restaurant in Florida, and because Bath, as Hunt said, "could stand a different kind of restaurant." It's proved true. "The regulars would kill us if we moved," Hunt said. One of them is a woman from Colorado who comes here for the chicken.

The wine list offers wines from Australia, France, Italy, and California ($18 to $30 per bottle). Everything is available by the glass ($5 to $7).

Tiramisu, made to order, chocolate chocolate pie, Swedish Cream (a *panna cotta* with a berry sauce), can come at the end of the good meals.

# Starlight Café
(207) 443-3005
15 Lambard Street
Open for breakfast and lunch Monday through Friday 7–2
Lunch $3 to $9

☛ *A great place for breakfast and lunch*

Almost everything here is made from scratch, including the vegetable soup with its huge list of ingredients, curried squash soup, spicy black bean soup with smoked ham, and the spicy chili. A turkey is roasted in the oven every day, and green onion garlic rolls and others are baked every day as well. Those and

*Starlight Café in Bath dresses up for Halloween*

Borealis Breads are used for the sandwiches. Desserts—bars and cakes and pies and brownies—are fresh, too. "Big as your head" cinnamon buns, always $1, are baked every morning. "They're our thing . . . they're not really big as your head, but big as your fist," Susan Cramey, the owner, said proudly. She's now in her eighth year running Starlight Cafe. "We think we're a community place," she said, with poet readings and fund-raising breakfasts.

## Market and Coffeehouse

### Bath Natural Market (207-442-8012), 36 Centre Street.
Open Monday through Friday 9–6, Saturday 9–5, and Sunday 9–4. With value wines at $3.99 a bottle and a wide selection of others priced not a lot higher, this store's wine section is a find. Also Borealis Bread, Black Crow Bread, and Tuva's Bakery products, Coffee By Design beans, and Oyster Creek dried mushrooms.

### Café Crème (207-443-6454), 56 Front Street.
Open Monday through Saturday 7:30 AM–8:30 PM, 8:30 AM–2 PM on Sunday. Serving Maine's Coffee By Design coffee, espresso, and Smiling Hill ice cream. Starfish Grill delivers cakes here, including their five-spice cheesecake and chocolate puddle cake. Every morning the Hardcover Café at Brunswick's Bookland delivers cookies, muffins, cinnamon buns, stuffed croissants, brownies, date bars, and dream bars; Mr. Bagel delivers bagels. Lunches from quiches and burritos to salads take care of the crowd at this busy place.

*Café Crème in Bath*

**The Bath Farmer's Market** is held Thursday 8:30–2:30 and Saturday 8:30–12:30 at Waterfront Park on Commercial Street, May through October.

# Brunswick

## Henry and Marty's
**(207) 721-9141**
**61 Maine Street**
Open for dinner Tuesday through Saturday 5–9; closed two weeks in January
Entrées $14 to $26
Reservations recommended

☛ *A hip place with ambitious dinners, growing to meet the demand*

Started by Henry D'Alessandris and Marty Perry, this restaurant has grown in reputation and popularity. It has also taken over the space next door and can seat more than 50, while including a small bar with four stools, and two tables that some people reserve for dinner.

This place has been making a stay in Brunswick a pleasure for people attending the Stonecoast Writers Conference, and all the other participants in programs held at Bowdoin College and everywhere nearby, for years.

Its head chef, Dana Robicheaw, has a degree from Johnson and Wales University in Providence, Rhode Island, and worked at Back Bay Grill in Portland for four years, joining Henry and Marty's in January 2004.

The menu is designed by D'Alessandris and Robicheaw, and one week in the fall included a grilled center-cut pork chop with a cider demi-glace and apples, dried figs, apricots, and other dried fruits ($22), and a whole roasted sea bass with arugula pesto and olive oil–poached tomatoes, slow roasted at 200 degrees for an hour ($24). "We try to stay in a rustic Italian vein, with some things with a Cuban influence," said Robicheaw.

A favorite appetizer is the pear salad with Gorgonzola and toasted pecans, and the kitchen also puts together sautéed calamari with garlic, herbs, white wine, and butter ($7).

During the summer and fall a lobster dish with capellini pasta and a white wine and garlic sauce makes one simple preparation in the rustic style the restaurant favors. A weekly vegan vegetarian dish, like stuffed acorn squash, or soy meatballs with pasta, is always on the menu. Bread is from Portland's Standard Baking Company.

The menu changes quarterly, and every week two to four new specials showcase seasonal foods.

Desserts play the same simple, homey notes, from a chocolate cake with ganache frosting to fruit cobblers with seasonal fruits, like an apple, walnut, and ginger cobbler served in the fall. All desserts are $6, and the cobblers are served with Shain's of Maine vanilla ice cream.

The wine list was being expanded in fall 2004, with 24 wines available by the glass. The price of a bottle ranged from $19 to $65, most hovering in the mid-20s, with a total of 50 to 60 wines from all over the map, along with 6 dessert wines.

# Richard's Restaurant
**(207) 729-9673**
**115 Maine Street**
**Open Monday through Saturday for lunch from 11–2 and dinner 5–9,**
**Friday and Saturday until 9:30**
**Entrées $11 to $21**

☞ *German entrées interspersed with Black Angus steak and other favorites.*

When you can get tournedos in three versions—the Wilhelm, with mustard and onions; the Karl, with asparagus and mushrooms with hollandaise; or the Erik, with béarnaise (all $17.95)—and German classics like Wiener schnitzel, jaeger schnitzel, zigeuner schnitzel, or paparika schnitzel, with a choice of *späatzle* (noodles), *klosse* (dumplings), *heisser Kartoffelsalat* (hot potato salad)—and more—you have a way to encounter a culture that is our source for romantic music and great art without crossing the sea. Rindsrouladen ($11.95), thinly sliced beef rolled with onions, bacon, mustard, and pickles, is a Thursday-night special year-round.

A taste of the *Sachertorte mit Schlag* ($5) might transport your taste buds back a century to an elegant café in Vienna.

## Scarlet Begonia's
**(207) 721-0403**
**212B Maine Street**
Open for lunch and dinner Monday through Saturday 11–8, Friday and Saturday until 9
Entrées $7 to $11

☛ *A Bowdoin College hang-out with pizza, pasta and sandwiches*

Scarlet's Harlot, linguini with a puttanesca sauce of garlic, olives, and capers goes for $9.95, and Stephen's Dilemma, penne with sausage, chicken, mushrooms, roasted garlic, and spinach in a marinara sauce, is $10.50. This casual place feeds its customers inexpensively on pizza too. The pie called Phoebe's Feast, with roasted garlic, red peppers, feta, kalamata olives, and cheese, is $9.25. Salads at the top of the menu include Caesar and a Cobb, with romaine, bacon, tomato, blue cheese, and chicken ($8.75, half for $6.25).

## Star Fish Grill
**(207) 725-7828**
**100 Pleasant Street**
www.starfishgrill.com
Hospitality—Capable, friendly service
Open for dinner Tuesday through Sunday at 5, closed Monday
Entrées $16 to $25
Reservations recommended, handicapped accessible

☛ *Good Mediterranean seafood dishes in a pretty room tucked into a strip mall*

The blue walls and the starfish hanging in the windows, and the orange glow of the heat lamp over the service counter, all contribute to a warm, watery atmosphere that prepares you for the seafood that is this place's specialty.

On our last visit, however, it was the locally made spicy chorizo ($7) that really starred.

The appetizer came in a bowl, with thinly sliced pieces of the rich sausage saturated by a big handful of chopped garlic, and bathed in a rich savory sauce. The taste was hot and bits of tomato jumped out with sweetness. My glass of Spann Vineyards Mo Zin ($8.75) stood up well to that strong flavor.

Egg foo yong ($8), a crisply browned eggy pancake of scallions, mushrooms, and soba noodles, held a spiral of hoisin sauce, the sugary Chinese condiment.

My seafood-phobic friend stuck with a dish of pasta in cream sauce with chicken ($8), and murmured contentedly to herself as she ate. I ordered a dish of halibut and Gulf shrimp in a *piccata* sauce ($18).

Passing up desserts like bananas Foster ($5.50) and a honey cake filled with fig spread and three-nut cream covered with vanilla buttercream ($8), we ended with a classic crème brûlée, and this one held its perfectly glassy crust of brown sugar until my friend's spoon smashed through it to the yolky sweet cream below. It was perfection.

## The Great Impasta
**(207) 729-5858**
**42 Maine Street**
www.thegreatimpasta.com
Open for lunch and dinner Monday through Saturday
Entrées $10 to $16

☞ *Well-loved Italian classics like spaghetti carbonara and stuffed manicotti*

This place has won several awards over the years, including best Italian restaurant on the Maine midcoast for nine years running and restaurateur of the year in 2004. The friendly welcome makes that understandable, and the great Italian food makes popularity inevitable. Sometimes the waiting list grows long, but the restaurant puts you on the list if you call from home. Pollo Mediterranean ($13), a chicken breast baked with a pesto cream sauce, prosciutto, and tomatoes is popular, and salmon poached in a white wine and served Tuscan-seasoned reduction and served over fresh spinach ($14) is one of the restaurant's several fish entrées.

Desserts include Italian classics, like cheesecake, tiramisu, and spumoni, along with an American special, like chocolate peanut-butter pie. "It's so loved that we have regular customers order them for birthday parties," said Alisa Coffin, the owner for 20 years.

## Morse's Lobster Shack
**(207) 725-2886**
**18 Bath Road (Old Route 1 right by Bowdoin College)**
Hospitality—The staff races to keep the customers happy.
Open for lunch and dinner daily 11–8 mid-April through mid-November
Entrées $1.50 for a hot dog to $15 for a pound-and-a-half lobster

☛ *A family business in inexpensive seafood that's expanded from Harpswell*

In a drive-in that used to be called Ernie's, Sheldon Morse, who is from a family that's been lobstering for generations, and his wife, Kathleen, are working out the kinks in their second seafood restaurant. The first is on the water, open only in the warm weather (see page 119).

Lobster stew, fish chowder, and clam chowder are accompanied by homemade biscuits at this place with a bigger kitchen. Waitresses can serve customers in their cars, but for those who don't want to endanger their car upholstery with a lobster dinner, there are picnic tables and 30 seats inside. The place has been decorated with fishing nets and nautical paintings that the Morse family has collected over the years. Morse still heads out in his boat to check traps four days a week, pulling up his traps the week before Christmas. They won't go back until June, if the weather is very cold; but if the winter is mild the traps can return to find some lobsters moving around and hungry for the bait as early as April.

A brownie sundae, blueberry crisp, whoopee pies, cheesecake, and strawberry shortcake are on the dessert menu.

## Lunch, Take-Out, Coffee, and Markets

### The Bohemian Coffeehouse (207-725-9095), 4 Railroad Avenue, next to Hannaford.
Open Monday through Saturday 7–7, Sunday 8–2. Selling espressos and brewed coffee as well as beans, this coffee shop has free wireless Internet access and smoothies.

## Morning Glory Natural Foods (207-729-0546), 64 Maine Street.

Open Monday through Friday 9–7, Saturday until 6, Sunday 11–5. This grocery store sells some prepared foods from Wild Oats (see below). A local Pakistani woman makes bread and dal that is sold here, as are muffins and scones from Zoe's Market in Belfast, which makes good cookies too. Wine and organic groceries are also offered.

## Wild Oats Bakery and Café (207-725-6287), 149 Maine Street.

Open Monday through Saturday 7:30–5, Sunday 8–3. This family-owned business is not connected to the big grocery chain. Bread is baked fresh five days a week, and the café includes a deli with pasta and sandwiches, soup, cakes, and baked goods like muffins and scones. This favorite stop for everyone downtown has about 10 tables inside and a porch with umbrellas outside; a hall in the mall offers more places to sit. Changing soups might feature fish chowder; the turkey BLT is a favorite ($5.50). But everyone makes their own sandwich combinations from the posted list of ingredients.

*Morse's Lobster Shack opened in the off season*

### Hardcover Café at Bookland (207-725-7033), Cook's Corner Shopping Mall, Cook's Corner.

Open Monday through Saturday 9 AM–8:45 PM, Sunday 9–5:45. With the added attraction of Maine's largest independent bookstore alongside, this place makes all its muffins, scones, cinnamon buns, and cookies from scratch. Soups, salads, and ethnic entrées, including lasagnas, burritos, and quiche are available. Dessert can be a pumpkin cake with a walnut topping, Heath Bar cake, Key lime pie, or strawberry or raspberry cakes. Espresso, of course.

### The Humble Gourmet (207-721-8100), 103 Pleasant Street.

Open Monday through Friday 8–6, Saturday 8–3, closed Sunday. Six-grain, buttermilk-honey, and oatmeal are a few of the breads baked here. Turkey and cranberry and the veggie Reuben with sauerkraut, roasted peppers, red onions, carrots, and tomatoes on rye both make great lunches. So does the chicken almond tarragon salad ($5.25). Chowders and other soups are also a source of pride. Desserts, morning pastries, coffee cake, and prepared food to go make this a great place to stop on the way up the coast.

### Tess's Market (207-729-9531), 54 Pleasant Street.

Open Monday through Saturday 8 AM–9 PM, Sunday 8–8. This market is known for its wine. Montepulciano d'Abruzzo sells for around $7, and Monte Antico for under $10. Wine tastings are offered once a month. A blend of provolone and mozzarella tops all the pizzas, made with fresh pizza dough from Sorella's in Portland. When this place started 50 years ago, with hot dogs, the next step was sub sandwiches; by the 1960s Tess's made its own pizza, but they recently outsourced the dough to Sorella's. Hot buttered crust—bare baked pizza dough—is offered with sugar and cinnamon, or garlic and oil. Homemade meatballs are used in the meatball subs, and a large variety of sandwiches is available.

### The Brunswick Farmer's Market

is held on Tuesday and Friday 8:30–3 at the Brunswick Mall and Saturday 9–12:30 at Crystal Springs Farm from May to the end of November.

# Georgetown

## Five Island's Lobster Company
(207) 371-2990
1447 Five Islands Road
www.fiveislandslobster.com
Open weekends for lunch and dinner 11–7 in spring and fall,
daily 11:30–8 Memorial Day through Labor Day
Entrées $12.95 for the fried clam basket or the lobster roll

☛ *Picturesque, of course, with fresh lobster off the boats and fried seafood*

The main things here are the lobster, the locally dug soft-shell clams, the fresh corn, and the farm-raised mussels. But the **Love Nest Grill** also serves fried clams, fried salmon, and a grilled haddock sandwich that can be ordered with some inventive sauces, like a fresh tartar sauce that uses fresh dill or cilantro mayonnaise. The crabcakes are touted to be without crumb filler, and the serving of homemade onion rings, made fresh, is generous ($3.95). Hot dogs, steak-and-cheese sandwiches, and even a veggie burger take care of the rest of us.

## The Osprey Restaurant
(207) 371-2530
Robinhood Marina, at 340 Robinhood Road
www.robinhoodmarinecenter.com
Open May through October, with a shorter schedule in the fall and spring
Entrées $15 to $22

☛ *A restaurant at a marina where you can dock your boat, with good chowder*

The osprey nest on a piling outside the windows has been here since long before our friends called for a rescue after the engine on their sailboat failed, and we drove to get them and revive ourselves with the lobster stew in this pleasant dining room. Now with a tavern open for drinks, the Osprey serves boiled lobsters and fried clams.

# The Robinhood Free Meetinghouse
(207) 371-2188
210 Robinhood Road
www.robinhood-meetinghouse.com
Hospitality—You are served with exquisite attention and care here.
Open mid-May through mid-October for dinner daily 5:30–9; and off-season
Thursday through Saturday 5:30–8
Entrées $18 to $25
Reservations appreciated

☞ *High-quality, unique, and inventive food in a lovely old building*

Robinhood Free Meetinghouse is a magnet on the coast, attracting people from far away for a special dinner on its dark and lonely peninsula, because the chef has been sending so many home with fond memories for so many years. Michael A. Gagne makes such good dinners that nowadays his restaurant is packed on holidays like Valentine's Day, Mother's Day, and Thanksgiving. You will definitely want to make a reservation if you choose a popular night.

The building will loom up out of the trees as you finally make the last turn in the road that brings you here. Resplendent and tall, this Greek Revival white-clapboard building housed prayers and services by both Methodists and Congregationalists beginning in 1855. It underwent a renovation after some years as a high school and as a library in 1995, and now is one of the classiest restaurants you can find. Drinking a large glass of wine in a pew upstairs can be startling, but soon the conversation at the tables up on the altar area and behind the pews puts you at ease. Or is it the great wine? The long list will please the most demanding customer, as I know from having accompanied him here.

Four mushrooms in puff pastry ($8), with button, shiitake, and oyster mushrooms lending their strong presence to cream, make a fine way to begin, as does the onion and goat cheese tart with tender flaky crust ($7.50). But Gagne's signature wide range fills the appetizer list, which leans toward Greece with *Kreatopitas,* phyllo pastry with ground lamb, feta, and onion, and veers south with grilled shrimp adobo on homemade tortillas with banana salsa ($10).

Entrées shift the globe-trotting into high gear. Wiener schnitzel ($22.50), Thai vegetables in green curry ($18), and Jamaican jerk shrimp ($21.50) all stare out from the top of the list on a menu that changes in a few items every day, but remains for the most part the same year-round. Tournedos with two sauces, béarnaise and roasted garlic, brought all the pleasure of that classic to my lips, and the beef attained a sublime tenderness. My friend submitted to being pleased by the pecan-encrusted haddock with a beurre blanc ($21.50) after sending back the bottle of Bordeaux. He found a cabernet sauvignon that pleased us both. Valentine's Day, always a prime time for a fight, slipped away without conflict, although we had to decline all the glorious chocolate desserts, devil's food cake and chocolate mousse with Grand Marnier, and even the profiteroles (all $7.50).

# Harpswell

## Holbrook's Wharf and Snack Bar
**(207) 729-0848**
**984 Cundy's Harbor Road**
Open end of May through mid-September for lunch and dinner daily 11:30 to sunset, Entrées $9 to $15, BYOB

☛ *Relaxed atmosphere and a great location for good chowders and seafood*

Now with a middle section that has lights and heat and carpet, this simple seaside restaurant is turning into more of a lunch and dinner place. But you can't beat the outdoor seating for 120 people, with a great view of Cundy's Harbor, and tuna fishermen unloading their big catch close to your table. Tie up in your own boat if you want, and enjoy homemade lemonade.

This place sells seafood fried and baked, a vegetarian sandwich, and BLTs and chicken sandwiches and organic burgers for those opposed to or overwhelmed by seafood. The fish comes from a nearby supplier. There are no clams, but you can dine on haddock, scallops, and shrimp, all from Maine—there's nothing from Canada here. The lobster stew and fish chowder, with creamy broth, please the customers. And the kitchen makes the desserts—homemade cookies, brownies, and a crisp of the season, with a rhubarb starting in the early summer, changing to blueberry, and to peach. It might be sold out, though, if it's been a busy day.

## Morse's Lobster
**(207) 833-2399**
**Off Route 123, Harpswell Neck**
Open, weather permitting, for lunch and dinner 11–8, July 1 through Labor Day; after Labor Day Friday through Sunday 11–7 until mid-September Entrées $1.50 for a hot dog to $13.50 for a pound-and-a-half lobster, BYOB

☛ *The epitome of a summer seafood place, with no frills*

Simplicity, simplicity, simplicity. The season is strictly allied to the good weather here, because meals are enjoyed outside at picnic tables on a wharf. The small place is just down a hill to an open deck with about 20 tables covered by green umbrellas that do not keep off the rain. If it's raining, the restaurant is closed.

A cooked lobster was $8.95 a pound in 2004. Locals love this place with reasonable prices. Lobster cookers are simmering most of the day; but at lunch lobster rolls ($11.95) are the favorite. Fried clams, a haddock dinner, and a haddock sandwich, a Caesar salad with lobster salad, crab salad, and chicken and hamburgers are all available. For desserts, the biggest sellers are whoopee pies. Sometimes there's cheesecake or strawberry shortcake, and 75 percent of the time there's a blueberry or apple crisp.

## Estes Lobster House
**(207) 833-6340**
**1906 Harpswell Neck Road**
Hospitality—Counter service with servers who bring out the meals and clean them up
Open daily for lunch and dinner 11:30–8:30 Mother's Day through mid-October, closed Tuesday and Wednesday after Labor Day
Entrées $8 to $30

☛ *A huge place that can seat 300 people inside, with more room on the deck*

Most people who come here love fried clams or the lobster dinner, with a pound-and-a-half lobster. Clams are bought from a local digger, haddock and scallops from Canada, and shrimp from the Gulf of Mexico.

A menu for seniors over 60 is served from 11 to 4 and features broiled scallops ($6.95) with eight different additions, like a beverage and sides. Small portions are perfect and very popular for the folks who come here after church on Sunday.

Blueberry and apple crisp, strawberry shortcake, and a brownie sundae are all made here; the popular blueberry crisp is served hot with vanilla ice cream ($4.25).

A Lazy Lobster—four claws and two tails, accompanied by corn on the cob and coleslaw ($29.95)—can make dinner easy. A lobster pie with 4 to 5 ounces of lobster meat in its seafood stuffing and lobster salad on romaine are also on the menu.

"We never have a wait," said Amber Crooker, the manager and daughter of owner Larry Crooker, who has worked here off and on since she was a kid. Over the years things have changed. Full service is no longer offered; after placing an order at the counter, customers get their meals from servers who find them by looking for a table flag. Everything is served on paper and plastic. Leftover lobster shells, especially from the jumbo lobsters, go into Crustacean Creations, lobstermen built by Larry Crooker.

The business plans to make its own lemonade by summer 2005.

## Dolphin Chowder House and Marina
**(207) 833-6000**
**515 Basin Point Road, South Harpswell**
www.dolphinchowderhouse.com
Hospitality—Friendly and outgoing
Open daily for lunch and dinner 11–8 from May 1 to October 31
Entrées $5 to $22

☛ *Well loved for its lobster stew and fish chowder; you can moor your boat here*

Both the chowder and the lobster stew here are accompanied by a blueberry muffin. A bowl of the rich milk and cream based lobster stew is $12.95; and many people make the journey here just for this. A bowl of fish chowder ($8.95) and a fried haddock sandwich are two of this well-known restaurant's other favorites. A haddock dinner, with the fish either fried or broiled, is $16.95. Burgers,

*Dolphin Chowder House is a warm refuge during a rainy day on the Maine coast*

grilled cheese, and chicken dishes are on the menu too. Desserts always feature pies. The selection changes with the season; apple, pumpkin, and five-fruit were up on the board in fall, for $3.95 a slice with a scoop of vanilla ice cream. Beer and wine are served.

## Moe's Country Store (207-833-5383), 1220 Harpswell Neck Road.

Open daily, usually 6 AM–8 PM. The only store out here with gas or anything else; you can also get pizza, hamburgers, and subs. Breakfast sandwiches, bagels, pancakes, and French toast run the gamut for breakfast. Raspberry and apple turnovers are made at the store. Coffee is made with Green Mountain Coffee beans.

## The Water's Edge Restaurant
(207) 389-1803
75 Black's Landing Road (take Route 209 to 217)
www.thewatersedgerestaurant.com
Open daily for lunch and dinner 11–9 May to September
Entrées $11 to $29

☛ *A fresh seafood place in an old clam depuration shed on the water.*

Maine shrimp scampi, with butter, garlic, and herbs on pasta ($14.95), vies with "Today's Fresh Fish" specials, like baked cod with crabmeat stuffing in a Parmesan cream sauce ($15.95). Some like the grilled kielbasa appetizer, and the industrious can opt for lobster legs ("the little ones") served with butter ($3.95). Crabmeat dip ($6.25) and steamed clams (1 pound with butter and broth, $8.95) are made with creatures that grew up nearby. Salads, sandwiches, and, of course, boiled lobster can be matched with beer and wine.

# Phippsburg

## Spinney's Restaurant and Guesthouse
(207) 389-2052
987 Popham Road
Hospitality—Enthusiastic service
Open daily mid-June through mid-October, 8 AM–8:30 PM; also open in May, but call for hours
Entrées $9 to $27

☛ *A classic restaurant for quality seafood in a lovely, informal setting*

Dinner here in this classic seaside restaurant features something called the Wood Island Wreck: 3 jumbo shrimp, 5 scallops, 4 hand-cut sirloin tips grilled "on the barbey, and wicked good," according to Glen Theall, who has owned Spinney's with his wife, Diane, for seven years. The restaurant started serving seafood dinners in the late 1930s, here next to one of Maine's most beautiful beaches, and Theall has tried to jack up the quality while keeping the theme fresh seafood and good beef. "Good coast of Maine home cooking," he called it. "We grind our own hamburger. We serve the freshest possible ingredients we can get our hands on."

The large fisherman's platter, with four different seafoods and all the other fried food, is made with 100 percent vegetable oil that's changed frequently. "There's no scrimping there," Theall said.

Lobsters come from the waters in front of the restaurant, and the clam flats where the clams are dug are visible from the restaurant—they're some of the best flats in the midcoast, Theall claimed. Homemade biscuits are fresh everyday, and the kitchen serves up three meals a day, seven days a week, except after Columbus Day and in May, when breakfast, with its homefries and corned beef hash, is made on weekends only.

Pies (blueberry, apple, strawberry-rhubarb) and cakes, brownies, sundaes, and blueberry shortcake are all made in the kitchen here, not bought frozen off a truck. Theall doesn't think much of the majority of Route 1 area restaurants, which rely wholeheartedly on the freezer and the Frialator. Although he does use frozen french fries, he gets the best he can find, he said, and the onion rings are cut and made fresh every day.

# Westport Island

## The Squire Tarbox Inn
(207) 882-7693, 1-800-818-0626
1181 Main Road (on Route 144, just south of Wiscasset off Route 1)
www.squiretarboxinn.com
Hospitality—Servers have been well instructed in taking care of their tables here.
Open for dinner 6–8:30, April 1 through December 31
Prix fixe $29.50 to $39.50 for five courses
Dinner is by reservation only

☛ Dinner in a handsome old house in a quiet green landscape, with good food and wine

After we drove around the twists and turns of Route 144, the inn appeared like a refuge. We arrived when fall was just starting to nip at our toes, reminding us of the end of summer. The inn's dining room, with dark, bare beams pulled from a ship's belly, copper saucepans, and a range of cowbells from tiny to enormous hanging from a rafter, gave me the feeling of an old cloak pulled up around my shoulders. The glass of Renwood Zinfandel added to the pleasant sensation, while my friend enjoyed her Castello Albola Pinot Grigio. We read the menu and ate crackers with goat cheese and olives from a tray set out for inn guests and diners.

My friend started off with a rich onion soup, served in a small bowl with the right amount of melted Gruyère and Appenzeller cheese. My own soup of pureed mushrooms had a rich strong flavor of its own, and preceded a tender filet mignon with Damariscotta morels in a delectable sauce. Asked where the mushrooms came from, innkeeper Mario De Pietro brought out his collection from a mushroom seller at the Damariscotta farmer's market, a big hunk of orange hen-of-the-woods and a fine bowl full of little oyster mushrooms.

My friend found the haddock moist and good, and was put off only by the large size of the serving. Crusted by a potato pancake, it filled her plate. Our soups had been on a friendlier scale.

Both entrées came with a slew of thin strips of squash, sautéed and crisp, with a baked tomato full of summer sunlight, topped with crumbs. Vegetables and salads were grown in the inn's own organic gardens. Frozen Grand Marnier soufflé made a delicate dessert. My Pavlova, a meringue crowned with lots of whipped cream and only a few pale strawberries suffering a bad case of jet lag, made me hanker after better strawberries than the supermarkets could provide now that berry season was past.

Our meals cost $35.50 for the beef and $34.50 for the fish, which included the soup and dessert, and to which a 15 percent tip was already added. "Don't you want more than that?" I asked our pleasant waitress, who smiled, and shrugged and surely didn't mind when I tacked on another 5 percent.

**CHAPTER 4**

# Wiscasset to Damariscotta

I**N THIS SECTION OF THE MAINE COAST** lies a town that has been a tourist destination for generations. Boothbay Harbor, crammed with shops and restaurants, fills up with crowds in the hot summer months. Sited in a lovely stretch of harbors and islands, it's a good place to start from, but a great place to leave, for a drive southwest to Southport Island, either for dinner at an old inn like the Lawnmere, over the swing bridge on Townsend Gut, or for lobster on a deck at Robinson's Wharf, overlooking an uncrowded harbor.

Or drive east and south to Ocean Point, another classic inn with simpler meals; there's a place for tea on the way.

Just around the harbor itself, down at the end of Atlantic Avenue, you can enjoy the most elegant meals in the area at the Spruce Point Inn.

But Boothbay, while many people's destination, shouldn't keep a visitor long. A drive farther up the coast leads to more charming stretches of windswept, granite peninsulas, ending in Pemaquid Point and its lovely lighthouse. Or wind around Round Pond, with its artists in residence and lobster served on a wharf. The peaceful loneliness of this landscape paradoxically draws those crowds, but a taste of the forests are at hand for anyone who cares to walk down the many land trust and park trails.

Wiscasset and Damariscotta, the former right smack on Route 1, to many of its inhabitant's dismay, and the latter smugly just off, on Business Route 1, are delights to visit, with good antiques shops, bookstores, and clothing stores, along with several fine places for good meals.

Wiscasset is also the site of a friendly rivalry that mirrors the coast-long competition to serve and sell seafood, in particular the predominate lobster rolls.

*The swing bridge on Townsend Gut opens for a sailboat*

A while ago a place in Damariscotta, Larson's, now closed, sold the biggest lobster rolls, with perhaps 6 ounces of lobster meat in each one.

Now the little toasted and buttered hot dog rolls with 4 ounces are considered the gold standard, and two businesses face off at the bottom of the hill in Wiscasset, by the bridge on Route 1. Sprague's Lobster and Red's Eats both claim to serve that fully adequate amount. It's easier to buy one from Sprague's, at least so far, because there is not usually a line.

# Boothbay Harbor

## Ports of Italy
**(207) 633-1011**
**47 Commercial Street**
Hospitality—Servers are eager to get you what you want,
but may not be smooth about it
Open daily for dinner 5–9:30 April through mid-October
Entrées $20 to $28
Reservations suggested

☛ *An adept hand in the kitchen makes great classy Italian food, with everything by the season.*

One of the best meals of my life was a risotto *alla pescatore,* eaten outside at a Roman restaurant. So when I saw the same dish offered in a place in the middle of Boothbay Harbor, I had to try it. It evoked all that memorable pleasure, its Arborio rice cooked to a creamy, chewy consistency, expertly combined with tender scallops, shrimp, and squid. Salty, with bits of tomato and a spike of rosemary, the big dish ($14) more than satisfied my hunger for both the recollected meal and the new one.

Christa and David Rossi (David is from Milan) opened this bright place in 2004 and managed to collect customers quickly, filling its bright yellow, second-floor room. Reservations are a good idea, especially on weekends.

*Astici della Maine,* Maine shrimp, could have been ordered in three ways on the day of our visit, with cherry tomatoes, celery, and red onions in a citrus vinaigrette; with julienned carrots and fennel with lemon dressing; or with baby arugula, potatoes, and pomegranates in citronette ($10 to $21). Filet mignon with a wild mushroom demi-glace was $26. A good simple dish of penne with a bright, flavorful tomato sauce and mozzarella ($10) made another good meal, but next time we want to try the gnocchi, or the spaghetti *alla vongole* ($16), with cherrystone clams, garlic, and wine. And we'll be sure to place another order for the great sabayon, made with egg yolks and Marsala and served with toasted slivered almonds over seasonal fruit.

## 88 Grandview and Bogie's Hideaway Spruce Point Inn

(207) 633-4152
88 Grandview Avenue, P.O. Box 237
Hospitality—Well-trained, accommodating staff
Open daily for dinner mid-May through late October
Entrées $24 to $30

☞ *Elegance and fine dining in a beautiful location at 88 Grandview; high-quality casual food in a stylish lounge at Bogie's Hideaway*

The long, pale cream dining room of 88 Grandview, the formal room in this resort, can fill with light reflected off the water just down the slope outside. Brown plaid curtains and room-dividing swags of brown linen keep the large space from seeming huge. We came in early summer, and were ushered in by a friendly hostess and soon supplied with a glass of Wild Horse Cabernet ($8.50). Then our server brought us an amuse bouche, free from the chef: a fried pork spring roll with a strong meaty flavor.

The next course I ordered myself, a napoleon of grilled portobello, Bermuda onion, tomato, roasted pepper, and fresh mozzarella ($8). Lovely to behold, it worked in the mouth too, the thick slice of onion sweet and fresh. Shrimp and lobster on wakame salad with pink horseradish sauce ($10) and a steak-house Caesar with caper berries, Asiago, croutons, and fresh anchovies ($7) also made the appetizer list.

The roasted sea bass entrée ($26), with miso butter sauce and served on a bed of wasabi potato with four teeny bok choy that had a sweet hot bite to them, held great moist white flakes of the fish in its large portion, tender and well contrasted by the brown sauce. The chef was clearly not shy of using ordinary sugar or chili pepper flakes, along with a lot of beurre blanc, to send the food into orbit.

A scaloppini of pork tenderloin with sage prosciutto and smoked mozzarella in a mushroom Madiera sauce ($26) also argued for complication.

*Spruce Point Inn looks out onto the ocean*

The crème brûlée, with tender custard, did not meet the density and richness required by my in-house crème brûlée expert, who nonetheless polished off every scrap. The chocolate oblivion torte formed a mass of solid chocolate, relieved only by the crème anglaise and some zigzags of raspberry coulis, and was perhaps too much. I could have had the four-berry pie instead, though no doubt the butterscotch and hot fudge sundaes would have been much of a sameness. Dense and rich were the themes of our fine meal.

Bogie's Hideaway serves more casual, less expensive food; it's where families dine, with hamburgers for the kids and more inventive food for the adults.

## The Lobster Dock
**(207) 633-7120**
**At the east end of the Boothbay Harbor footbridge**
www.thelobsterdock.com
Open for lunch and dinner 11:30–8:30 early June through early October
Entrées $12 to $25

☛ *Famous for doing lobster rolls hot with butter and cold with mayo*

Sometimes when you mess with a classic it works out. This place has won attention and praise for messing with the lobster rolls, serving them warm with melted butter or cold with mayonnaise, and their customers love them both. The lobster stew is made with all the knuckle and claw meat left from the busy business in lobster rolls. You can be assured there's no frozen meat being used here. A seafood *fra diavolo*—scallops, shrimp, mussels, and a whole lobster cooked in a spicy tomato sauce full of herbs, garlic, and bay leaf, served on linguini ($24.95)—made one customer exclaim it was the best he'd had.

But seafood lovers can explain to their reluctant children and spouses who can't stand shellfish that there's a nice strip steak here, or some crunchy garlic lemon-butter artichoke hearts ($5.95).

# Casual Meals, Take-Out, and Treats

### Blue Moon Café (207-633-2349), 54 Commercial Street.
Open Monday through Saturday 7:30 AM–2:30 PM, Sunday 8–2. Best to hit this popular spot after the height of lunch hour. Order the perfect crabcakes ($7.95) at the counter, or the splendid chicken quesadilla with melted Boursin, tomatoes, and big chunks of chicken ($7.95). Lots of wraps and grilled sandwiches, clam chowder, and high-quality deli sandwiches and salads. If you're lucky you'll snag a table on the deck over the water.

### Chowpaya Thai Restaurant (207-633-7272), 28 Union Street.
Located on the way to the other side of the harbor, this Thai restaurant came well recommended and serves all the Thai food you might suddenly be craving after too many lobster rolls with mayonnaise. *Chaoprya,* "a special curry," could do the trick, with scallops and shrimp in red curry, sautéed with red peppers, onions, green peas, and served on a bed of spinach ($15.95).

### Eastside Market (207-633-4616), 26 Atlantic Avenue (across the footbridge).
Open daily Memorial Day through Columbus Day, this place can make your picnic lunch with crabmeat rolls or any of a dozen special sandwiches and salads. For breakfast it serves egg sandwiches and wraps, including three eggs with salsa and sour cream ($3.75). Pizza is made on focaccia, and wine, beer, and champagne complete the feast.

### Ebb Tide (207-633-5692), 43 Commercial Street.
Open 6:30 AM–9 PM daily, closing at 9:30 on Friday and Saturday, closing one hour earlier all days off-season. Fresh peach shortcake and a scallop stir-fry were the specials on our visit, when these pine walls and booths were full up with happy tourists. Homemade pies, Grapenut pudding, and a hot fudge brownie sundae vied with the chocolate, vanilla, strawberry, and coffee frappes for our allegiance, after the fried clams and fish entrées.

## 88 Baker's Way (207-633-1119), 89 Townsend Avenue.

Open daily 5:30 AM–10 PM; Vietnamese menu available from 11 AM. Many people never get farther than the baked goods ranged in the glass cabinet in front, and the standard menu of ham and cheese or breakfast eggs. But lemongrass stir-fries, ginger stir-fries, and beef and shrimp curries are on the "other menu" just as ably prepared by the Vietnamese owners as the doughnuts and apple dumplings Boothbay teenagers scarf up by the dozen.

We enjoyed a wonderfully tender dish of stir-fried squid ($8.25). Scored in a crisscross, this local seafood came richly flavored with lemongrass and garlic in a spicy sauce that turned chunks of celery, strips of carrot, and pieces of broccoli, into exotic foreign vegetables. The vermicelli rice noodles with thin-cut pork, crumbled bacon, shredded lettuce, onion, and bean sprouts topped with chopped peanuts and hot chili sauce was another surprising delight unanticipated in Boothbay Harbor. We enjoyed both in the simple back garden, surrounded by small maple, dogwood, and magnolia trees, and our waitress was wonderful.

*Making apple dumplings at 88 Baker's Way*

## MacNab's Premium Teas & Tea Room (207-633-7222, 1-800-884-7222), 5 Yu Yu Tea Lane (off Back River Road).

Open Tuesday through Saturday 10–5 in July and August, 10–4 from September to June. Pots of tea come in a variety of patterns, and the cozies are phenomenal, the knitting creativity of a resident genius. Our Darjeeling, steeped before it was brought to the table, tasted like the best tea I make for myself, and the cookie medley with an apricot bar was delightful in the midafternoon, as it's meant to be. Cock-a-leekie soup ($5 a bowl), scone sandwiches, and highland pie, with ground beef, in an oat-and-onion crust ($10.95) cover some of the savories, and sweets of cake and blueberry scones with lemon curd cover some of the rest. Tea paraphernalia, and tea itself, are for sale in this charming little house in the country.

### Type A Café (207-633-2020), 29 McKown Street (Route 27).

Open daily 10–6 in summer. Turnovers, shortbread and macaroons, and an apple pie made with very thinly sliced apples pull in the customers here. Prepared foods are sold, like "gâteau" of crêpes with alternating layers of spinach, béchamel, and cheese; also pâté, and steaks, chops, and ribs can be bought for the grill. Breakfast baked goods, too.

### Boothbay Region Lobsterman's Co-op (207-633-4900), Atlantic Avenue.

Open from 11:30 mid-May to mid-October. A retail business, selling lobsters, clams, and mussels, is open year-round, and they can cook the seafood to go. In-season, this is the place of choice for discerning visitors interested in an annual lobster dinner. The picnic tables inside and out are informal and comfortable, and you won't need to worry about the liquid squirting out of the lobster claw you just cracked open. Crabmeat rolls, corn on the cob, and a few seafood alternatives make the menu work for families.

### Down East Ice Cream and Yogurt Factory (207-633-3016), the By-Way.

Open 10:30–10:30 in the height of summer. Make your own sundae here with hot fudge and other toppings, and homemade hard ice cream.

*MacNab's Tea Room serves restorative tea and many accompaniments*

**Daffy Taffy and Fudge Factory (207-633-5178), the By-Way.**
No credit cards. Open daily 10–10 in-season, making candy every day except Wednesday. The taffy is pulled, and cut and wrapped, and fills up the little skiff inside the store for the passing children to bail out.

**The Boothbay Harbor Farmer's Market** is held on Thursday 9 AM–noon at the high-school ball field on Route 27 from mid-June to the end of August.

# Damariscotta

## Andrews' Pine View Restaurant
**(207) 563-2899**
**769 Main Street (by intersection of Business Route 1 and Route 1 at the north end of Damariscotta)**
Open daily for lunch and dinner 11–8, Saturday and Sunday for breakfast 7–11 and dinner 11:30–8
Entrées $9 to $20

☛ *A casual family place with lunch or dinner available from 11 to 8*

The menu for lunch and dinner is the same and all items can be ordered at any time. Pasta Alfredo with marinated grilled chicken ($15.25) comes with a salad and homemade bread. Haddock Lester ($9.95 small, $15.95 large; most entrées are available in two sizes), baked haddock with crumb topping with Parmesan, lemon, and garlic, is the most popular choice on the dinner menu.

Craig Andrews had his own restaurant in Boothbay Harbor, Andrews' Harborside, for 17 years before he moved out to Route 1. With a degree from the Culinary Institute of America, and in spite of a slow start in 2003 (which might have been because previous restaurants at this location were bad), things are starting to pick up with more and more locals choosing the Pine View for a night out. Steaks, seafood, and salads, and a children's menu, make this a fine stop for travelers.

Homemade desserts include blueberry cobbler, apple crisp, lemon cake pudding with raspberry sauce, brownie hot fudge sundae, Grapenut pudding, chess pie ($2.75 to $4.50).

# Backstreet Restaurant

(207) 563-5666
**Elm Street Plaza, 17 Elm Street**
Open in summer Sunday through Thursday 11:30–8:30, Friday and Saturday
until 9; call for winter hours
Entrées $13 to $20

☛ *Casual dining and good food with a water view*

Look for this place off Main Street, in the Elm Street Plaza behind the Radio
Shack. It's right on the river, with views of the water from all of the approximately
100 dining-room seats, and was redecorated in 2004. You won't forget where it
is once you find it, like the locals who return for a good, casual dinner, you will
want to come back.

You can find vegetarian dishes, like a penne pasta and green salad, and sometimes the chef can provide a vegetable platter or another choice if you don't see
one that works. Bistro steak ($20), a cut off the shoulder that's very tender; lob-
ster dishes in the summer; rare seared tuna ($20); and a haddock napoleon lay-
ered with spinach, bacon, potato, and aged cheddar sauce ($18) come on and
off the changing menu.

A variety of red and white wines are paired with foods and range from $4.25
to $6 a glass, with most bottles in the $20 range.

Desserts are all made here and change every week, from crème caramel to
cheesecake ($4.25 to $6); they vary according to the season.

# Damariscotta River Grill

(207) 563-2992
**155 Main Street**
Open daily 11–9:30 (closing at 8:30 in winter), Sunday brunch 9–2:30
Entrées $14 to $22

☛ *Well-made meals that cater to everyone who likes good food and
reasonable prices.*

This hopping place with exposed brick and two floors offers pan-seared scallops
with a balsamic reduction, spinach, and roasted tomatoes; a risotto and a roast
of the night; and prime rib every Friday on a menu that changes seasonally.
Favorites are the lobster cakes with hand-picked lobster, and oysters on the half-
shell or baked oysters topped with bacon, spinach, and Pernod cream sauce. Three
sauces accompany the raw Pemaquid oysters, brought up from the water less than

10 miles away, and they are always popular.

Now under the same ownership as the Anchor Inn at Round Pond (see page 142), this place in the middle of town offers a lot of fresh seafood and grilled meat.

With a very reasonably priced wine list—20 wines available by the glass and about 60 bottles, many under $20 and the most expensive $47 (this one seen listed at another restaurant for $70)—the grill sells a lot of wine, as well as beer and cocktails from the full bar.

A baker makes all of the homemade desserts and bread. Eight to twelve desserts are offered every night and include crème brûlée, different cheesecakes, bread pudding, and chocolate peanut-butter torte (all about $4).

## King Eider's Pub
(207) 563-6008
2 Elm Street
www.kingeiderspub.com
Hospitality—Bustling staff usually handles the busy meals well
Open daily 11:30–11
Entrées $9 to $19

☛ *Longer hours make this the place to go early and late for seafood, soup, and desserts*

"We're the home of New England's finest crabcakes," Todd Maurer, one of the owners, told me, a claim under local, not to mention statewide, dispute. He also said the crabcakes are made following a secret recipe, and with the freshest local ingredients, he continued. Downstairs is a cozy pub, outside are tables for warm-weather dining, and upstairs is a restaurant. After eight years in business on Main Street before moving to Elm, this place does catering too.

Breads, including baguettes and rye and corn bread, are made by the restaurant, come with the meals, and are used in the sandwiches. A fall menu offered a variety of Reubens made with Morse's Sauerkraut (see page 190), and homemade Thousand Island dressing. A smoked salmon BLT, teriyaki beef salad with spinach and cucumbers, and chicken potpie are also on the menu.

"Molly's famous homemade desserts" are another of Maurer's selling points. They could include a bread pudding with Irish whiskey sauce, toffee apple pie, or Guinness chocolate cake. The locals like this place, and we loved its clam chowder late one cold night, when everyone else had shown up and the place was like a warm bright hearth sheltered from the night.

# Ice Cream, Groceries, Breakfast, and Lunch

**Round Top Ice Cream (207-563-5307), Business Route 1.**
Open from the first weekend in April to Columbus Day for retail sales, this Round Top provides many coastal businesses with their ice cream and makes the stuff year-round. Brenda and Gary Woodcock have owned this business for 18 years, but worked at it for 34. The business has been established for 80 years, and started at the nearby Round Top Farm. With 15 percent butterfat, the product is properly called a super-premium ice cream. Over 52 flavors are made, as well as sorbets, sherbets, and frozen yogurts. Fall flavors include pumpkin, Indian pudding, ginger, cinnamon, and apple cinnamon; all are made with cream from Maine's three biggest dairies. Different creams goes into different flavors, because the cooks here are very alert to the creams' tastes. In the summer, try the red raspberry swirl.

**Rising Tide Natural Foods Co-op (207-563-5556), 15 Coastal Marketplace Drive.**
Open daily 8–7. Rising Tide sells Rosario Vitanza's Italian Bread (see page 139), Tuva and Black Crow breads, and Café Miranda focaccia, pizza, dips, and sauces. Organic local produce in-season, local organic eggs, Morse Farm raw whole milk. and Wicked Joe's roasted coffee are also available. There's a café offering sandwiches, muffins, cookies, and soups made here everyday with all organic ingredients.

**The Breakfast Place (207-563-5434), Main Street.**
Open 7–1 for breakfast only in summer, and for lunch as well in winter. Anything customers want they can have at this accommodating place, or they can choose from a menu that lists a Toad in a Hole, among many other things. The wide selection of baked goods, all made fresh each morning, included muffins (blueberry, raspberry, blackberry, banana-nut, corn), cinnamon buns, cheddar biscuits, English muffins, and white, wheat, oatmeal, cinnamon-raisin, anadama, rye, pumpernickel, and cheddar breads on the day I visited. Homemade crabmeat and cream cheese omelets ($7.50) are often ordered, as is a popular shrimp Creole omelet made with Maine shrimp ($7.50).

**Weatherbird Café (207-563-8993), 72 Courtyard (just off Main Street).**
A small café with good lunches, including paninis with prosciutto and a wide range of ingredients. Soups like an asparagus with wild rice often sell out. Fresh-

-baked scones might include mascarpone-filled and ham-filled, or ginger-pear and raspberry. Pecan brioche are also available, and coffee comes from Rock City Coffee Roasters. Linzer tortes are from a local baker, and lavender-lemon and rosemary-lemon pound cakes and great gingerbread with crystallized ginger are also available. Gelati from New Hampshire are featured too.

Produce, local and imported cheeses, eggs, a great wine section, and prepared foods to go, some from Café Miranda (see page 173) are sold. Outdoor seating is available in summer.

**The Damariscotta Farmer's Market** is held Monday 9–noon from late June to late August at the Assembly of God Church, corner of Business Route 1 and Belvedere Road, and Friday 9 to noon mid-May through late October at the same location.

# East Boothbay

## Tea by the Sea
**(207) 633-9996**
**18 Sunset Rock Road**
Hospitality: Brisk and competent
Open for lunch Tuesday through Saturday 11–3in summer, Thursday through Saturday in winter
Lunch $6 to $8
Reservations advised

☞ *A sweet small teahouse with a view of Linekin Bay and good food*

High tea is served with a prior arrangement, but a lunch of asparagus and leek quiche with a side salad ($7.95) or a turkey Reuben on pumpernickel with coleslaw ($6.95) makes a high point in a day spent driving around the coastline's hidden nooks and crannies. Tuscan tomato or ginger-carrot soup ($3.95 a bowl) can be ordered in a cup with half a sandwich ($5.95).

Desserts could be a chocolate terrine with raspberry sauce ($4) or ladyfingers with ice cream topped with strawberries ($3.25), depending on the season and whim of the owner, who also makes good berry and Boston cream pies, ($3.50 or so a slice). You'll enjoy this bright, cheerful place far from the crowds.

# Lunch and Take-Out

**East Boothbay General Store (207-633-4503), 255 Ocean Point Road.**
Open daily year-round. Pizza and deli sandwiches and subs, baked goods like cookies and bars. A big wine and beer selection.

# Newcastle

## Lupines Restaurant
**(207) 563-5685, 1-800-832-8669**
**At the Newcastle Inn, River Road**
www.newcastleinn.com
Open for dinner Tuesday through Saturday at 6, Columbus Day through May
Friday and Saturday only, closed January
Prix fixe dinner $55

☛ *Elegant meals with ingredients culled from surrounding sources*

A five-course dinner is served here, with hors d'oeuvres enjoyed together at 6 and dining starting at 7, when an appetizer or soup, salad, sorbet, entrée, and dessert are enjoyed at the table.

Nine wines can be bought by the glass. A long wine list lingers in France and California, and the wines are sometimes chosen to particularly complement the menu.

Start with the local favorites, Damariscotta River oysters, served with lemongrass mignonette, or a Swango Farm green salad with chervilly beans, or roasted Long Island cheese squash with curried crème fraîche. Dinner entrées could be long-simmered beef short ribs with leek puree and fall vegetables; a grilled buffalo hanger steak with red wine, thyme, and shallots accompanied by a tomato, olive, and onion tart; or a roasted duck breast with plums, ginger, crisped semolina, and haricots verts.

Everything is baked on-site, from the bread to the cakes. Josh DeGroot, the chef since 2003, was named one of the top 12 chefs of 2004 by the Maine Organic Farmers and Growers Association. He makes butter as well as ice cream and sorbet, and favors local and organic foods, including Maine artisan cheeses.

The rich desserts include German chocolate torte with dried cherries and white chocolate ice cream. Warm blueberry buckle, a hot cobblerlike dessert served with a blueberry buttermilk ice-cream sundae, and lemon-herb sorbet all on one plate celebrated Route 1 blueberries. An apple crêpe with orange-caramel sauce and cranberry-honey ice cream was also all made by DeGroot.

# New Harbor

## Bradley Inn
**(207) 677-2105, 1-800-942-5560**
**3063 Bristol Road**
www.bradleyinn.com
Open daily except Wednesday from the end of May through October, Thursday through Sunday off-season
Entrées $23 to $28

☛ *A pleasant ambience with candlelight, with elegant food to match*

At the tip of the Pemaquid peninsula, this old sea captain's home has weathered more storms than any of us and wraps itself around diners with a congenial atmosphere. Meals could include a pecan-crusted lamb loin or sea scallops with pasta in a cognac beurre blanc.

## Rosario's Café and Pizzeria
**(207) 677-6363**
**Southside Road**
Open in summer Tuesday through Sunday 4–8, Saturday 12–8; closed Tuesday Labor Day through October and mid-April to June, closed November through mid-April
Entrées $4 to $18

☛ *Welcome to the best pizzeria north of Boston*

Pizza, salad, and homemade cannolis, and biscotti from Dina Lattauzi in Cumberland are sold here. Rosario Vitanza owns and cooks at this 6-year-old café; he made Italian bread for 12 years before opening up this restaurant and still sells bread from the café. The pizza is made with tomato, pesto, or a creamy Parmesan sauce, with homemade dough, and toppings could include portobellos, eggplant, red pepper, many other vegetables, pepperoni, sausage, Virginia-baked ham, salami, bacon, prosciutto, anchovies, grilled chicken, and meatballs.

But Rosario makes specials that have been so successful they don't change. A popular red pizza, *Melanzane e Funghi,* uses eggplant and portobellos, roasted red pepper, fresh garlic, fresh mozzarella, and shredded Parmesan ($6.25 for the mini, good for one person; $15.25 for a large good for three to four people).

The Pollo Pesto Pizza features chicken, pesto, grilled portobellos, red pepper, mozzarella, and Parmesan ($6.95 mini, $16.75 large). Prosciutto *Bianco,* with creamy Parmesan-garlic sauce, shaved prosciutto, grilled portobellos, mozzarella, and Parmesan, has been called the best pizza in Maine by at least two professional travel writers ($5.95 mini, $14.95 large). Bring your own wine to this casual place without waitresses. Pick up at the counter, and enjoy, and end the great meal with an espresso and one of those supernatural biscotti.

## Samoset Restaurant
**(207) 677-2788**
**2477 Bristol Road**
Open daily in summer 11:30–8:30, until 9 on weekends; in winter nightly for dinner, Friday through Sunday 11:30–8
Entrées $11 to $18

☛ *The only place around here that stays open in winter, with a simple and popular menu*

This local favorite makes shrimp scampi and chicken Parmesan (both $9.95), and stir-fries with vegetables, chicken, or shrimp served with rice or tossed with noodles ($9.95). Also available are smothered chicken ($10.95), liver and onions ($8.95), 14-ounce rib-eye steak ($14.95), and meat loaf ($6.95); all come with baked, mashed, or fried potatoes or rice pilaf. Soups, salads, appetizers, and a cheap kid's menu keep this a popular stop. Wednesday night is Italian night, with 10 entrées and a free salad, and on Sunday the turkey dinner starts early—roast turkey, stuffing, winter squash and other vegetables, mashed potato, cranberry sauce, and gravy ($8.95). The pub next door is open every night from 4 to close, and you can eat the full menu there until the kitchen shuts down.

Homemade desserts include apple, blueberry, and pumpkin pies every day ($3). Some cakes come from Sam's Club, like the triple chocolate fudge cake ($3).

## Shaw's Fish & Lobster Wharf
**(207) 677-2200**
**129 State Road (Route 32)**
www.shawsfishandlobster.com
Opens daily 11–9 from the Thursday before Mother's Day until the Sunday after Columbus Day

Entrées $10 to $30

☞ *One of the great, huge, seafood restaurants on the coast*

A triple lobster can be over $30 when lobster prices are high, other times around $25, but most people go for the twin special at this huge seafood restaurant. One woman from down south of here extolled its true Maine flavor, downscale and straightforward.

With counter service and paper and plastic, the kitchen serves customers their orders when their numbers are called. Three hundred people, 100 inside and 200 out, can make this a crowded spot; Lloyd Mendelson, one of the two owners, estimated he serves 100,000 people in a summer. I've known it to look decidedly weary after a busy night. It's set where the Hardy Boat Cruises depart to take folks out for a glimpse of the repopulated puffins, and is therefore perfect for a casual meal before or after a cruise. You may have to walk down from a parking lot set up the road in the busy season.

The place has a raw bar underneath the deck, right by where the boats come in. Pemaquid ale made in North Whitefield, Maine, by Sheepscot River Brewery is the most popular ale, and goes well with the revered Damariscotta oysters, $1.40 each with lemon and cocktail sauce. Fried clams, shrimp, scallops, and haddock, all from Maine, are the most popular items on the menu, but broiled halibut and swordfish ($12.95) can be enjoyed here too. Homemade chowders and stews are well loved. Full bar available.

Homemade strawberry and blueberry pies, among others, range from $2.25 to $2.75.

# Pemaquid Harbor

## Pemaquid Fisherman's Co-op's Harbor View Restaurant
(207) 677-2642, (207) 677-2801
Co-op Road
www.pemaquidlobsterco-op.com
Open daily 11–8 from Memorial Day weekend to Columbus Day
Entrées $7 to $17

☞ *Picnic-style dining indoors or out, in a spot that looks out on the Pemaquid River*

These picnic benches are a fine place to enjoy chowders, and the fresh oyster stew ($6.95 a bowl) is made with the oysters that grow under the water you can see from your seat. Forgo the hot dogs and burgers for the crabmeat roll ($7.95) or the lobster roll, or indulge in some very fresh seafood, such as a crabmeat melt ($6) or fried haddock, clams, shrimp, or scallops. A shore dinner with a 1-pound lobster, steamed clams, corn on the cob, coleslaw, and a roll was $16.95 in 2004. The lobster tastes great here, at the oldest continuously operated fishermen's cooperative in the United States.

# Round Pond (in Bristol)

## Anchor Inn
**(207) 529-5584**
**Anchor Inn Road**
Open daily Mother's Day through Columbus Day for lunch and dinner in summer, closed some days off-season
Entrées $13 to $22

☛ *High standards set this casual seaside restaurant up on a level with its lovely harbor view.*

Run for 17 years by the same family and the same chef-owners, this restaurant set on beautiful Round Pond Harbor serves great crabcakes and seafood. Fresh boiled and baked stuffed lobsters are popular, and the chowder makes us all happy. Steak and chicken are on the list that also includes five dinner specials, two of them fresh-fish entrées. One pleased customer enjoyed a crab melt, and recommended the Italian seafood stew and seared scallops with red and yellow tomatoes. The restaurant seats 100 with room at the bar for a dozen more and has a wine selection with a few unusual white varietals, modestly priced.

Desserts are homemade, and may include Bailey's Irish Cream cheesecake or Kyle's killer chocolate cake, with white chocolate ganache filling, dark chocolate ganache on the outside. There's a large variety of fruit and mixed-fruit pies, and Swedish almond cream with fresh berries runs $4.50.

# Southport

## Lawnmere Inn
**(207) 633-2544, 1-800-633-7645**
**65 Hendricks Road, P.O. Box 29**
Hospitality—Our server went out of her way to make our meal good.
Open for dinner Memorial Day weekend through Columbus Day, daily until
Labor Day, closed Monday thereafter
Entrées $16 to $25

☛ *Old-fashioned seaside hotel dining; a comfortable atmosphere with wonderful food*

The glassy water of the inlet reflected the stroking wings of the gulls moving across, close to the surface. We were looking at a cove off Townsend Gut from our chairs in the Lawnmere's knotty pine dining room. A lawn sloped down to the water from the inn, and children ran across the grass while a couple paddled to shore in a kayak.

We started with a grilled bruschetta with portobello and porcini mushrooms and chèvre ($8.50), and enjoyed the savory dark mushroom and tangy cheese. My glass of wine wasn't much, since the inn doesn't offer much by the glass, but a Renwood Viognier ($21) and a Faustino Rioja ($17) were on the longer wine list.

A fresh white roll like the old Parker House rolls and banana bread were served with butter. Entrées like garlic-lime pork tenderloin, with red onion marmalade and roasted red potatoes ($17.50), and tuna steak with Cajun rémoulade ($17.50), give an idea of the direction the kitchen is headed. My choice, seared scallops in red pepper sauce, came with the scallops perfectly tender, and the sauce was a delightfully sweet match. My friend opted for the mozzarella and tomato salad with balsamic vinaigrette and a smattering of pine nuts ($9.50). It was too early for good tomatoes, but the dish was otherwise good, if a bit large.

Strawberry ice cream with whipped cream was offered as the homemade flavor of the day ($3.50). But when I begged instead for a plain bowl of berries, because it was the right time for them, the waitress offered to get one for me. They were the real thing, truly ripe and plainly good, with fluted spots of whipped cream. The maple crème brûlée ($4.50) made a good dessert for my companion.

You can come out here for breakfast, too, in-season, and try their corned beef hash, blueberry pancakes, and homemade granola. Better yet, just spend the night. The inn is being renovated, slowly but surely, while keeping its old charm.

# Robinson's Wharf
(207) 633-3830
Route 27 (just across the swinging bridge over Townsend Gut)
www.livelobstersfrommaine.com
Open daily for lunch and dinner 11:30 to close mid-June through Columbus Day
Entrées $4 to $16

☛ *Away from Boothbay Harbor crowds, on the peaceful coast,
with good seafood*

Lobster dinners, fried seafood plates, and seafood rolls are the highlights at this classic lobster shack, where the lobstermen make deliveries, and the restaurant fills what was once the island's bowling alley. Outside dining in good weather puts you right on the water.

Clambakes for 20 to 25 people can be arranged here in the restaurant, in the main dining room.

Desserts include pies made by a woman on the island; strawberry shortcake and brownies are made at the wharf. You can buy live lobster and clams here year-round; a small fish market is planned for 2005. Cooked lobsters and clams can be purchased from the retail side in the summer.

# Wiscasset

## The Black Hawk Tavern at the Ledges
(207) 828-8118
211 Main Street
Hospitality—Friendly and accommodating
Tavern open Wednesday through Sunday 5–11, dining rooms open Thursday through Saturday 5–9
Entrées $7 to $22
Reservations unnecessary, handicapped accessible

☛ *Moderately priced good food in beautiful Georgian dining rooms*

There's a curse on the building, some people say, with restaurants coming and going, and the whole place once landed on the auction block. But with the latest renovation, the Black Hawk Tavern, the building can lift up her head again and smile.

The front dining rooms are handsome, one an olive-toned green with off-white trim, English hunting prints, and brass sconces. The table for five in a bay window, framed by slender fluted columns, is elegance defined. The opposite parlor has been painted white, a red-and-orange-toned abstract hangs over the black fireplace, and round, white Japanese lanterns shade the ceiling lights. Our food was brought quickly to our table, which was the only one occupied.

Our chef offered a half-dozen grilled Damariscotta oysters, dabbed with a chipotle chili sauce ($10) that were utterly delicious. Their heat, both in temperature and spice, livened up the delicate oyster flavors, and the tiniest bit of cooking left the oysters themselves tender and sweet.

Braised pork dumplings, meaty and folded in a tender wrapper ($8) pleased a dumpling fan at the table.

The haddock, scallop, and shrimp entrée ($20) came swimming in butter, a lovely element for things from the sea, and rather rapturous for the first moments of my enjoyment, but also quickly too much. The four spears of asparagus hailed from far away, always a pity in late summer in Maine when the local harvests are brimming over in the farmer's-market stalls.

A cheese and red pepper quesadilla ($13), its chicken happily subtracted at a diner's request, was suspiciously oozing orange cheese. But it pleased, with a cup of sour cream and a cup of slightly hot mango salsa (the mango unripe), and though more than half of it was uneaten, that is so typical of this particular customer it hardly counts as a criticism.

Dessert was great. Key lime pie ($4) was intensified with a scattering of lime zest over its creamy rich filling and cream topping, and blueberry crisp ($5) used the Maine blueberries then in-season, keeping them whole and sweet in a light sauce, with a browned sugary oat topping all bathed in a melting scoop of Round Top vanilla ice cream.

The Black Hawk's menu mixes casual and more ambitious food, making this a good place for families to try, and for groups with varied resources. The glass of Renwood Zinfandel ($6) was one of only a few offered by the glass, but the wine list also featured modest prices. A hamburger with fries ($7) would make a visit to the elegant dining rooms the economic equal of some meals at Red's Eats down the hill, where you have to stand in a line along noisy Route 1.

George Freeman and Bill Waters, the owners, also own Lilac Cottage Antiques next door.

# Le Garage

(207) 882-5409

**15 Water Street (at the town dock, one block south of Route 1)**

Open daily in summer for lunch and dinner, closed Monday from Labor Day to June

Entrées $9 to $22

☛ *Casual down and more elegant up with a view of Wiscasset Harbor; well-made entrées*

Light dinners are offered at this popular restaurant, like a charbroiled lamb and vegetable kabob ($12.95) served with a fresh vegetable, coleslaw, and potato or rice; add a chowder or dinner salad and the price is $16.95. A regular dinner might be walnut-crusted fillet of haddock with vegetable, baked or mashed potato, or rice; $20.45 includes a chowder or a dinner salad. The wine list is long, and several wines are offered by the glass.

Lunch brings fans of the sandwiches and salads, and a big assortment of omelets, like ham and cheese and a creamed finnan haddie.

Rolls are made here, as are the desserts—fruit cobblers, apple crisp, dessert crêpes.

# Red's Eats

(207) 882-6128

**Water Street (Route 1 just south of the bridge)**

Open April through September 11 AM–2 AM Friday and Saturday, until 11 PM Monday through Thursday, and noon–6 on Sunday

Lobster rolls about $14.95

☛ *The famous place with a line serves big lobster rolls with melted butter, and hot dogs.*

Few people around here understand why people stand in long lines to order the food at this little roadside stand. In the hot sun such behavior seems downright pathological, but it certainly ranks as one of the sights to see—a line alongside Route 1 all summer long—when you are driving through Wiscasset. There is a reputation here, an allure, some buzz about the best lobster rolls, and that accounts for the patient waiting. You can get the lobster roll with just melted butter; and a big bunch of lobster meat does come on the toasted bun, $14.95 in 2004. Also, there are hot dogs.

# Sprague's Lobster
## (207) 882-1236
## Route 1 (on the wharf at the western end of the Wiscasset bridge)
Open 11 to sunset mid-June through the weekend after Columbus Day
Entrées $2.25 to $15

☛ *Take-out, inexpensive great shore dinners with fresh boiled lobster, and big crab and lobster rolls*

Lobster rolls here cost $10.95, a haddock sandwich $4.95 in 2004; the shore dinner, with steamers, a boiled lobster, corn on the cob, a hard-boiled egg, a roll, and melted butter, was $14.99. There is a shorter wait, less expense, and a better view here than just up the road at Red's Eats.

Lobster and clambakes are offered by this operation whenever and just about wherever a customer wants to have it—including Virginia. But most are held here in Maine. For their take-out business, owners Frank and Linda Sprague are hoping to add more room on their corner of the Creamery Pier, a town dock, with a few more picnic tables. Frank Sprague makes clam fritters fresh from chopped clams without the bellies, but wanted to emphasize this is his business's 16th year, and that the centerpieces of his meals are the cooked lobsters. They each have their own timer when they go into the pot for your dinner.

And he fills his rolls with 4 ounces of lobster meat, the same weight used at Red's.

*Simple fare at Sprague's Lobster*

Hamburger - $2.25
Royal - $2.75
Bacon Hamburger $2.75

Grilled cheese $1.95
w/ Bacon $2.95

Lobster Roll $10.95

Cheeseburger - $2.75
Royal - $3.25
Bacon Cheeseburger $3.75

Fresh Cut Fries

Haddock Sandwich w/ cheese + tartar sauce $4.95

# Sarah's Café

(207) 882-7504
**45 Water Street (corner of Main and Water)**
www.sarahscafe.com
Open Monday through Friday 11–8, open at 6:30 AM Saturday and Sunday,
until 9 PM in summer and on winter weekends
Entrées $10 to $18

☛ *A good place for a meal on the road, with hot soup and fresh baked goods*

Sarah Hennessey, owner of Sarah's Café for 24 years, uses all her own recipes. She started a restaurant in Robinhood when she was 15, making pies, burgers, and fries, and hasn't stopped since. In 1981, her vocation was a home-delivery business in Boothbay Harbor; she moved to her present location in 1987. She bought and renovated the present restaurant in 1997, when the pub was added.

All along she's been serving meals made from scratch; homemade soups and chowders are made from a list of 578 soups developed over the years and accompanied by homemade bread. The owner's little brother, Howard, is the lobsterman who provides the lobsters, Swango Farm in Woolwich is the biggest supplier of vegetables, and herbs come from Sarah's own garden in Georgetown.

Lobster cooked 12 different ways and haddock Mateys, fresh baked haddock in lemon butter and wrapped in a fresh dough blanket and baked, are some of the favorites on the menu. There are always lots of specials, with seafood, salads, many vegetarian items, and Mexican dishes filling the list.

There are 120 seats with two outside decks, with an engaging view of the water and the traffic on the bridge.

# The Sea Basket

(207) 882-6581
**Route 1**
Hospitality—Counter service in an immaculate, cheerful dining room
Open Monday through Saturday 11–8 June through August, Tuesday through
Saturday in the off-season, closed mid-December through most of February
Entrées $3 to $14

☛ *A local favorite for lobster stew, fabulous scallops, and well-made fried fish*

Following the white arrows painted on the pavement makes walking into this bright, cheerful restaurant as easy as pie, and the perfectly trimmed shrubs and window boxes are signs in themselves of the well-organized, tranquil efficiency reigning inside. Blue molded wood benches fill the floor, and murals of green fields along the sea fill the walls with color.

The menu over the counter offers the classic favorites—chowders ($5.95 for a bowl of fish chowder), dinner baskets, and jumbo platters of fried fish. Single servings are thoughtfully available, without fries, rolls, or coleslaw ($6.25 for fried Maine shrimp), and all the offerings also come in sandwiches or rolls, like a big haddock filet sandwich ($5.75).

A kid's menu with penne pasta with Parmesan ($3.50) and peanut butter and jelly sandwiches ($3.99, with fries) makes this place work for any family.

Scott Belanger works here now, a part-owner along with his mother and father; the Belanger family started the business in 1958. He said his folks put a lot of money into the place, and are proud to be using only canola oil for the frying, with absolutely no hydrogenated fats.

He also extolled a woman who comes in at 6:30 AM every day to wash the place clean, from the ceiling to the floors, and trim those perfect bushes. The business is closed for only a short spell in winter because, Scott said, they want to keep the staff they depend on to run the restaurant so well, and they have a loyal local clientele who pop in to keep things going even in dreary March.

The restaurant is well known for its lobster stew, which can be purchased frozen and brought back home, and for its great scallops. Belanger said, "We know the boats," and they know him.

Among several options for dessert, the rainbow of whoopee pies stands out, from blueberry and raspberry "fruit 'n cream" to peanut butter to classic chocolate, all $1.85 each. This place is a favorite and many Mainers know just where it sits, on the inland side of Route 1 south of the village of Wiscasset. The extensive parking lots are ready to accommodate everyone. You can also bring your own beer or wine to enjoy with your meal—the restaurant does not have a liquor license.

## Lunch and Take-Out

### Treats (207-882-6192), 80 Main Street.
Open Monday through Saturday 10–6, Sunday 12–5. This gorgeous food store makes Wiscasset a lucky place, but knowledgeable travelers can visit it easily. The interior, with its old butcher-block table, stone counters, and array of appealing food will rouse an appetite as you contemplate what to buy.

*Fresh baked goods beckon from the top of Treats'*
*display case*

Little pies—strawberry, blueberry, peach, and raspberry ($5.95 each)—sometimes sit elegantly on top of a glass display case that holds little chicken potpies ($5.50), along with big platters of stuffed eggplant and roasted veggie pasta salad.

People sit along a long table in the rear of the store to drink the strong coffee and eat blueberry muffins in the morning, or enjoy the sandwiches for lunch. The store makes the different sandwiches every day, rearranging its turkey, roast beef, salami, and ham with Boursin and goat cheese on bread from Black Crow and Borealis delivered fresh in the morning.

Teas, jams, maple syrup, chocolate, marzipan, and a fetching tower of homemade cookies beckon along the way through the store. In a neighboring area another glass display case is stocked with cheese, including Hudson Valley Camembert, and along the walls filled with wine you can find a $20 bottle of D'Arenburg Footbolt Shiraz from Australia.

I can't imagine not stopping here on the way through town, to get the last details of a picnic or a fabulous house present; it's on the right when you drive north, two blocks before the bridge out of town.

**CHAPTER 5**

# Western Penobscot Bay

**T**HRIVING TOWNS LINE UP in this wonderfully mixed section of the coast, the site of what some call the state's best restaurant: Primo's, in Rockland. Here Route 1 gets to hug the water, turning north in Rockland, and crawls through the crowded streets of Camden. Camden has been an upscale tourist stop for a long time, but Rockland seems to be the place on the move now, with several good restaurants, bakeries, and cafés. This blue-collar town is vital year-round; Camden seems more livable after the summer season is over.

Belfast sustains its energetic mix of high and low, with Chase's Daily overflowing with the most beautiful produce you've ever seen in the summer and an elephant trumpeting from the roof of the Colonial Theater.

Of course there are always changes going on in the restaurant scene. With the growing tourist business here, some places are able to succeed and thrive. Francine Bistro, a small and completely admirable restaurant in Camden, makes the most sophisticated happy year-round. Farther up the coast Jesse Henry and Tim and Joan Porta bought an oceanfront house just south of an inn they own in Lincolnville. They plan to open a 70-seat restaurant there by the time this book is published; I mention it here because their intention is to make a place that can rival Primo's, with food, an ocean view, Maine produce, and fish and meat filling the menu. Henry and the Portas have been working with Rob Evans and Nancy Pugh, owners of the brilliant restaurant Hugo's, in Portland. They will build a pier so a water taxi from Islesboro and private boaters can access this still nameless restaurant. A soft opening is scheduled in May, in time to get down to serious business in the summer. Call the Inn at Ocean's Edge (207-236-0945) for information.

# Belfast

## Chase's Daily
**(207) 338-0555**
**96 Main Street**
Hospitality—Busy, but the service is up to speed and accommodating
Open Tuesday through Saturday 7–10:30 for breakfast, 11:30–3 for lunch,
Friday 5:30–10 for dinner, Sunday 8–1 for brunch
Entrées $9 to 14
Reservations necessary for Friday-night dinners

☛ *A beautiful vegetarian paradise (especially during harvest season)
with great soups, salads, and lunch and breakfast, and Friday dinner
feasts*

The Chase Farm in Freedom stocks the back room of this high-ceilinged space;
on my visit in August, the crates of tomatoes, baby artichokes, French filet beans
and long, snaky pale purple Japanese eggplants filled that space with their glamorous shapes and colors. Those vegetables were on the menu in front, in the
roasted eggplant sandwich with peppers, fresh greens, and walnut sauce, on
grilled white sourdough bread ($7.50), and in the heirloom tomato salad ($9),
worth every penny.

*The produce section at Chase's Daily overflows in late summer*

Some people have been known to complain about not being able to get bacon with their breakfast here. But when you can order a Swiss chard and feta omelet ($6.50), or buttermilk pancakes with fresh blueberries ($6.25), you can put off bacon for a day.

The bakery makes anadama bread, rye walnut loaves, and semolina bread, and bakes fresh ginger-cream scones and pear-almond muffins. Cheeses like Manchego from Spain and Great Hill Blue from Marion, Massachusetts, are available at the counter. Dinners range from enchiladas and Middle Eastern specialties to other vegetarian tarts and baked dishes, with prices around $14.

This is a place to seek out, especially in the late summer and fall, and enjoy.

## Darby's Restaurant and Pub
**(207) 338-2339**
**155 High Street**
Hospitality—Friendly and helpful
Open daily for lunch 11–3:30, dinner from 5
Entrées $8 to $19

☛ *An old-fashioned space with a wide-ranging menu, burgers to pad Thai to fish-and-chips*

There are so many different things to eat here, under the tin ceiling or alongside the old bar, both of which have been restored and preserved since this place opened in 1865. Macaroni and cheese, made with Gruyère and cheddar ($11.50), comes with a small salad, and makes eating this supreme comfort food a little more respectable. The portobello sandwich is served on the restaurant's own bread with sautéed onions, roasted garlic mayonnaise, and fresh mozzarella ($7.95), and hand-cut french fries are included. Big salads, pad Thai, enchiladas, and sweet potato raviolis give a glimpse of the range here, and I shouldn't omit the potato latkes with sour cream and applesauce ($6.50).

# Seng Thai

**(207) 338-0010**
**160 Searsport Avenue (Route 1)**
Hospitality—Quick, attentive, and perfect
Open Tuesday through Sunday from 11:30 for lunch and dinner
Entrées $9 to $14

🐖*A great Thai place with spicy dishes and fresh ingredients*

I had the Japanese eggplant special ($7.95) for lunch; it came with red and green peppers, shrimp, and chicken all in a black bean sauce. Given a scale from 1 to 5, I asked for the spice level of 2. Brown rice was another $2, and white an extra $1. My friend ordered the pad Thai, which arrived with a carved white radish rose, lots of green scallions and bean sprouts, and a good, clear flavor not unduly adulterated with sugar.

My eggplant was one of the same pale purple, curved, slender beauties I would later encounter in the produce section at Chase's Daily (see page 153). Decorated with a beet rose, the plate gave off an enticing aroma of garlic, and I enjoyed every bit. I'd been warned the spiciness levels were serious; level 2 was perfect, giving me just the slightest heat and mildest perspiration.

A couple of beautifully arranged platters of spring rolls were ready for an incoming customer who was throwing a party. You could call ahead and bring one to the house you've been invited to some summer weekend.

# Young's Lobster Pound

**(207) 338-1160**
**Mitchell Avenue**
Hospitality—The efficient counter service dispenses hundreds of lobsters to customers.
Open from 7–7 in summer, open in winter for take-out only, closing at 5:30
Entrées $10 to $17 and up for lobsters

🐖 *A big lobster pound and take-out place with views of Penobscot Bay*

This place keeps thousands of lobsters in its tanks—and as many as 500 people can find a place to sit and eat them, either upstairs or outside at a picnic table. Good weather is everything, because there is no heat in the big inside dining room; after the warm weather goes, the place is open for take-out only. You can always buy lobsters, clams, mussels, and crabs here, either fresh or cooked to go. An 8-ounce cup of clam chowder is $4.95, a lobster roll is $11.95, and a crab roll costs $9.95.

# The Twilight Café
**(207) 338-0937**
**70–72 Main Street**
Hospitality—Willing to go out of their way to accommodate you
Open for dinner at 5:30 Monday through Saturday
Entrées $16 to $25
Reservations recommended

☛ *Somewhat upscale fish and beef dishes in a friendly, casual atmosphere*

With a short wine list that nevertheless spans the globe, the Twilight Café sets out to do a little more than its neighbors while at the same time keeping its food to a fairly narrow path. Appetizers include mussels steamed with white wine, with a little cream and Dijon mustard ($9.50), Ducktrap smoked salmon ($10.50), and a plain classic, shrimp cocktail ($10.50). Pecan-crusted lobster cakes with pumpkin-ginger crème fraîche ($21) headed up the entrées, and beef tenderloin with port wine mushroom sauce followed. The large room with a storefront window on the street has a good local base and does more business, of course, in summer.

## Lunch, Take-Out, Coffee, and Ice Cream

**Bay Wrap (207-338-9757; www.baywrap.com), 20 Beaver Street.**
Open Monday through Saturday 11–7:30 in summer, closes at 7 Monday through Friday and at 4 on Saturday in winter. Walk through Hobbledehoy Toy Store to find this spot from Main Street. Try the daily soups, including turkey, black bean, and vegetable all stars (no meat). Or enjoy the popular wraps—maybe the Wraptor, with roast turkey and garlic aioli, greens, tomatoes, onions, sprouts, and cucumbers in a flour tortilla ($6.35). A list of eight vegetarian choices includes Delhi Delight, with curried cauliflower, carrots and lentils, jasmine rice, Asian slaw, garlic yogurt sauce, and mango salsa in a tortilla ($6.35). All were available in a small size for one dollar less.

**The Belfast Co-op Café (207-338-2532), 123 High Street.**
The store is open daily 7:30 AM–8 PM; grilled sandwiches and lunch specials available 11:30–2:30. Order from the chalkboard menu in this big health-food store. Roast beef and honey ham sandwiches were $4.95, and veggie and cheese $3.95. A vegan chef salad and a chef's salad (both $5.95) could be eaten in the café, with its

blond wood, golden walls, and green railings and cornice. Sticky buns and chocolate chip cookies are from Zoe's, cakes from Cedar Street Bakers. The curried cashews are wonderful.

### Bell the Cat (207-338-2084), 1E Belmont Avenue, Reny's Plaza, Route 3.

This place has a very laid-back atmosphere and serves as a reading corner for a big paperback and music store. The long list of sandwiches

*The Belfast Co-op Café is a good place for lunch*

sticks to the tried and true, from BLTs to German bologna. They use good Borealis bread, and you can get one with hummus, roasted red peppers, and melted provolone cheese (hold the sprouts) ($5.25).

Or get a pecan bar, or a lemon-raspberry cream cheese bar (both $1.75), or a cookie from a range of glass jars (55¢ each) to go with a cappuccino. Sundaes and milkshakes too.

### The Gothic (207-338-4933), 108 Main Street.

Open Monday through Friday 7:30–5, Saturday and Sunday 8:30–5; closed Sunday between Labor Day and the July 4th weekend. This little coffeehouse is stunning, with Valentine red walls and brilliant white pressed-tin wainscoting and ceiling, added during the 1993 renovation by owner Lisa Whiting. Red teapots serve great organic Assam and other teas; and espressos, cappuccinos, and lattes steam out of the machine in the back all day long, made with Rock City Coffee Roasters organic coffee (the company that owns Second Read in Rockland). Ginger scones and cranberry-lemon coffee cake were available on our visit. You can also get a scoop of ice cream, in flavors like espresso, crystallized ginger, and black raspberry ($2.76 for a single scoop, $3.27 for two).

*The Gothic is painted in glamorous shades of red and white*

## Scoops (207-338-3350), 35 Lower Main Street.

Open Monday through Saturday 12–10, Sunday 12–6 in summer; Thursday through Sunday 1–10 in winter. Round Top Dairy in Damariscotta makes the ice cream, which is outstanding, and sundaes and other specialties can be enjoyed in the big comfortable room at tile tables with wooden chairs. The back wall is covered with owner Karen Rak's brother's caricatures. Chuck Rak has depicted folks from the renovation crew,

*Scoops serves Round Top Dairy ice cream*

regular customers, the mayor of Belfast, and others, and might be able to do an amusing drawing of you for about $20 if you see him. But in any case you can always order "Kate's Ireland Cure," ginger ice cream with hot fudge sauce, which sounds just right, if somewhat obscurely Irish ($3.95 for a small portion).

## Three Tides (207-338-1707; www.3tides.com), 2 Pinchy Lane.

Open Tuesday through Saturday 3 to late closing (bar hours), Sunday 1–8 in summer, later opening in the off-season. A place for a good drink, and a fun place to hang out and eat good bar food, either at the serpentine polished concrete bar, or in tan vinyl booths, or in warm weather on an outdoor deck overlooking the river. Small plates include crabmeat-stuffed mushrooms ($6.50), little pizzas ($8.50), pear, goat-cheese, and greens salad with toasted pine nuts ($7), and Pemaquid oysters ($11.50 for six, $19 for a dozen).

## Wasses Hot Dogs, in Reny's Plaza on Belmont Avenue (Route 3).

Open Monday through Saturday 11:30–4, Friday until 5, closed Sunday. A kraut dog is $1.85, and so is a bacon dog, and a cheese dog, at this small white building on the side of the Reny's Plaza parking lot.

# Food and Wine

## Perry's Nut House (207-338-1630, 1-800-6PERRYS; www.perrysnut house.com), Route 1 just north of the Belfast Bridge.

Open Monday through Saturday 8–6, Sunday 9–5 in summer; Monday through Saturday 9–5 in winter. This place was once the biggest and best tourist trap on the coast, with a collection of nuts from all over the world that has since gone to the Smithsonian, and a big collection of animals and creatures on display after a taxidermist preserved them. The new owners, George and Ellen Darling, want to bring back some of the old attractions, and have plans for a second-floor display in 2005, near the 1947 wall mural of Africa. An albatross with an 11-foot wingspan will be there, as well as an 1893 wild boar, and a lion and a cheetah, but the man-eating clam from the Philippines cannot be found. This was the Belfast Cigar Factory before it became a nut house, and it started in 1850 as a ship captain's house; its roof ridge is built like the keel of a ship.

Nowadays there's an array of candy, dried blueberries, maple syrup, and honey for sale. A rare find is the chokecherry jelly from Colleen's in Searsport.

### The Clown (207-338-4344), 74 Main Street.
A branch of the Portland store. The manager here said, "The people who run the store in Belfast cater to the Belfast customers," ordering wines especially for the town. You can also pick up a $370 custom picnic basket, made of wicker, with cutlery, dishes, and a thermos.

**The Belfast Farmer's Market** is held Tuesday, Friday, and Saturday 9–1, from early May to late October at Reny's Plaza parking lot at the junction of Route 1 and Route 3.

**A second Belfast Farmer's Market** is held Tuesday 3–6 and Friday 9–1 in the municipal parking lot in downtown Belfast, on Lower Main Street.

*Classic buildings in Belfast*

# Camden

## Atlantica

(207) 236-6011, 1-888-507-8514
1 Bay View Landing
www.atlanticarestaurant.com
Hospitality—Long waits have been an issue here.
Open for lunch and dinner Wednesday through Monday
Entrées $17 to $27
Reservations advised

☞ *Popular for its good food; you might want to go on an off-night and avoid the crowd*

Chef-owners Ken and Del Paquin run this upscale place on the water, and don't serve the same old fried clams. You can order interesting dishes like a marinated grilled lamb chop with poached pear ($12) or roast wild salmon with cranberry horseradish butter ($24), and eat them on the deck that stands over the water.

Starters, like black bean cake served hot with eggplant caviar and basil-walnut pesto, make this spot a possibility for vegetarians. There's lots of good wine by the glass, including Cline Pinot Gris ($5) and Sterling Merlot ($11), along with eight half-bottles of wines a little more special, like Wild Horse Pinot Noir ($19). Full bottles range from downright cheap and up, with lots to choose from.

But reports of long waits here suggest it's a good idea to come on an off-night, or early or late. Or ask how things are when you call to make reservations. Staffing issues caused the restaurant to stop serving lunch in fall 2004 but were expected to be overcome by spring 2005.

## Cappy's Chowder House

(207) 236-2254
1 Main Street
www.cappyschowder.com
Open for lunch and dinner daily in summer,
closed one or two days a week in winter
Entrées $9 to $17

☞ *A big place dedicated to inexpensive seafood*

Seafood pasta and specials, like fresh swordfish, are the top-priced items on the menu, at around $16.95. But the mainstays are chowder and fried fish. The hard-working staff serves as many as 1,000 meals a day at this spot that's good for lunch entirely without a view. You can take home cans of chowder from the store and pastries from the bakeshop.

## Francine Bistro
**(207) 230-0083**
**55 Chestnut Street**
**Hospitality—Great service from servers proud to work here**
**Open for dinner Tuesday through Saturday 5:30–10**
**Entrées $22 to $25**
**Reservations recommended**

☛ *A fabulous place to eat*

After being told over and over to try Francine, I could only imagine it must be good. When I dug into my redfish with foraged mushrooms, crab, and green tomato chutney, with potatoes dyed green by parsley ($24), I understood that word-of-mouth spoke the truth; the food is a wonder.

A corn soup with scallops and a circle of basil oil ($6) also pleased the whole table, though we could have done with a cup instead of the big bowl we were served. Beside us the chef's parents were enjoying an anniversary dinner, and his mother, sounding bemused, said, "That's the best soup I've ever had."

Another entrée, roast pork loin with apple rosemary puree, pistachio slaw, and beets ($23), was also built too large, making the desire to consume it all a painful conflict between discomfort and greed. It looked great too, with a ring of parsley cream so green it was psychedelic. Maybe it's not the chef's problem if his food is so good you eat too much of it. The combination of flavors in every dish made the best gustatory sense, persuading us all that we were getting to know a place we'd want to return to. The lemon cake with lemon icing ($6) jumped on to our taste buds with singing lemon, and the roasted figs with butterscotch pudding ice cream that our friends had decided not to order—imagining they could restrain themselves—suffered repeated attack from every spoon at the table.

Chef-owner Brian Hill and his partner, Lindsey, who took Francine over after working here for a year, have made their bistro a place to travel to. Their chewy, dense homemade bread makes it all obvious from the first bite.

# Frogwater Café
(207) 236-8998
31 Elm Street
Open daily for dinner May through mid-October, Tuesday through Saturday
mid-October through April
Entrées $10 to $18

☛ *Casual, high-quality meals in the middle of Camden*

This little restaurant on Camden's main drag makes an appetizer, sweet-potato cakes, of shredded sweet and "chef" potatoes topped with sautéed shrimp in vermouth cream sauce. For an entrée you might find braised lamb shank with onion, tomato, and rosemary in a brown sauce ($18). The desserts are all made from scratch—even the ice cream is homemade—and they follow the season: berry pies in summer, and apple tarts and pumpkin pie in fall on a dessert menu that changes every two weeks.

# Hartstone Inn
(207) 236-4259, 1-800-788-4823
41 Elm Street (Route 1)
www.hartstoneinn.com
Hospitality—A family-run room, with your host and server and your chef the married couple who own the inn
Open for dinner Wednesday through Sunday July through October, Thursday through Sunday in the off-season
Prix fixe $42.50
Reservations recommended

☛ *The small menu gives few choices, but what is made here is highly praised.*

Up to 20 people at nine tables are all taken care of by Mary Jo Salmon, owner with her husband, Michael, who is the chef. He was awarded a medal for being the best chef in the Caribbean in 1996 before he became a chef in Camden. Reservations here are important, since it's rare that a table can be had at the last minute, especially in summer. Every evening they prepare just a couple of choices, all high quality.

The five-course menu, changing every day, could start with Caribbean pork tenderloin with mango salsa, go on to a local greens salad, then strawberry sorbet followed by the pistachio-crusted rack of lamb with Pommes Anna, and finish with blueberry and hazelnut soufflé with toasted hazelnut crème anglaise. Only a few wines can be had by the glass, but the list of bottles is long, and don't forget that Maine law allows you to take what's left in the bottle home with you. Frei Brothers Reserve Pinot Noir, 2000, is $34, and many others are in this price range.

## The Waterfront
**(207) 236-3747**
**Bayview Street on Camden Harbor**
www.waterfrontcamden.com
Open for lunch, light lunch, and dinner 11:30–11 in summer, shorter hours off-season
Entrées $11 to $25

☛ *A great view, and good food with a low-key, casual atmosphere*

This place is our New York friends' favorite; they ate lunch here every day during a Camden stay, content with the salads and sandwiches and happy that their little girl felt just as at home as they did. You can get a steamed lobster for lunch or dinner, but the lobster roll, crabcakes, and haddock fish-and-chips ($13.95) compete with the fried haddock sandwich ($8.95) and a big hamburger ($8.50) for the most attention.

Dinner gets a little more elaborate, with oysters, steamers, and mussels on the appetizer list, and entrées like salmon with roasted garlic and chive aioli ($17.95); a fisherman's platter with fried haddock, scallops, clams, and shrimp ($18.95); and a baked stuffed lobster with crab and shrimp ($24.95). A low-carb dish was on the menu in 2004—it might not survive into 2005—pan-roasted lobster and shellfish ($22.95), lobster, clams, mussels and scallops with crème fraîche, spinach, Asiago cheese, and a Romesco sauce.

Seventeen wines were offered by the glass, and over 20 beers and ales. Some of the items on the bigger menus are served between lunch and dinner and after hours, like grilled panini sandwiches, a hamburger, and an herbed salmon burger with caper-basil aioli ($8.50), and the lobster or crab roll.

# White Hall Inn

(207) 236-3391
52 High Street (Route 1)
www.whitehall-inn.com
Hospitality—This inn makes sure everyone is well taken care of.
Open for dinner Tuesday through Sunday mid-June through mid-October
Entrées $18 to $28

☛ *An old-fashioned inn moving slowly but surely into updated dining*

A couple of generations are in charge here. The folks at this big, white-clapboard inn focus on the needs of people who have been loyally returning for summer vacations for years. One guest napped in the lobby on our visit. We all love the candlelight, classical music, and white linen tablecloths in the dining room, a big, red-carpeted space bordered on one side by windows overlooking the back of the inn and its leafy woods.

But with head chef David Grant, former owner of Portland's Aubergine, cooking and Chip Dewing, one of the owners, making the wine list ever more elaborate and special, the ground here may be just slightly shifting, now and in the coming years.

The duck breast with ruby port, orange zest, and currants ($23) and a roast pork tenderloin with green apples and local cider would please any generation. Haddock *piccata* with lemons and capers ($18) was one of several seafood entrées; the menu also included a lobster taken out of the shell and served with a saffron sabayon ($25), a daily fish special, and a plain boiled lobster.

Some really interesting wines can be enjoyed by the glass, including a Chilean merlot from Marques de Casa and an Amano Primitiva from Puglia (both $5.75).

Chip Dewing worked in the wine business and has assembled the four-page wine list; he can recommend a good wine for any meal here. You could enjoy some of the great wine in the bar called the Spirits Room, a small, red space, and ask for a plate of duck liver pâté ($8) or smoked salmon ($9) from the appetizer list.

## Take-Out, Ice Cream, Breakfast, and Bakeries

### Scott's Place (207-236-8751), Elm Street, in the shopping center off Route 1 south of downtown Camden.

Open daily 10–7 in summer, 10–4 off-season. This is a little place in a parking lot that's stayed in business over 30 years by selling inexpensive hot dogs, lobster rolls ($6.99), and fries. The tiny little hamburgers are great.

### The Camden Bagel Café (207-236-2661), 25 Mechanic Street.

Open Monday through Saturday 6:30 AM–2 PM, Sunday 7:30 AM–2 PM. How pleased we were to arrive here after a long trip farther Downeast, far, far from any good bread and even farther from a decent bagel—these will set you up. Chewy and freshly made here, you can order them toasted with butter, cream cheese, or in sandwiches with a big range of fillings. But it's the bagel itself that makes it all worthwhile. The space is plain, with white shutters keeping out the sun, but the hummus is spicy. No credit cards.

### The Cedar Crest Restaurant (207-236-7722), 115 Elm Street (Route 1).

Open daily for breakfast and lunch 7–2, for dinner 5–8:30, closed Sunday evening. A local favorite for breakfast, with thermos urns of coffee left obligingly on the tables. Homemade breads make the toast a good thing, but the frozen non-homefries need to go. Lunches here include wraps and sandwiches. You might also be in the market for the $12,000 nautical painting hanging on the wall by the cash register. The service here is excellent.

### Camden Cone (207-236-6448), 33 Bayview Street.

Ice cream in a wide range of flavors.

### Meetingbrook Bookshop and Café (207-236-6808, 1-800-510-MEET; www.meetingbrook.org), 50 Bayview Street.

Open Tuesday through Saturday 10:30–7, Sunday 11–4:30. This small bookshop serves delicious Austrian desserts, like *Pflaumen Kuchen* (plum cake). There are brownies, pain au chocolat, and much else. With Gregorian chant singing out of the speakers, wafts of chocolate and fruit from the baking, the tapping of the dog's claws on the floor, and the welcome fire in the fireplace on a winter night, this is a refuge for all. It also hosts wide-ranging conversation on stories in the books and the state of the soul.

### The Camden Farmer's Market is held on Wednesday from 4:30–6:30 mid-

June through September on Colcord Street, and on Saturday from 9–noon mid-May through the end of October, at the same place.

# A Lobster Primer

by David Corey

**H**ere are a few rules about eating lobster that will make your visit to Maine a more enjoyable and tasty one.

• **Get your hands in it.** Make sure you remove all jewelry from your fingers and wrists; this includes watches. Lobster has a strong odor that might take a day or two to get out of your skin, so if you want to keep your jewelry clean, take it off. The same holds true for clothing. I've seen one or two Mainers actually turn their shirt inside out or remove it altogether. At least roll up your sleeves.

• **Get to know your lobster.** Menus may try to lure you into ordering a 2-pound or more lobster, but if you're looking for the most tender and sweet meat, order one between 1 to 1½ pounds; 1¼ pounds is the ideal weight, and also the most common. There are two general types of lobster: hard shell and soft shell. Soft-shell lobsters—also known as shedders—are what most summer visitors will eat and are usually much sweeter and tastier than hard shells. (Lobsters molt. When they outgrow their shells, they shed them away, leaving only a soft membrane beneath. This membrane eventual firms back to a hard-shell form.)

Despite the availability of nut crackers and picks to eat a lobster with, a good soft shell can usually be taken apart by hand, peeled like an orange.

• **Dig in!** The claws are the easiest "get." Stress the joint and twist. Then do the same with the remaining joints of the claw. Meat abounds. Remove the tail by bending it back toward the lobster's back while twisting your wrist. Then remove the tail fins (there's small flakes of meat in here too) and use your thumb to push the lobster meat out of the tail in one big piece. Peel back a thin strip of meat along the length of the tail meat to reveal the intestinal tract. Pull this out and discard.

• **Finish the job.** First, peel the legs off one at a time. Place one in your mouth as far as you can, then clamp your teeth down. Slowly pull the leg from your mouth, keeping your teeth clenched, and work the meat out. As the juices trickle from the open end of the leg, suck the juice and meat into you mouth. They're wonderful, sweet little treats. Next, using the "stressed joints" method mentioned above, slide a thumb into the cavity at the base of the body where the tail once was. Pull the rounded red shell away from the spider-like entrails. The first thing you'll notice is a greenish, soupy ooze called tomalley. It will look like nothing you would ever want to eat, but, again, keep an open mind. Using your pinkie finger, scoop up the tomalley and suck it off the tip of you finger. If you've gotten this far (many don't), and if you're pleasantly surprised (many are), repeat this process until the tomalley is gone. Next, take the spiderlike entrails in both hands and bend back the tops of the legs, exposing tiny pockets of meat. Using your fingertips, work the small bits of meat out and pop them into your mouth.

Once you're satisfied that all the meat is gone, lick all your fingers—one at a time—in a hedonistic manner, then let out a long groan and ask the person sitting next to you if he's going to finish his. After all, you're learning a process, and eating lobster takes practice.

# Islesboro

## Dark Harbor House

(207) 734-6669

Main Road, P.O. Box 185

www.darkharborhouse.com

Hospitality—Our waitress, an island woman, took wonderful care of us.

Open daily for dinner 5:30–8:30, May through October

Entrées $18 to $21

Reservations required

☞ *A ferry ride to a Georgian Revival mansion and a great meal make the evening memorable.*

You really have to spend the night here—or possibly at one of the two B&Bs, or at your Islesboro friend's house—to eat a meal here, so it's an investment. Our room had a balcony overlooking the lawn and distant water, and the next morning osprey wheeled overhead calling, between fishing trips.

The hot summer day of my visit I walked down Pendleton Point Road, past all the elaborate summer places of the very rich people who get here in their own boats and planes, and developed a good appetite for dinner. I asked for a drink at the door to the dining room and carried a glass of Fundacion Argen-

*The Dark Harbor House has a collection of masks on the walls beside the stairs*

tinean Malbec out to the long porch.

The inn is full of the innkeepers' odd collections: mounted, tiny European antelope antlers hang in the library; masks from around the world overlook the beautiful double stairs. That ambience of eccentricity promised well for our dinner, and there was no disappointment. The kitchen uses a

Dacquoise, *a light and luscious dessert, from Dark Harbor House*

lot of local produce from a farm on the island and made a salad of greens ($5) that were impeccably fresh. We could also have started that night with organic red lentil soup with kale and garlic sausage ($6) or a caramelized onion, Swiss chard, Gorgonzola, pine nuts, and olive tart ($6.50).

I switched to Rock Rabbit Syrah from California ($5.50) for the main course; the slightly sweeter wine matched up with the perfect piece of king salmon I'd ordered ($20). Poached, with a rare interior, the fresh fish lay in a rim soup bowl in a savory broth, surrounded by new green peas and semolina gnocchi. Every mouthful brought pleasure, with its cracked pepper and minimal addition of oregano.

The barbecued duck breast ($19) that my friend chose seemed on the sweet side, her preference but not necessarily mine. Its fragrant sauce gave off hints of cardamom, coriander, cumin, and cinnamon. A flatiron steak au poivre, and a vegetarian platter with stuffed eggplant, grilled portobellos, and tomatoes with talegio ($18) were also on the menu.

Distant steel-gray water glimmered through the wisteria vine next to our window, where birds were feasting at a feeder. They didn't have our luck, though, with dessert. We ordered a *dacquoise* with orange and Grand Marnier buttercream. The nutty texture of the hazelnut meringue and the tangy buttercream introduced us to this classic dessert, and made converts of us all. The homemade mango sorbet tasted of the fresh fruit. It's unfortunate we could not have eaten the vanilla ice with fresh strawberries, or the other sorbets, including watermelon, lemon, and grapefruit. Next summer, perhaps.

# Lincolnville

## Chez Michel
(207) 789-5600
**Route 1, Lincolnville Beach**
Open April through mid-November for dinner Tuesday
through Sunday, lunch and dinner Sunday
Entrées $12 to $28
Reservations advised

☛ *Popular for its mussels mariniere and lamb shanks; classy dishes
with French roots*

This restaurant serves a duck au poivre ($18.95) and a steak au poivre ($19.95)
(12 ounces of either rib eye or sirloin) that is served on a green-flowered Walker
china dish and makes a superb French meal.

The rabbit pâté and fisherman's stew are also well loved.

One local fan asked the chef to make up 18 orders of the lamb shanks,
cooked with herbs from the chef's garden and from local farms, to be frozen and
heated up in the long winter while Chez Michel is closed.

And people consistently praise the raspberry-glazed pie made every summer
as the raspberries ripen, topped with a glaze made from the raspberries and
Chambord. Some people reserve a slice of that pie when they call and make their
reservation. The crème brûlée has made another good impression. The classic
version ($5.50) is sometimes layered with a chocolate–Grand Marnier crème
brûlée to make what they call a Tuxedo ($6.50).

# Winery

## Cellardoor Winery and Vineyards (207-763-4478;
## www.mainewine.com), 367 Youngtown Road.
Open May through October, 10–5. Stephanie and John Clapp have planted
many acres with vines behind the barn that shelters the daily free wine tastings
in the summer and fall; look back out on the rolling hill, and you'll feel trans-
ported to another place. The wine tastings are fun, with a variety of bottles
offered. This is the only vineyard in Maine that makes wine from its own grape
harvest, but it makes wines from grapes and fruit it purchases as well, including
a semisweet blueberry wine that Stephanie Clapp says tastes like blueberry pie

($7.99 a bottle). The Cayuga White has a big taste, full of oak and spice ($12.99). They make a semisweet Riesling, as well as a dry Riesling, and many other bottles that are a pleasure to sample.

# Monhegan Island

## The Monhegan House Dining Room
(207) 594-7983
www.monheganhouse.com
Open May through October for breakfast and dinner
Entrées $15 to $28
BYOB

☛ *A fine place for dinner on an island renowned for its artists*

The food at this faraway inn impressed our sources as the best on the island. With lobster spring rolls, tuna carpaccio, and lemon-basil shrimp risotto as possibilities on the changing menu, it's easy to see why. The meals use whatever ingredients from the sea and land are fresh and in-season. Also offered might be a Boursin-stuffed tenderloin of beef, boneless roasted chicken breast with pork and apple stuffing, or house-made beet pasta with artichokes, olives, kale, and sautéed onions in a cream sauce.

The inn has its own salad and vegetable garden. It does not serve wine—the island is dry and doesn't issue liquor licenses—but wine and beer can be bought at island stores, and enjoyed here with the meals.

Behind the inn is **The Novelty,** a take-out shop for pizza, sandwiches, baked goods and drinks. Ice cream cones and sundaes, too.

# Port Clyde

## The Harpoon
(207) 372-6304
**Drift Inn Road (just off Route 131)**
Open May through October, daily for dinner in summer, Wednesday through Saturday off-season
Entrées $12 to $21

☞ *The locals like to eat here, and so do the visitors.*

Blackened Cajun scallops, popcorn-fried Maine shrimp with Cajun batter, and crabcakes with dill sauce star on the appetizer menu. Chowder and French onion soup lead up to broiled, baked, or fried seafood, or a linguini dish with clams in a red or white sauce. A cioppino with clams, lobster, scallops, and shrimp, and a seafood platter, show the seafood range here. You can also order grilled steak or fried chicken, and all meals come with a salad. House-made desserts.

## Take-Out

**The Dip Net** (207-372-6307), 1 Cold Storage Road.
Open in-season 11–10. This take-out place makes a variety of items to eat on the wharf, including pizza, crab and lobster rolls, and whole steamed lobster.

# Rockland

## Amalfi
(207) 596-0012
**421 Main Street**
www.amalfi-tonight.com
Open for dinner Tuesday through Saturday 5–9
Entrées $15 to $18
Reservations recommended

☞ *The brilliant flavors of the Mediterranean, in a sleek space*

The inspiration here comes from Spain, Italy, France, Greece, and Morocco, but the BLT salad with Gorgonzola vinaigrette comes straight from the chef's imagination. David Cooke has a loyal following here, where customers sit in the yellow-painted wood booths on plush blue and purple cushions, and the rosy glow is from the light bouncing off the exposed brick and the good food and wine.

Spinach manicotti with three cheeses ($14.95 as an entrée or $6.95 as an appetizer), moussaka ($16.95), and the signature paella show some of Cooke's range.

The paella comes in several versions, tailored to a customer's taste. With fish, shrimp, and mussels ($17.95); with chorizo, chicken, shrimp, and mussels ($15.95); and with vegetables only ($14.95); all versions accentuate the pleasures of saffron and short-grain rice.

Duck risotto and braised lamb shank are also on the menu, and all find a match in the mostly Spanish and Italian wine list; most of the whites and half of the reds are priced around $25 or less.

## Café Miranda
**(207) 594-2034**
**15 Oak Street**
www.cafemiranda.com
**Open for dinner daily at 5:30 in-season, Tuesday through Sunday off-season**
**Entrées $17 to $20**
**Reservations advised**

☛ *The eclectic menu ranges world cuisines, and the kitchen delivers delicious meals.*

The red neon sign looks fine on the gable-end of the clapboard house that is Café Miranda, on a side street in Rockland. A checkered linoleum floor and old Formica tables fit with the two flamingos in the windows. A side terrace with a parabolic tarp and black metal tables fills with patrons on warm nights.

You can't eat here many nights without a reservation, so be sure to make one. Café Miranda is so successful that it is now selling its focaccia, pizza, fresh pasta, hummus, and salsa at markets around Rockland. But coming to the source gives you a chance to enjoy the full range of skill here, from pierogi to Armenian lamb-stuffed peppers to Thai pork to scallops and mussels with creamed leeks on fresh pasta.

The long menu is crammed on one side with 35 appetizers. Gnocchi with tomato-sage butter ($9.50) make the long winter endurable, and so does the Squash O'rama, mashed butternut squash with farmer's cheese ($7.50). Fried oysters with arugula ($9) leap to the eye, and into the mouth. Salads and seafood and New Age chowder compete on this attractive list.

Mexi Beef is a hanger steak seasoned with cumin and coriander, with red peppers, black bean and corn salsa, and yellow rice ($19.50). There's "Chicken Fried Chicken" with creamy gravy, grilled rare tuna with pineapple salsa, roasted polenta, and duck confit. Part of the pleasure in dining here is getting through this list, but maybe you'll have to get a job as one of the kind staff people to manage to taste them all. Wines, of course, come from all over, and the list encourages customers to try a "nonconformist blend" by putting these wines at the top, with quick descriptions on most bottles (prices in the $20s).

The casual humor in every aspect of this place makes for a fun dinner, and no one kids around with the well-made food.

## Conte's
**No phone**
**Harbor Park, Main Street**
**Hospitality: Gruff, occasionally stern, always capable**
**Open year-round**
**Entrées $17 to $19**
**No credit cards, no fried food**

☛ *Ferocious integrity here, with no menus, and enormous portions*

Finding this place on the wharf, behind its very authentic nautical detritus, starts off the evening with a sense of adventure. Inside the door are the paper lists of what's cooking that day, from which you order.

Then you go to your butcher-paper-covered table, where salad and bread are already set out. In 2004 the oil and vinegar bottles were gone, and missed, since all that was offered was a mayonnaisey salad dressing with dill, on one visit at least.

The salmon *pomodoro* that night ($16.80) was too plain, and the sauce too meager for the masses of spaghetti, even if it did turn into three meals, carted home in one of the Styrofoam containers pulled from the stack sitting behind the table.

But the ravioli with lobster in a Gorgonzola cream sauce ($18.90) was delec-

*The menu at Conte's*

Conte's rough exterior

table, obviously rich as sin, and included whole lobster claws and lots of tail meat, though the mix of ravioli, tortellini, spaghetti, and linguini seemed a little odd. Gnocchi with sauce ($9.80) and eggplant Parmesan with extra ricotta on top of the Parmesan ($12.80) were good choices too.

## In Good Company
**(207) 593-9110**
**415 Main Street**
Hospitality—Fine service and no airs
Open for dinner Tuesday through Sunday 4:30–10 or 11, depending on business
Entrées $10 to $15

☛ *A fun place to drink wine, eat a little food, and nurture friendships*

The sign that hangs in front of the door says WINE. FOOD. FRIENDS. The friendliness of our welcome bore it out. This big, white room with a lovely, ornate plaster ceiling (with Hermes and an American Indian among the carvings) filled up with groups who said hello across the room to others and settled at the tables, the couch, and the bar. Our glass of Renwood Zinfandel ($7) came with its own little carafe of extra wine, a happy touch that allowed the lovely large glass to be filled to a low level twice. I loved the big, hem-stitched white cotton napkins.

The scallops with pancetta were perfectly cooked, and the thin watercress aioli made a great dipping sauce for the bread. Roasted green beans and pizza with smoked salmon, cream cheese, and caramelized onions ($10) rounded out our little, delicious dinner.

White roses on the tables and crammed together in a big bouquet in the back room, where a large table accommodated a big party, imbued the scene with the same elegance as the pretty upholstery—coral and green fabrics, almost as pretty as the strawberries with cream in a wine glass that came for dessert.

With more than 30 wines by the glass, a big selection of wines by the bottle, beer, and aperitifs, the drink is a focus, and the food, prepared in a tiny kitchen, remains intentionally simple. It seems like a great concept, a whole business based on the idea of going to a good restaurant and eating an appetizer at the bar. Everyone seemed to be having a great time, so maybe this place is on to something.

## Primo
**(207) 596-0770**
**2 South Main Street (Route 73)**
www.primorestaurant.com
Hospitality—Great, friendly service, with lots of napkin folding
Open for dinner Wednesday through Monday at 5:30
Entrées $23 to $32
Reservations recommended

☛ *Exciting, inventive meals with very fresh ingredients have made a big impact, drawing in customers and inspiring accolades.*

The gardens are the first thing you might notice on a summer visit, laid out with charm and burgeoning with stuff for dinner. Primo has a big reputation these days for its fresh food, clarity of flavors, and delicious combinations—and pulling some of it out of the garden at the last minute has a lot to do with it.

We ate in the front parlor on our last visit, in a room on the second floor the time before; both rooms, filled with only a few tables, are good looking and comfortable. There is a view out to water in the front. But who's looking out there?

Actually, I was, because a huge dark storm seemed to be sweeping in. It never did, and meanwhile we had swallowed our first sips of specialty drinks—a Bellisima, with peach nectar and vodka, and a Key lime mojito. My uncle loved his blue martini and was rather annoyed that his companions ate his Gorgonzola-stuffed olives, so the waiter obliged him with a few more he refused to share.

I commiserated with the waiter, Aron, as the evening went on and I heard his recital of the many specials to new guests at other tables. He never faltered—until they said, "Could you say that again?" to a roar of laughter.

He recommended a wine for us, at our request. We splurged on a $64 bottle of Chalone Vineyard Pinot Blanc, 2003, that was promised to "knock our socks off," and was something chef and part-owner Melissa Kelly had just found. I loved its dry, musky fruits and wood, but I think my friends weren't so sure, or were a little appalled at the price. The food distracted them, a little freebie of crisp, oily bruschetta with tomato and salty tuna filling out mouths with good-ness. We proceeded to up the salt with a shared appetizer of home-made *sopressata,* onions cooked in balsamic, smoked Manchego, and hot cherry tomatoes that did fire-works in our mouths.

*The garden at Primo*

Pemaquid oysters roasted with deviled Jonah crab ($16) and foie gras three ways ($16) glittered on the appetizer list that held less expensive pleasures like a roast Vidalia onion with Manchego ($9).

And you can also dine on a variety of pizzas: one with prosciutto, tomato, arugula, and Parmesan is $14.

I could not resist ordering the same thing I'd had on my last visit—although the menu changes weekly, some things are often on it—the wild striped sea bass Livornese. Perfectly cooked, in a sauce of tomatoes, olives, and caper berries, the dish now included Swiss chard and was served on Israeli couscous. I would not object if that couscous, overused on the coast, dropped from such prominence. But the meal was wonderful anyway, the sauce flavorful, the hot olives a joy to break with my teeth. A grilled duck breast with grilled Pluots ($25) and grilled chicken breast with chanterelles, Swiss chard, and fava beans ($24) were other pleasures among the entrées.

Our cannoli, crunchy and perfect, inspired my aunt to say of pastry chef and part-owner Price Kushner, "I think he's improved the recipe." They came with a few preserved Amerone cherries that were great.

Then we were served some pecan shortbread and cocoa-covered truffles that bloomed in our mouths—really, the evening was full of this kind of moment, when the gorgeous taste of something took up all of our pleased attention.

# Salt Bay Café
**(207) 563-3302**
**277 Park Street**
Open for dinner 5:30–9 Monday through Saturday
Entrées $7 to $22

☛ *A big vegetarian menu, and many good meat and seafood dishes, with low prices*

The Rockland version of this successful restaurant from Damariscotta has its own salad bar, with carrot-raisin salad, potato salad, baked beans, and green salad. Consistency has made this place successful; almost everything is made on the premises, said Peter Everett, who now owns this one. He's owned the one to the south for six years.

Crab cakes, fresh seafood, steaks, and seafood pastas are offered, with a full vegetarian menu of 20 to 25 items making this a favorite establishment for vegetarians. Roast duck, chicken Florentine, and many other things make up the four-page menu. Fried oysters would make a good choice, or try the Gaelic steak, an 8-ounce tenderloin with Irish whiskey and hot heavy cream.

# The Water Works
**(207) 596-2753**
**7 Lindsey Street**
Open daily at 11:30 for lunch and dinner, late pub menu till 10, earlier close in winter
Entrées $9 to $24

☛ *Casual food, fine beer and ale, in a place built for good times*

The atmosphere here is fun, and the meals casual and well made, including a house sirloin ($14.95), lobster dinners in summer, and a shepherd's pie with layers of ground meat, corn, parsnips, and mashed potatoes with a cheese topping ($9.95). You can also enjoy salads, including Caesar with chicken and steak, and a hot spinach salad also with steak or chicken.

But this place is best known for its in-house microbrews from the Rocky Bay Brewing Company. All of the brewed beer and ale here, seven taps, comes from the brewery. A light summer ale, an India pale ale called White Cap, and a blueberry wheat beer are made in the summer. In the fall there's an Oktoberfest lager, and in the winter Viking Plunder, a caramel beer with a toasty flavor. The winter brew goes best with any sort of meat dish, and some specials are tailored to make it sing.

Apple crisp and peach cobbler are perennial favorites ($7), and dessert specials are always offered.

# Lunch, Take-Out, Coffee, and Provisions

### Atlantic Baking Co. (207-596-0505; www.atlanticbakingco.com), 351 Main Street.

Open Monday through Saturday 7–6. A great source of *ciabatta,* and whole-grain and rye breads, among others. Soups, sandwiches, salads, and pastries and cookies are also available. With several tables, and stools along the windows, all the better for you to enjoy a savory bacon, cheddar, and scallion scone, or a twice-baked croissant.

### The Brown Bag (207-596-6372), 606 Main Street.

Open Monday through Saturday 6:30–4. The Brown Bag is packed at lunch because, as Ellen Barnes says, it does what it sets out to do excellently. The great homemade breads, whole wheat, oat, rye, and sometimes Parmesan-basil and a seven-grain, make good sandwiches, and the soup and chowder are always top quality. Order at the counter, either breakfast or lunch, and carry it to a table or a picnic spot. A full breakfast and lots of baked goods; the Congo square with coconut, chocolate, and butterscotch flies out the door.

### The Second Read (207-594-4123), 328 Main Street.

Open Monday through Saturday 7–6:30, Sunday 8–6. This is the best place for a cup of coffee, made with beans roasted by **Rock City Coffee Roasters;** it can be served in a press pot, drip brewed, or as espresso. Tea and chai are available too, along with bagels, muffins, croissants, scones, and cookies. But stop reading that good book you just found in the stacks here to savor these things. Chocolate-dipped macaroons need total attention. Daily sandwich specials.

### Market on Main (207-594-0015), 315 Main Street.

Open Monday through Saturday 10–8, Sunday 9–8, with earlier breakfasts in summer. This cavernous place with galvanized steel tables and a cool clientele (yes, that's you) serves pasta tossed with mushroom cream sauce, called Fungus and the Forest ($9) and eggplant *rollatini,* ($10) from 10:30 AM until closing. Other possibilities on the long, narrow menus are mac and cheese for kids, haddock and spinach cakes for breakfast, flapjacks of joy, with or without blueberries, omelets, and eggs "how ya want 'em." Salads, sandwiches, including a hot ham with apple chutney, and a daily calzone. Prepared foods to go.

### The Thorndike Creamery (207-594-4126), 385 Main Street.
Open daily 11–9 or 10. This ice-cream parlor with marble tables and wire chairs sells Annabelle's Ice Cream from Portsmouth, New Hampshire. A wild blueberry sundae with blueberry syrup and vanilla ice cream is $4.85.

### Wine Seller (207-594-2621), 315 Main Street.
Open Monday through Saturday 10–6. Next door to Market on Main, this is the place to pair the meal you've bought to go with a good bottle of wine.

### Jess's Seafood Market (1-877-219-8653; www.jessmarket.com), 118 South Main Street.
Open year-round during business hours. Tanks of sea water are filled with lively lobsters at this great, family-owned seafood market. You can also buy clams, oysters, mussels, crabmeat, shrimp, scallops, and fresh fish. Everything can be shipped. Diver-harvested scallops are available from December to April.

At the Web site www.lobstertales.com, sponsored by the Island Institute, you can enter the number on the band that circled the lobster claws of the creatures you bought and learn who caught them.

### Wasses Hot Dogs, Route 1.
Keith Wass has become a legend, serving millions of hot dogs from his stands in Thomaston, Belfast, and Rockland since 1972.

### The Rockland Farmer's Market is held on Thursday from 9–1 from the end of May to mid-October at the Public Landing, downtown Rockland on the waterfront.

# Rockport

## The Gallery Café
**(207) 230-0061**
**297 Commercial Street (Route 1)**
www.prismglassgallery.com
Hospitality—Eager and attentive service
Open for lunch Wednesday through Saturday 11–3, for dinner 5–9, Sunday brunch 10–3
Entrées $17 to $35

☞ *Well-made meals in a handsome new space, with a bonus of glass blowing*

This restaurant opened in summer 2004 to praise, but its high prices put off some of us not quite ready for an expensive lunch. Still, when the air is warm and the back patio is open, the taste of the Macadamia nut crust Key lime pie ($7) did away with any of our complaints.

The brunch has featured a seared scallop salad with roasted figs, spiced nuts, and peach vinaigrette ($13), and steak and eggs with black trumpet mushrooms and mascarpone ($18). They dare to mess with the lobster roll here, serving it with roasted corn and romaine in a thyme roll ($13). You be the judge. Lunch could consist of chicken muffuletta ($8) with capers, olives, chicken, and provolone, or a mushroom tart.

Dinners work with wild ingredients like striped bass, served with tomato tapioca and cucumber coulis ($31), as well as a seared (and domesticated) filet mignon with buttermilk onion rings ($35).

## Bakeries, Markets, and Ice Cream

**The Market Basket (207-236-4371), Route 1.**
Prepared foods, muffins and pastries, sandwiches, and a wide range of cheeses, including many from Maine, can be found here. Wine, coffee, and fresh hot chocolate are also for sale.

**Sweet Sensations (207-230-0955; www.mainesweets.com), 315 Commercial Street (Route 1).**

Open daily 9–5:30, January through April 10–5. The almond and coconut macaroons, plain or drizzled with chocolate, taste luscious with a cup of coffee or tea. Made with high-quality ingredients, the pastries and baked goods here are wonderful. Fudge cake, lemon-lime tart, whiskey-pecan tart, and peach cream cake are all good reasons to volunteer to bring dessert.

### Miss Plum's Ice Cream (207-596-6946), 599 Commercial Street (Route 1).

Open in summer. A restaurant serving breakfast. lunch, and possibly dinner (undecided at press time), Miss Plum's stands out in the landscape with its shades of purple. The more than 30 flavors of ice cream made here range from coconut hash, to grapenut, to peanut butter cup swirl. Of course, there are vanilla, chocolate, coffee and strawberry. But why not try the devil's mint chocolate chip?

**The Rockport Farmer's Market** is held on Saturday 9–noon November to April at the State of Maine Cheese Company Store, 461 Commercial Street.

# Searsport

## The Rhumb Line
**(207) 548-2600**
**200 East Main Street (Route 1)**
www.therhumblinerestaurant.com
Open daily in summer, fewer days off-season
Entrées $21 to $28

☛ *Searsport's top-of-the-line, popular restaurant*

Entrées at this restaurant in a white house along Route 1 include orange-glazed roast duck with lentils and ginger-peach chutney ($25) and curried Contessa shrimp with sweet potato ravioli with sweet olive chutney ($23). The four ravioli on the plate were filled with sweet potatoes with spice, and occasional raisins and walnuts, and were perfect with the curry; this dish has been on the menu for several years. Contessa is a brand of shrimp that has great flavor, consistently fresh, with never any odor, according to Diana Evans, who owns and runs the restaurant and cooks the meals with her husband Charles. Both are trained "roundsmen" who take care of any part of the meal, and they serve as many as 45 to 50 people a night.

The chocolate–Grand Marnier mousse cake and lemon cream cake with fresh berries (both $8) are homemade.

In its seventh year, the restaurant has several staffers that are original. Melinda is the head waitress, the only year-round original waitress, and is often asked for by grateful customers.

# Spruce Head

## Craignair Inn
**(207) 594-7644, 1-800-320-9997**
**5 Third Street**
www.craignairinn.com
Open May through October for dinner
Entrées $19 to $24

☞ *An old inn on a lovely point of land, with good dinners*

The inn's homey dining room is filled with wooden chairs and tables and has a fabulous view of Clark Island. The food on the plates is good looking, too. Crab-cakes the restaurant prides itself on ($8.95) are among the appetizers, which also include a wedge of iceberg lettuce with blue cheese and caramelized onions, crumbled bacon, and Italian dressing ($6.50). Entrées might be a shrimp and scallop scampi on linguini ($18.95), haddock stuffed with shrimp, crab, and bread-crumbs ($18.95), or grilled filet mignon with brandy and peppercorn sauce ($23.95).

## Miller's Lobster Company
**(207) 594-7406**
**38 Fuller Road, on Wheeler's Bay**
Open for lunch and dinner June through September
Entrées $7 to $40 (for a 3-pound lobster)

☞ *A seaside shellfish restaurant*

Long, low red buildings stretch down to the open deck on the wharf at this simple, beautiful location, making fresh seafood all ways except fried. But there are some times some spectacular lobsters. A 3-pound lobster special on our visit was going for $39.99, a 2-pound creature cost $29.99, and a 1¾-pounder was $25.99. Lobster salad ($10.75), crab salad ($8.25), and shrimp salad ($7) were

*The Craignair Inn looks out onto Clark Island*

specials on the simple menu. Bring your own bottle of wine, or six-pack of beer. Homemade pie for dessert.

# South Thomaston

## Waterman Beach Lobsters
**(207) 596-7819**
**359 Waterman Beach Road**
Hospitality—Order at the kitchen window,
and the server will bring you your meal
Open for lunch and dinner Thursday through
Sunday 11–7 in summer
Entrées $2.25 to $25

☛ *Classic seaside dining, simple and beautiful, with no fried food, and homemade pie*

This traditional place has a big outside deck with picnic tables for enjoying the lobster dinners. A twin lobster special (no sharing) with chips, a roll, and butter, was $25.95 in 2004. Big servings of steamers, 1¾ pounds, were $12.50 with melted butter and broth. Wine and beer are served along with lobster rolls ($11.95). The place is well thought of for the good homemade pies. Blueberry and raspberry, pecan and other ($3.50 a slice, $4.25 with ice cream). You could eat on the wide porch if it rained, but this is clearly a spot for a gorgeous day.

# Tenants Harbor

## Cod End Cookhouse
**(207) 372-6782**
**Commercial Street**
www.codend.com
Open daily 11–8:30 Memorial Day through September (market open 7–7)
Entrées $9 to $22

☛ *A "cookhouse" that grew out of the present market to its own building serves fresh seafood and burgers at tables with great views.*

Fresh seafood specials, like broiled salmon, tuna, and halibut, come along with the regular fried seafood offerings here—clams, shrimp, and scallops, and steamed clams and mussels. Lobster dinners, lobster rolls, haddock rolls, and Mediterranean seafood stew along with clam and fish chowder are on the menu.

Desserts are pies, brownies, blueberry cake, and ice cream. And all of it can be cooked and packed to go for a supreme seafood picnic at a cove of your own choice.

## East Wind Inn
**1-800-241-8439**
**21 Mechanic Street, P.O. Box 149 (bear left**
**just past the post office on Route 131)**
Hospitality—Great service from a reserved and attentive
Maine native at a place with a lot of tables
Open daily April through November for breakfast 7:30–9:30,
for dinner 5:30–8:30
Entrées $16 to $26

☞ *Good basics and fabulous desserts here*

The inn's porch makes a fine place for a glass of wine before dinner, but you may have to search it out for yourself as we did, since there was no service outside on our visit.

Once in the dining room with its sailing ships on the walls, we started with mussels steamed with sake, cilantro, coconut milk, and Thai red curry, but the spices didn't make themselves obvious and we wanted them to. The crabcakes ($9.95), however, were filled with lots of fresh crabmeat, wonderfully satisfying with greens and dill and sherry aioli.

Lobster steamed in seawater was perfectly cooked. An order of the halibut special, served with a sesame sauce, pleased with, again, perfectly cooked fish; but the sweet sauce overwhelmed the subtle flavors of the fish, which came with a rice mold. A third entrée, scallops broiled in sun-dried-tomato butter with Pernod and lemon ($18.95) could have benefitted from stronger flavoring.

But our good waitress, Judy, had forewarned us to save room for the homemade desserts, and her advice was a pleasure to follow. The bread pudding tasted good, the blueberry buckle was fantastic, homemade and infamous, with Maine blueberries, and a crisp crust that exactly balanced the tart and the sweet. The apple crisp came warmed, with coconut, and was also delightful.

# Sul Mare

(207) 372-9995
13 River Road
Open for dinner daily 5–10
Entrées $8 to $18

☛ *Grilled meat and fish, prime rib on weekends, with an Italian respect for straight flavor*

Kevin Kieley took a cement block building in St. George, just north of the village of Tenants Harbor, and gave it a makeover. Now it resembles an Italian trattoria, complete with stuccoed walls. Kieley himself is, he said, "100 percent Irish," but a few years in school in Italy put a new face on food that he makes his living from. He grills pork, lamb, and three kinds of steak, serving dishes from a regional Italian menu and wines from a mostly Italian list. Five can be bought by the glass; the bottle price ranges in the low $20s.

After an appetizer like grilled calamari with smoky chipotle mayonnaise and lemon oil ($10), an entrée like spit-roasted lamb with Chianti, tomatoes, and rosemary would be welcome. Kieley also roasts prime rib on the weekends; that combined with Budweiser is the preferred meal for the lobstermen that are his

*Sul Mare has the look of an Italian building*

guests. They've eaten enough fish, he said, and don't want to eat it for dinner when they go out.

But with fresh fish and lobster from local waters, a risotto with lobster, artichokes, and Parmesan ($18) would sound awfully good to anyone else.

Desserts ($6 each) are always homemade, and might include tiramisu, chocolate cream pie, or individual bananas Foster tarts.

Kieley had caught a big tuna the week before we spoke to him. Asked if it was on the menu he said no, "It goes right to Japan." He got $7,000 for the 711-pound fish, and could never have made that serving it in his restaurant.

# Thomaston

## Thomaston Cafe and Bakery
**(207) 354-8589**
**154 Main Street**
www.thomastoncafe.com
Hospitality—Friendly, warm, quick service
Open for breakfast and lunch 7–2 Monday through Saturday, for dinner
5:30–8 Friday and Saturday, for Sunday brunch 8:30–1:30
Entrées $12 to $25
Reservations recommended for dinner

☛ *A favorite neighborhood place with a reputation for wonderful food*

The lobster ravioli with lobster sauce ($25) has been praised to the skies by many of the customers of this comfortable, casual restaurant. Although it fulfills its role as a neighborhood place to a T and gives our friends who live a few blocks from the door something to feel quite smug about, the quality of the meals makes it worth a trip from farther way.

One visitor from the southern end of the coastline extolled the diver's scallops. "The food was just unbelievable," she said. If the scallops aren't on the menu—and they will be there only if the restaurant has a fresh supply—there is plenty to tempt you, off the plainest piece of white paper, like the baked fresh haddock with crabmeat, crabcakes with rémoulade, fresh tuna with wasabi ($25), and broiled lamb chops ($22). All dinners come with a salad and two sides. A vegetarian entrée, one night Israeli couscous with wild mushrooms and vegetables ($12), is part of the evening menu.

But dinner is served only Friday and Saturday. Breakfast, lunch, and Sunday brunch are made just as well, and could also be a destination meal. Lunch includes crabcakes, bratwurst with sauerkraut, a bison burger, a Reuben sandwich, chowder, and a daily special soup.

For breakfast the orange juice is squeezed to order, the best way to serve it ($3.25 a glass and worth it). Haddock fish cakes, cheese blintzes, omelets, and pancakes all beckon. The Thomaston special is two eggs any style, choice of bacon, ham, or sausages with homefries and toast ($5.75). Bagels come from the Camden Bagel Café and are good (see page 165), and many other products come from local farms and waters.

# Fish and Ice Cream

## The Fish Truck.
Alvin Dennison's colorful truck is parked on Route 1 across from the cement plant and is the source of great fresh fish for many loyal customers.

## Dorman's Dairy Dream, Route 1.
Open mid-April till mid-October. Closed Sunday. Ginger is the best, some say, but with many flavors, and years of experience making them here, this locally loved ice-cream stand has many "bests."

# Vinalhaven

## Annabelle's
**(207) 863-2789**
**250 Main Street**
Open daily 8 AM–9 PM in summer, closing at 10 pm on weekend nights
Entrées around $6

☛ *The place for good sandwiches, coffee, soup, and salads*

This new place on the island gets good supplies from the mainland, like Atlantic Baking Company bread, Willow Bake Shoppe doughnuts, and Rock City Coffee Roasters coffee. They bake their own muffins and cookies. Good burritos, and a Tacchino, a turkey panini with pesto, roasted red peppers, and provolone ($5.95). Annabelle's Ice Cream is sold here.

## The Harbor Gawker

(207) 863-9365
Main Street
Open daily for lunch and dinner 11–8 in summer, closed Sundays in spring and fall
Entrées $6 to $12

☛ *Counter service for chowders, fried seafood, lobster rolls, and blueberry pie*

Wait for your number to be called after you decide on the seafood of the day, and enjoy the view of Carvers Pond. Finish up with ice cream from the dairy bar.

## Market and Wine

**Downstreet Market (207-863-4500), Main Street.**
A bakery, café, and whole foods store, with espresso and baked goods in the morning, sandwiches and soup later.

**Island Spirits (207-863-2192), Carvers Harbor.**
Open Monday through Saturday 11–6:30 in summer. Good wine, good cheese, beer, olives, and freshly ground coffee.

## Waldoboro

## Morse's Sauerkraut

(207) 832-5569
3856 Washington Road (Route 220)
Hospitality—Overwhelmed sometimes (don't go on Saturday), otherwise fine
Open daily 9–5 (9–6 at the store)
Entrées $7 to $9

☛ *Too small for the extent of its business, but offering good German food and great kraut*

In the fall, when the newly harvested cabbages completed their fermentation and were transformed into fresh sauerkraut, the former owner of this Germanic outpost would put an ad in the paper: "Kraut's ready." Everyone who cared knew what that meant.

Today Morse's still makes sauerkraut all year long, and still sells the most in the fall, made with the new cabbage crop. Some customers wait until November to get the kraut made with cabbage that's been sweetened by the frost. But whatever they prefer, there is always kraut here, made fresh with all its beneficial bacteria, now understood to be a crucial part of a healthy human being. Articles about that are on the walls.

And now, with new owners, the business has expanded into a store and delicatessen crammed with German breads, chocolate Babka from Brooklyn, and Schaller and Weber sausages. You can eat sauerkraut served up to you in the four-booth restaurant, another addition, or buy it to take home.

When we visited, unfortunately a Saturday, we encountered a restaurant that cannot take care of its customers with any real cordiality. A line had formed outside the tiny dining room by the time we finished; the hostess was frantically attempting to take orders in advance while the patrons grew surly, and we were stared down for having the bad manners to have left something on the table we needed to go back and get. Although we felt we were in the way, we thought the meal was good. My huge piece of kielbasa and another of bauerwurst, served hot with sauerkraut, were both too much to finish. The bauerwurst, a farmer's sausage made with pork, beef, mustard seeds, and marjoram, was smoother in texture than the garlicky, great-tasting kielbasa and disappeared more rapidly. Other sausage could be chosen instead for this sampler plate ($6.95), like bratwurst, smoked Hungarian sausage, or an Irish banger.

A chicken potpie ($5.95) consisted of a mélange of chicken, potato, carrot, and mushroom under a square of browned puff pastry. Side orders of red cabbage with apples; German potato salad made with slices of red potato, bacon, onion, sour cream, and vinegar, served warm; or Maine baked beans made with heirloom yellow eye beans tempted from another part of the menu. But what we really wish we'd ordered was the liverwurst sandwich and the homemade pierogi.

Choucroute garnie ($8.95)—sauerkraut braised in wine with sausages and a pork chop—was on the menu. Sauerbraten and Wiener schnitzel could be ordered too, and there was German chocolate cake and apple strudel ($3.95) available for dessert.

We thought the anomalous Key lime pie was just great.

Visit on a weekday if you want to eat here, or go at an hour that isn't lunch, since you can eat anytime between 9 and 5.

# Moody's Diner
**(207) 832-7785**
**Route 1**
www.moodysdiner.com
Hospitality—Swift and skilled in this busy, busy place
Open Monday through Friday 4:30 AM–11:30 PM, Saturday 5 AM–11:30 PM, Sunday
6 AM–11:30 PM

☛ *A gorgeous landmark with diner food and a devoted following*

The lure of the blinking red neon sign, hypnotizing everyone driving past at dusk, may have something to do with this place's enduring and flourishing business.

The meat loaf, turkey roasted upside-down, and cream pies at this 1930s diner have pleased so many customers that by now over a million have eaten here. In 2002, at the 75th-anniversary celebration, 31 members of the extended Moody family were involved with running this place.

The food is basic, mostly homemade plain fare, modest sandwiches and traditional dishes. That explains the reasonable prices, perhaps the main reason local patrons fill this place, with its long menu, for early suppers. A souvenir store for T-shirts and cabin rentals have succeeded here too.

## Bakery

### Borealis Breads (207-832-0655), Route 1 (across from Moody's Diner).
Open Monday through Saturday 8:30–5:30, Sunday 9–5. Moist, chewy, and crusty, is how the company describes its own breads; and we know that is the exact truth. The *ciabatta* is tender as well, an object of worship fresh from the oven. We love the rye and the multigrain. The slow-rising technique Borealis employs gives every loaf a distinctive flavor.

**CHAPTER 6**

# The Blue Hill Peninsula and Deer Isle

**I**T SEEMS AS IF THE PEOPLE THAT LIVE on this strangely beautiful stretch of the coast have a special intensity about their food—more of them are starting food businesses, growing produce, or baking bread with more skill and more attention than on other parts of the coast.

The good fortune lies on both sides. The bakers can make a living, because the customers are there to buy what they make. The farmers can sustain their farms, because the people around them want to eat what's growing on their neighbor's land.

Nancy Veilleux and Chris Hurley live in Brooklin and lease land in Penobscot that they have worked on for eight years, land they call the Lazy C Farm. Hurley brought a crop of melons to the Deer Isle farmer's market late last summer, and one of his assistants explained some melon facts.

The little dark-green round melons sound hollow when they are thumped. If you hit them too hard, they'll break, he said. "And then we eat them."

We laughed to hear the pleasure in the young man's voice. One of the market's elderly customers bought one of the little round melons so she could eat her own.

She and Hurley were participating in a program called Senior Share. "It brings out crowds of seniors," he said gleefully. They love to get the produce and can use some state funding to buy it up. The program benefits the seniors' diet, helps farmers like Hurley pay expenses, and keeps one more stretch of dirt alive for crops.

That farmer's market was jammed, with people lined up and waiting to make their purchases, the kind of line you might see at a vendor's truck in New York City's Union Square. It was a sight to give you hope, to make you wonder if we could, someday, share a culture that loved good, fresh, flavorful food, and that could leave behind a sorry indulgence in junk food that has no taste worth talking about, and no nutritional value beyond sheer calories.

If you're going to indulge, after all, why not indulge in something delicious? Why not trade in the can of soda for a piece of pie, at the very least. There are several ladies on Deer Isle than can make you a pie worth the eating.

The people in this neck of the woods already know that.

# Blue Hill

## Arborvine Restaurant and The Vinery
(207) 374-2119
Main Street, Tenney Hill
www.arborvine.com
Open for dinner Tuesday through Sunday 5:30–9, July through Labor Day,
Wednesday through Sunday until New Year's Day, Friday through Sunday until
May, Wednesday through Sunday in May and June. The Vinery has the same
summer hours; closed after Labor Day until Memorial Day weekend.
Entrées $18 to $22

☛ *A very popular fine-dining place with consistent, quality food and
lovely grounds and rooms*

The handsome old, beamed dining rooms here were filled up every night of our
visits, and the parking lot was overflowing, and we never managed to snag a table.
We'll try again next year, and meanwhile regale you with the menu; confident
from all the praise we heard bestowed on this restaurant's hospitality, that you
will enjoy a meal here.

Noisettes of lamb *chasseur* with shallots and mushrooms ($22) and medallions
of pork with pears and a Calvados-maple glaze ($18.50) give a glimpse of the direc-
tion of the meat entrées. I would probably start with the Damariscotta River oysters ($9.50), but then I'd do that anywhere they had them. More unique to
Arborvine would be the smoked scallops and trout with horseradish cream
($9.50) or a salad of melon, grapefruit, mango, and smoked salmon ($9.50).

A chocolate gateau with raspberry puree ($6.50) and a pear crisp with
whipped cream ($5.50) are one the dessert menu.

The Vinery, open only in summer, can take care of some of the overflow at
the Arborvine, although you may have to wait a while for a table. With white
walls and a bar, this place is more casual. Friends of ours did not like the fact
that they had to pay for bread. Wines start kindly down at $14, and the list is
long enough for some intriguing bottles between the high-priced greats and those
economical good-enoughs.

# The Gourmet Lobster Restaurant at the Captain Isaac Merrill Inn

(207) 375-2555
**On the green**
www.captainmerrillinn.com
Hospitality—The Eastern European staff are extremely polite and helpful.
Open for lunch Monday through Friday, for dinner Monday through Saturday, June through October 15
Entrées $16 to $28

☛ *A lovely inn and terrace serving lobster at least seven ways*

This old, charming inn, with the captain's chest and pewter dishes in the front hall, has been updated with modern amenities and is adorned with a pretty brick terrace in back, a perfect spot for a nice lunch. The parlor, with its handsome white mantel, would be a good place to enjoy dinner and settle down to some serious meditation on the meaning of lobster. The menu, challenged by the restaurant name it must live up to, bristles with the creature, from lobster cocktail ($9.25) to mango tango lobster salad ($21)—all the meat from a 1-pound lobster plus mango, tangerines, walnuts, blue cheese, cranberries, and greens. Then come the entrées: lobster bake with corn on the cob; lobster asparagus puffs; lobster Merrill, with Boursin and Roman cream sauce on fettuccini; lobster beurre blanc; and lobster ravioli.

Lobster haters, have no fear. Roast duck breast with honeyed pears ($18.50), rack of lamb, and Caribbean pork tenderloin are also on the dinner menu.

Lunch offers lots of good salads, like the mango tango above, some of the lobster pasta dishes, and a lobster roll, with a BLT and a Merrill club to give the theme a rest.

## Lunch, Pizza, Take-Out, Wine, and Bakeries

### The Pantry (207-374-2229), Water Street.

Open for breakfast and lunch 7–2 Monday through Friday. This tiny pink place has staying power, making eggs and omelets, bagels with cream cheese and smoked salmon, and Belgian waffles for breakfast, and more for lunch, since 1988. The Melina-PMS Crab sandwich intrigued me, but the Reuben, the turkey sandwich with Swiss cheese, and the good chowders might have more mass appeal. Crabmeat and lobster rolls too. There's outdoor seating, and all orders can be wrapped to go. Blueberry shortcake for dessert, and self-serve coffee at the counter.

*Go through the tiny door to the left to enter the Fishnet's tiny dining room*

## Ovenworks (207-374-5775), 37 Water Street.

Open Memorial Day through Labor Day Monday through Saturday 7 AM–9 PM, off-season Monday through Wednesday 7–4, Thursday and Friday 7–8. Known for its good pizza, this place is a recent addition to Blue Hill. The Nadia has prosciutto, olives, onions, roasted garlic, fresh tomato, and mozzarella ($17 for a large, $14 for a small). A white pizza is made with artichoke hearts, feta, mozzarella, olive oil, roasted garlic, and fresh tomatoes ($16 large, $13 small).

The eggplant parmigiana sub ($5.75) was "an all day sandwich," we heard, with some for lunch, some for a snack, and some for supper, and still enough left to make a fine late-night snack. Stuffed quahogs with salad ($12) and mac and cheese with prosciutto or broccoli ($12) were two specials.

New York–style bagels are 75¢ each, $6 for a baker's dozen, and $2 with cream cheese. Breakfast offerings also include eggs and homemade breakfast sausage and various pastries from a local woman's kitchen.

## The Fishnet (207-374-5240), Main Street, P.O. Box 720.

Open in summer Sunday through Thursday 11–8, Friday and Saturday 11–9; in fall and spring daily 8–4; closed from the end of Septtember through March.

This is the drive-in and take-out place the locals recommend for fried seafood, with hamburgers and hot dogs for the kids. It's been in the same family for years and is known for good fish-and-chips. A scallop dinner with french fries and coleslaw was $11.95, and a dinner with all the seafood fried here—scallops, clams, haddock, and shrimp—would have cost you $16.95. Live lobsters and steamers, side orders of fried fish, and ice cream and homemade desserts. A tiny dining room with five gold-wood booths is to the left of the order counter.

## Blue Hill Food Co-op Café (207-374-2165), Main Street (Route 172), P.O. Box 71.

Open year-round Monday through Friday 7 AM–2 PM, in summer Saturday and Sunday 8 AM–1 PM. Some people say this is the best place in town for lunch. Considering the taste of the delicious golden seafood stew, with crabmeat and lemongrass, that seems about right. Robin Byrne learned about cooking at the Natural Gourmet Cookery School in Manhattan, and her partner in the business, Joe Porada, grew up in a restaurant in Binghamton, New York. Between them the café is turning out high-quality soups, baked goods, and three standard salads, as well as daily specials. Many dishes are vegan; all use organic ingredients. Sesame noodles, red curry chicken salad, and fine hummus are a few of the choices, and dessert could be a strawberry bar.

## The Blue Hill Wine Shop (207-374-2161), Main Street, P.O. Box 71.

In addition to a large selection of wine from around the world, this 25-year-old shop sells a full range of teas and coffee, cigars and tobacco. The 90 varieties of wine are sold in an old stock barn—penciled descriptions of the cattle sold there are on the wall. Port and sherries are available too.

## Pain de Famille (207-374-3839), Main Street, P.O. Box 1437.

Open in summer Monday through Thursday 7–6, Friday 7–7, Saturday and Sunday 9–2; in fall Monday through Thursday 7–5, Friday 7–7, Saturday 9–2, closed Sunday. The plain room of this bustling bakery is filled with goodness; a counter and baskets are filled with the creations of the women working across the room. *Pane stirato,* a stretched, chewy loaf from Lombardo, focaccia, and field wheat loaves (all $3.50) are a few you can find here. The counter is laden with Creole pecan bars ($1.50), Blue Hill Dream Bars with coconut and pecans ($1.50); shortbread, macaroons, rugelach, and biscotti tempt from glass jars. The Nutty Bird Bar ($1.85) did resemble something from the bird feeder, but it was fabulous, with pumpkin seeds, walnuts, pecans, almonds, sunflower seeds, flax seeds, tahini, and honey, and I wish I had one right now. Sandwiches and wraps are stocked in the cooler, and pizza is in a rack. Friday night is pizza night.

**The Blue Hill Farmer's Market** is held Saturday 9–11:30 late May through Labor Day weekend at the Blue Hill fairgrounds, and then at the Union Trust Bank parking lot.

# Brooklin

## The Brooklin Inn
**(207) 359-2777**
**Route 175, P.O. Box 25**
www.brooklininn.com
Hospitality—Obliging and charming on our visit
Open for dinner daily except Tuesday
Entrées $18 to $34

☞ *An inn with a welcoming, casual atmosphere and well-made dinners*

The old rooms here have seen years of hospitality, something host and innkeeper Chip Angell, who led us to our seats, excelled at himself. He made us all comfortable with a little banter, returning to open the bottle of Navarro Correas Malbec ($25) we ordered at his recommendation, and it did the trick with its dry, intense flavor.

Since the menu mentioned the possibility of children's portions, or a special dish, we asked, and the chef offered to make a dish of tricollatura pasta with butter and Parmesan, to our young guest's delight. The adults were off and running with appetizers. Peekytoe crabcakes ($10) with chive-cilantro mayonnaise and

*The Brooklin Inn bouillabaise comes with crisp garlic toast*

pineapple salsa were packed with crab, crusty, and well flavored. A large, poached pear sat on a bed of spinach leaves with slices of Manchego, sweet pecans and maple vinaigrette ($8); all together on a fork the salad made a wonderful mix of salt, sweet, toasted nut, and fresh greens. Paul Brayton's mussels, a full pound with Dijon sauce, kept one of us busy for a long time as she savored the mustard's sharpness against the plump, fresh Blue Hill mussels' salty sweetness. She reluctantly gave up that big bowl only when the entrées could not be delayed any longer because the rest of the table might mutiny.

There were ships around us, ships' flags, and photographs, and models. Brooklin has some fame as the base for *WoodenBoat* magazine and its related boat-building school.

The sea was nearby, certainly, in the bouillabaisse put in front of me, with halibut, haddock, clams, scallops, and mussels in a clear broth with tomatoes, and wonderful grilled lengths of crusty bread, well buttered. The shellfish and fish were all tender, the flavor of the broth echoing the sea and warmed with garlic.

Wild salmon ($23) slightly too cooked for my taste, came with forbidden rice, a black, chewy grain that made a good contrast with the sweet flesh of the fish that also gained with a horseradish sauce. A special shiitake mushroom risotto pleased with its melting texture.

For dessert, the chocolate seduction cake seduced. "It's like eating fudge," one of my companions said, so be forewarned. A strawberry napoleon with layers of shortbread and whipped cream made a light confection, the cream not over-sweetened, and the shortbread crisp and thin.

The menu credits the suppliers of most of the meals' ingredients, letting you know that Johnny White caught the lobster yesterday, and Ivan Keniston grew the strawberries. I credit the inn with doing right by them, and chef Elaine Randall for making that night out a pleasure for us all.

# Brooksville

## Oakland House Seaside Resort
**(207) 359-8521, 1-800-359-7352**
**435 Herrick Road, Herricks Landing**
www.oaklandhouse.com
Hospitality—Outgoing and warm
Open daily from the end of June through September for dinner
Entrées around $20

🐖 *Fine food and wine served in a lovely old inn*

This wonderful place, a family resort with elegant old cabins set along the sea, serves dinner to its own guests and to the public during the summer months. With a dining room reserved for families and another for people without children, you can find the right spot for yourself. And then settle in to enjoy the mussels, or the creamy chicken, prosciutto, and pesto soup.

After an organic salad made with the inn's own garden produce, a meal of sesame-seared tuna with soy and ginger sauce, or roasted vegetable ravioli with the house marinara, would be welcome. A fine selection of wines is available to accompany the good food. And dessert might be lemon cheesecake, homemade peach ice cream, or orange custard tart.

We rely on the report from fellow travel writer Chris Tree, who extolled her dinner here, calling the lamb chops the best she'd ever had. Wine dinners and other special occasion meals are sometimes held in the spring and fall.

## Bagaduce Lunch (207-326-4729), 19 Bridge Road (Route 176).

Open daily 11–7 from May to the second week of September. This take-out place is set beside the Bagaduce Falls, where a reversing tide rips up and down its narrow channel at the ebb and flood. The area is famous for its horseshoe crabs and haunted by beautiful birds—eagles, ospreys, and herons among them—looking out for their own lunch.

I enjoyed a crabmeat salad made with local greens and tomatoes. The crabmeat, mixed with mayonnaise, was delectable. The onion rings were a different matter, not elegant, but delicious all the same, thin, crisp, hot, and oily. An overflowing paper dish of fried scallops ($8.95), with perhaps 16 big scallops and good tartar sauce, were succulent and tender, and the clean picnic tables scattered along the waterside make for lovely alfresco meals. Ice cream and sundaes, too.

*Bagaduce Lunch offers picnic tables overlooking reversing falls*

# Buck's Harbor

## Cafe Out Back

**(207) 326-8683**
**Route 176**
Open for dinner 5:30–9 Wednes-
day through Monday in summer,
Wednesday through Sunday off-season
Entrées $12 to $28
Reservations advised on weekends

☞ *Ingredients full of integrity, put together by a chef with imagination*

This out-of-the-way café doesn't benefit from any helpful signs on this area's winding roads, but Eric Czerwinski isn't bothered by that. "People who come are coming for the food," he said, and they get directions. Since 1999, when lunch was first offered in the market his restaurant lies behind, the place has been building a reputation for good meals.

Czerwinski's menu accommodates customers interested in a single course, and always offers a $12 hamburger, made with naturally raised beef. From October to May, most of Café Out Back's produce is provided by Eliot Coleman's Four Seasons Farm, grown miraculously through the dead of winter with Coleman's moving hoop houses and shelters. In summer the café has a harder time getting consistent good produce, because Coleman's harvests only in the off-season, but Czerwinski seeks out as much local stuff as he can find.

Wild king salmon with rice and grilled vegetables ($22), rolled pork with an apple-pecan filling served with mashed potatoes ($20), and duck three ways, with a roasted duck breast, duck confit, and foie gras ($28), are listed on the menu, along with suggested wines from the café's single vineyard bottles, several organic.

The burger might taste great with the Cinquante Cinq Merlot ($22), for instance, a wine you can also buy at the market if it pleases you. Just over 20 wines are on the list, with many priced in the $20s.

Czerwinski said he tries to keep the quality of the meals high and consistent. He has his own loyal following, and many enjoy the crusty calamari, raw oysters, and mussels, sometimes in Dijon cream sauce, that figure as appetizers.

The restaurant space was originally a bakery, started by Steve Lancelotta, who now continues his artisan baking at Sophia's in Portland. A giant mural on the restaurant's white walls shows a wheat harvest, Pan playing his pipes, and the Grim Reaper strolling the horizon. The black metal chairs sit on a green linoleum floor, and the ambience is casual and fun.

### Buck's Harbor Market (207-326-8683), Route 176.

This general store has a bakery that's got the best pizza on the peninsula, according to one food lover in Blue Hill. Former Standard Baking Company baker Michael Sheehan is in charge of baking here now and turns out wonderful bread as well, along with morning croissants. Groceries and produce, fine wines, some from the Café Out Back, and beer.

# Castine

## Dennett's Wharf Restaurant and Oyster Bar
**(207) 326-9045**
**Sea Street**
**www.dennettswharf.com**
**Open spring through fall daily for lunch and dinner**
**Entrées $9 to $17**

☛ *An old sail and rigging loft now brews beer and serves lunch on the waterfront*

The bar is made with Georgian lumber shipped here for a bowling lane, rediscovered under the linoleum during a renovation, and transformed into the world's longest oyster bar, now the site of Maine's oyster-eating contest. Oysters are shucked to order ($11.95 for six, $20.95 for a dozen); you might as well get some practice in.

Steamers, lobster cakes, and fried clams are also on the appetizer list. Seafood lasagna, scallops and shrimp with cheeses in a white sauce, sounds rich ($14.95). You can get a steamed lobster, or barbequed ribs and steaks, or roast chicken. Burritos, BLTs, lobster rolls, and a crabmeat melt for lunch.

# Pentagöet Inn

(207) 326-8616, 1-800-845-1701
Main Street, P.O. Box 4
www.pentagoet.com
Hospitality—Well-trained staff do a great job serving dinners.
Open daily for dinner at 5:30 May through October
Entrées $18 to $24

☛ *One of the best meals on the coast of Maine, for ambience, service, and great food*

We had our best meal of the summer here, and that happened not because the food was well made and delicious, although it was, but because everything seemed to come together, as it sometimes does. There was a dish that my companion loved, and one that made me just as happy. The glass of Jacob's Creek Merlot I drank on the porch at the end of a long day of traveling put me in the right mood, to be sure. And there was the wonder at the folded terry-cloth towels in the bathroom, in a stack waiting for use, with a basket to drop them in. How could they keep up? I wondered. But they did; on my last visit as well as the first, the room was impeccable.

Castine's elms still tower over Main Street, and you can admire them from the Pentagöet's porch, or attend a fund-raiser at the inn to help take care of them. Our visit was strictly selfish.

A puree of artichoke hearts, garlic, and oil came with warm focaccia to get us in the mood to eat. The salad with Gorgonzola toasts, port-pickled grapes, and olive oil ($7.50) had a fascination; the grapes were a cross between a raisin and a fresh grape, tasting more of fruit than wine, but delicious and a lovely contrast with the Gorgonzola. A glass of Spy Valley Sauvignon Blanc, from New Zealand ($6.50), fruity and intense, kept pace with the strong flavors.

A lobster tail and claw meat, mussels, and scallops, all tender, lay bathing in a dark rosy broth in the bouillabaisse I ordered, a special that night; flakes of luscious cod lapped in the peppery, fennel soup and filled my mouth with its perfection, and a long piece of crouton with lobster butter kept up the pleasure. The whole production demanded that I slant the bowl and scoop out the last spoonful.

My friend's enormous plate of gemelli pasta with pulled Smithfield ham, peas, and shallots in black truffle cream could not be devoured so thoroughly, but she loved it just the same and put down her fork with regret.

Yellow chintz wrapped around cream poles at the windows, and red walls negate the feminine assault of the china knickknacks here, where the décor is balanced and still almost giddy with ornamentation. As with the over-the-top towel service, the place pulls it off. The fabulous desserts, a blueberry cobbler with homemade ice cream ($6.50) and a chocolate *budino* (warm Italian pudding cake) would have been our destiny if we hadn't gone with the pecan pie with maple ice cream and a Maine blueberry tart with lemon curd. The tart triumphed with a preponderance of berries over curd, and the pecan pie's light filling stood well with the sweeter maple ice cream.

A glass of port, or single malt scotch, would have gone well, but they will have to wait for another night. Eight wines by the glass, and a good range of reds and whites, many around $24, satisfy the thirst; and the champagne was popping on the porch early that summer evening.

*The old facade of the Pentagöet Inn looks out onto an elm-lined street*

## Bakery and Lunch

### Bah's Bakehouse (207-326-9510), Water Street.

Open Monday through Saturday 7–5, Sunday 8–5 in-season. Delicious danishes and raspberry scones are made here, where a customer can put together a meal to carry out in a wicker basket to a table with an umbrella in the yard on a fine day. Soups and sandwiches and creative salads. Hot coffee.

### Castine Variety Store (207-326-8625), 1 Main Street.

Open 5 AM–9 PM in summer, 5 AM–8 PM in winter. Inexpensive crabmeat or lobster rolls, pizza, and a big collection of videos for rent. The old, unrenovated counter from a long time back in this old-fashioned store makes a good setting for a milkshake.

*Castine Variety Store's counter service brings old Maine to mind*

**The Castine Farmer's Market** is held Tuesday 9–11:30 at Bah's Bakehouse, Water Street.

# Deer Isle

## The Pilgrim's Inn
**(207) 348-6615, 1-888-778-7505**
**20 Main Street, P.O. Box 69**
www.pilgrimsinn.com
Hospitality—Excellent service
Open daily for dinner mid-May through mid-October, closed Monday off-season
Entrées $21 to $26

☛ *Sophisticated and fabulous food in a handsome old room*

You are invited to begin a meal here in a room with a huge Colonial fireplace, downstairs from the front entrance. Hors d'oeuvres set out on a table, hummus, salsa, and a crust with a cheese filling and diced vegetable topping went nicely with the glass of Drouhin Beaujolais Villages ($5) I'd gotten from a tiny bar through a doorway. In a few minutes, after guests awkwardly began their introductions, we were called to sit in the beamed dining room, a warmly colored room that was once an old barn. The day's menu took our intent attention for a few minutes, then we ordered and enjoyed the bread already at the table, very good, freshly baked rosemary focaccia. A different kind is baked every day, our server said.

Peekytoe crabcakes with red pepper rouille ($8), which soon appeared in front of me on a cobalt triangular plate, had a crisp crust and tender interior dense with crabmeat and nothing, so far as I could tell, else.

A Parmigiano-Reggiano flan with tomato basil coulis ($8) had the subtlety of a savory custard. The cheese flavor was too faint for a neighbor dining alone, who amiably began a conversation with us, but I liked its delicacy.

A glass of Liberty School Cabernet Sauvignon ($7) warmed my palate as I contemplated my plate of duck breast in pomegranate, cranberry, and orange sauce, which proved the best duck I'd ever tasted, and kept me engaged from first taste to last with its flavor, so very piquant. Meanwhile, my friend savored her penne pasta with pesto, cherry tomatoes, zucchini, and cream, all adorned by a big nasturtium. It was cooked al dente, and the tomatoes did their proper fireworks for the taste buds, with their warm intense red flavor. But, oddly, she became really excited about the side dish of zucchini and yellow squash strips with green beans. Finished in a maple vinaigrette those veggies were so good she asked for a second serving, brought quickly along by our waiter.

Ale-braised lamb shank with maple barbecue sauce ($24), a filet mignon with Gorgonzola nut butter ($26), and poached Atlantic salmon with cucumber dill sauce ($21) glimmered on that good menu.

Part of the elegance here has to do with the reasonably sized portions that however rich and pleasurable had not at all overwhelmed. We ordered the warm apple crisp, accompanied by vanilla ice cream made by a woman in Orland, and a parfait of vanilla ice cream with raspberry sauce. Red rose petals surrounded our dessert plates, and the smooth, vanilla-scented ice cream, clear raspberry of the parfait, and warm comfort of sweet apples made a graceful, delicious conclusion to our fine dinner.

Jonathan Chase is the executive chef here, as I'd been told over and over around Blue Hill, where he is well-known for his own former restaurant, Jonathan's, a place everyone loved.

# Take-Out, Lunch, Pies, and Ice Cream

**Susie Q's (207-348-6013), 17 Sunset Cross Road.**
Open Monday through Saturday 9–3 in summer, call for hours after Labor Day. Fresh-baked pies from Susan Scott, owner of the Fisherman's Friend Restaurant (see page 215). Blueberry, raspberry, and strawberry-rhubarb pies are $16. Muffins, cakes for parties, and blueberry and raspberry crisp are also available. Crab quiche. And gifts and mementos, too.

*The Deer Isle Farmer's Market*

**Harbor Ice Cream (207-348-9360), 11 Main Street.**
Open Monday through Saturday 11–8, Sunday 12–8, May through the end of September. This place sells Gifford's ice cream in cones, sundaes, and frappes. The food otherwise isn't anything to write home about, or hear about either.

**The Deer Isle Farmer's Market** is held 10–noon on Friday from May to October in the Congregational Church parking lot.

# Isle au Haut

## The Keeper's House
(207) 460-0257
www.keepershouse.com
Open late May through late October
Entrées are included in the price of a night's stay.

☛ *A trip to a beautiful island where the innkeepers' dinners have been delighting visitors for years*

Jeff and Judi Burke, the hosts at this restored lighthouse station, feed their guests wonderful meals. The adventure of making your way out here and staying in the living museum of the lighthouse station no doubt sharpens the appetite, but their meals are praised by all our friends who have had the pleasure of enjoying them. You might start with a hot lobster dip, or six-onion soup, and a garden salad, then enjoy grilled salmon with herb butter and roasted red potatoes along with fresh-baked bread. End with fresh peach pie and coffee or tea, and then it's time to listen to the surf outside your inn window.

# Little Deer Isle

## Eaton's Lobster Pool
**(207) 348-2383**
**Blastow Cove Road**
www.eatonslobsterpool.com
Hospitality—Helpful and experienced at this traditional lobster place with salads
Open for dinner 4:30–9 mid-June through Labor Day, weekends from Mother's Day and until Columbus Day
Entrées $8 to $39 (baked stuffed lobster)

☛ *The view off the porch of a nearby island and distant hills makes all the fresh seafood delicious.*

There is full service here nowadays, with starters like lobster stew ($17 a bowl), steamed clams ($14), and a garden salad ($4). You can also enjoy lobster salad ($19) served with lettuce, tomatoes, and cucumbers, or a lobster roll ($12) served with french fries.

The peaceful setting at the end of the winding Blastow Cove Road, with a

*Eaton's Lobster Pool stretches out over the water's edge*

chorus of crickets in late summer and stretches of water leading to the area's thematic softwood-covered hills, makes this spot one of the best settings in Maine. I guess that's why the prices are a little higher than elsewhere. A baked stuffed lobster ($39) or a twin lobster, served with salad and french fries, or a baked or mashed potato ($32), would be worthy of this landscape.

Fried fish and shellfish dinners would be too ($16 for either clams or scallops, with a salad and choice of potato). Broiled scallops or haddock can be ordered, and strip steaks, grilled chicken breast, and crabcakes are offered as well.

*Crack open a lobster on the deck at Eaton's Lobster Pool*

# North Brooklin

## The Lookout
(207) 359-2188
**Flye Point Road (2 miles down)**
www.acadia.net/lookout
Hospitality—Miraculous, on our visit, when one man took care of eight tables
Open for dinner 5:30–8:30 Tuesday through Sunday, June through Labor Day;
Wednesday through Sunday until mid-October
Entrées $18 to $32

## ☞ A flirt with chaos, worth it because sometimes the kitchen is brilliant

This beautiful setting, in an old white farmhouse above a long stretch of rolling grass and lines of Queen Anne's lace that trail to the blue water, with a large white tent glimmering down there, may present one of the most picturesque views around. It's too bad the windows were a little dirty in this still thoroughly casual place. It was also too bad the restaurant was out of both Italian reds listed by the glass, but a request for the Clos du Bois Merlot, not listed by the glass, produced a glass anyway, full almost to the brim. I didn't mind that it wasn't elegant.

The scruffy ambience softened as darkness fell and vanished altogether while I ate from a plate of seven or eight small scallops ($9) browned to a dark crust, in aioli with greens. But I hankered after an aioli powered by more garlic, like the one I'd first tasted at Bread and Puppet Circus. My friend's ricotta and spinach ravioli, with prosciutto and sage butter ($7), had a filling touched by cinnamon, and the salty prosciutto really jazzed up the flavor.

When my entrée arrived I got my wish. The salmon fillet, covered by a thick crust of crumbs and onion ($21), was accompanied by a roasted tomato absolutely stuffed with garlic, along with a little feta and spinach. It was just the supercharged garlic overdose I was hungry for. I was lucky enough to eat the tomatoes that came with my friend's dinner too. Those hot tomatoes weren't particularly civilized, or American, but how I loved them. A potato gratin with cubes of potatoes in a rich cheese sauce was well made, and tender duck sat well in its ginger-rhubarb sauce. But it was the side dishes that really impressed, evidence of an active mind in the kitchen getting excited by all the good stuff coming out of the garden that night in late August.

The plain, wood-paneled porch we sat on, in cheap restaurant chairs, lacked pretension, and the piano jazz on the speakers barely registered, while all around us people seemed to revel, caught up in the pleasure of the food and oblivious to the rest. Others were enjoying rack of lamb (a half for $22), a roasted and boneless free-range chicken ($18) with roasted vegetables, or maybe the scampi Napoli ($22), shrimp sautéed with garlic, butter, and lemon, served with Parmesan and Romano on angel hair pasta, or the filet mignon with béarnaise ($26). It was also pleasant to ignore the challenge our good-tempered waiter, Ryan, faced, taking care of us all by himself. A little waiting was required, as we considered ordering either chocolate-chip cookie à la mode or blueberry crisp.

But really, they were beyond us, and it must have been the garlic, calming our appetites, making us peaceful, and leaving us happy.

.

# Sedgwick

**Blue Poppy Garden (207-359-2739), Reach Road.**
Open July and August 12–2:30 for lunch, 2:30–5:30 for English cream tea. A beautiful garden is the setting for lunches of hummus, chicken salad, lentil salad, and quiche. Teas are the traditional time to enjoy scones with clotted Devonshire cream and jams. Sandwiches and pastries turn it into a high tea. If the blue poppies are blooming, you'll wonder if you've arrived in Tibet.

# Stonington

## The Cockatoo
**(207) 367-0900**
**24 Carter Lane**
Hospitality—Whatever you want, someone here will help out, including dancing with Peaches, the cockatoo
Open for take-out in the summer 12–8
Entrées $11 to $22
BYOB

☛ *On a warm night, the outside patio is a kind of heaven overlooking Webb Cove; the spicy seafood heats up your mouth, and the party around you inspires salsa dancing*

Suzen Carter was Suzen Diniz before she married a fisherman and moved to Stonington six years ago; she's Portuguese, from New Bedford, Massachusetts, with ancestors from the Azores, and she loves to cook. She loves to cook so much that when she first moved here she would bring her food to the bank and to the gas station, just to share it and because she didn't know anyone on the island. "Why don't you open a restaurant," people told her, and her husband said the same thing. He had expanded his fish store just down the hill from their house. She started out small one summer and by the end of the season was amazed.

"It was all word of mouth," she said. Remembering the previous Saturday night when the tables in the outside patio were full, and a line of 14 people waited for take-out, she felt confident that she would be mixing up more of her shrimp Mozambique ($12.95), a garlicky, pungent dish, and her Portuguese sole ($12.95), full of saffron and rice, for seasons to come.

*The Cockatoo's terrace has a magnificent view and an eclectic decor*

"We don't have anything frozen," she said. Her husband's three fishing boats bring in supplies for the little fish store, and a day-old harpooned swordfish sat in the cooler. Clams are dug, shucked, and fried within a day.

"You don't even need any seasonings," she said, even though she'd shown off the bag of Portuguese salt, Peniche, a moment before—it adds "fresh out of the water flavor," she said.

The clams are part of the word going from resident to visitor and back as people turn in on the dirt driveway off Oceanville Road to Carter's Seafood and the Cockatoo. The only seating is at the outside tables, where you carry your order from the take-out window. Bring your own bottle of wine to this party.

People also talk about the nine-year-old dancing cockatoo, Peaches, who favors a Latin beat and sings to the music, crowing with her gray tongue and bobbing with evident delight, ruffling her white feathers and the few orange ones, and then studying you intently with her round black eyes.

Suzen makes a dish called a snake, a spiral of tender crust filled with mild cheese, a few chopped vegetables, and crabmeat or yellowfin tuna ($14.95). The mild cheese and the simple flavors make it a delicious meal, with some left over to snack on later. She'll make it a "cobra" to serve more than one, if you ask.

Also on the dinner menu are Spanish clams with linguine and salad ($12.95), steamed clams, and lobster. Two pounds of clams steamed in beer and seasoned were $13.95, and 2 pounds of mussels with garlic and oil were $7.95.

Suzen plans to keep baking Portuguese sweet breads and pastry through much of the winter, but whether Stonington's 1,200 year-round residents can keep her busy is doubtful. Only so many of them will have a birthday over the winter and order one of her cakes.

*Peaches dancing with Suzen Carter, Portuguese chef of The Cockatoo*

But as we watch her clap and dance with Peaches, it looked like they will both have the spirit to sustain them through the harsh island winter and be ready for more garden parties among the torches and the hot pink petunias next summer.

# The Harbor Café
**(207) 367-5099**
**Main Street**
Open for lunch and dinner year-round, with early closing on Sunday in winter
Entrées $7 to $17

☛ *An informal restaurant with friendly service and simple meals*

The Harbor Café sits up over Main Street in a clean, light-filled room, with a a view of the water, pine booths, and white walls stenciled with ivy. Specials, like scallop chowder, were up on the board, and the day's vegetables included pickled beets, corn, stewed tomatoes, and coleslaw. Standard sandwiches and seafood rolls, with hamburgers and salad plates, provide lunch. Dinners are a variety of fried fish and shellfish, and a ham steak or sirloin.

Homemade desserts included apple-raisin, Toll House, blueberry, and raspberry pies, and Key lime cheesecake.

# The Fisherman's Friend
**(207) 367-2442**
**School Street**
Open for lunch and dinner in summer, closing earlier in winter
Entrées $6 to $12

☛ *Local favorite for simple cooking and outstanding pies*

The lobster stew and chowders are always ready here in this old Maine seafood restaurant. Crabcakes, lobster rolls, and other things to eat in-between, like hamburgers and grilled cheese. The pies, over 20 listed on occasion, can really get your heart beating. Owner Susan Scott sells pies on the side (see Susie Q's on page 208), as well as supplying them to the restaurant, so you can buy one to take home. Blueberry, raspberry, and strawberry-rhubarb pies are just a few you're likely to run into here.

*The Fisherman's Friend Restaurant has a reputation for fine seafood*

# Lily's Café

(207) 367-5936

**Route 15, P.O. Box 653**

Hospitality—Quick and cheerful service

Open in summer for breakfast and lunch Monday, Tuesday, and Friday 7–4, Wednesday and Thursday until 8, for dinner; in winter Monday, Tuesday, and Friday 7–3, Wednesday and Thursday until 7 for dinner

Entrées $7 to $13

☞ *A charming, casual spot for good food; organic ingredients in the recipes*

Smells of baking fill this old gray-clapboard house on the corner of Route 15 and the airport road. The tendency is toward organic, with a produce stand open in the summer for vegetables from places like Brooklin's Carding Brook Farm; a lot of their produce is used in the soups and other dishes in the restaurant.

Breakfast starts with eggs, moves on to a big assortment of pancakes, and includes bagels, homemade granola with Greek yogurt ($4.95), and hot organic oatmeal with raisins and maple cream ($4.95). Island Acre Farm breakfast sausage is $2 a link, and organic coffee is $1.50, with free refills.

Lunch could be Ethel's pork BBQ sandwich, boneless pork simmered in a raspberry barbeque sauce on French bread ($7.95), or crabcakes made with island crabmeat and served with salad, bread, and curry-mayo dipping sauce ($12.95). There's a vegetarian burger made from scratch with nuts, cheese, and brown rice ($6.95), lentil salad, Chinese noodles, and a baked fish sandwich on rye ($7.95). Apple pie, chocolate cake, and blueberry muffins are all made here.

*The farmstand outside of Lily's Café is another reason to stop by*

# Maritime Café

**(207) 367-2600**
**27 Main Street**
www.maritimecafe.com
Hospitality—Local talent makes for quick, intelligent service
Open daily 11:30–2:30 for lunch, 5:30–8:30 for dinner, in-season
Entrées $6 to $20

☞ *A stylish café with upscale prices and a great deck*

The outside deck over the water, with tables under umbrellas, is the favorite spot here, but the inside dining room looks sleek, with taupe-and-black-striped upholstered wall benches, dark wood tables, white walls, and rope-encrusted sconces.

Dinner specials, like grilled salmon, add a few more choices to the short menu, with crabcakes, barbequed ribs, baked haddock, and lobsters for dinner.

Lunch is pretty much the same, with a lobster roll ($11), a crab roll ($9), a very ordinary hamburger with flavorless meat, chips, lettuce, and tomato ($5.50), and haddock, turkey, and veggie sandwiches.

My lobster salad ($16) satisfied with a generous amount of lobster mixed with mayonnaise, but there wasn't much to like about the greens, a grocery tomato, and cucumbers too familiar with a refrigerator. A side dish of roasted creamed corn held some interest, with the toasted corn kernels in creamy sauce. And the glasses of ginger lemonade ($2) were full of fresh lemon and the astringent sharpness of macerated ginger.

We went a little crazy about the blackberry pie ($4); sweet and dark, with a crisp and chewy topping, it was served hot with ice cream and whipped cream and woke us up from our lunchtime ennui to start enjoying ourselves.

## Coffee, Take-Out, Wine, Smoked Seafood, and Lobsters

### The Espresso Bar at the Inn on the Harbor (207-367-2420), Main Street, P.O. Box 69.

Open Memorial Day through Columbus Day, 11–4:30. You can get an espresso made with Lavazza coffee and sip it on the back deck over the water. Accompany it with peanut-butter cake ($2), blueberry scones ($1.50), or Chastity's superb peanut-butter balls (60¢ each).

## The Take Out (207-367-6363), Atlantic Avenue.
Open in-season Sunday through Thursday10:30–8, Friday and Saturday until 9. This place has the best crab rolls around.

## Penobscot Bay Provisions (207-367-5177), West Main Street.
Fresh baked goods, bread, and terrific sandwiches.

## The Clown (207-367-6348), Main Street.
Open mid-May through mid-October. A branch of the Portland wine store, you can buy wine here, along with some items of European kitchenware.

## Carter's Seafood (207-367-0900), 24 Carter Lane.
This is the source of the great fresh fish and shellfish at the Cockatoo (see page 218). All types of fresh fish, clams, mussels, lobsters, and shrimp are sold here.

## Stonington Sea Products (1-888-402-2729, www.stonington seafood.com), Route 15.
Open Monday through Friday 10–5 and Saturday 9–2 in summer; Monday through Friday 10–4 in winter. Fresh fish is sold here—tuna, swordfish, and lobster—as well as an array of smoked seafood, from salmon, to mussels, to fish, and other products, including smoked fish pâtés, flying fish roe, and seaweed salad.

## Stonington Lobster Cooperative (207-367-5564), Indian Point Road, Sunshine Seafood (207-367-2955), Old Quarry Road, Fifield Lobster (207-367-2313), Fifield Point Road, and Greenhead Lobster (207-367-0950), Ocean Road, all sell lobsters.

# Sunset

## Goose Cove Lodge
(207) 348-2508, 1-800-728-1963
300 Goose Cove Road
www.goosecovelodge.com
Hospitality—Local college students can be a little overwhelmed, but they are kindness personified.
Open for dinner Tuesday through Sunday from early June to early October
Entrées $16 to $20

## A perch over a classic view of islands of pointed firs, with high-quality meals

The end of the season is always a roller coaster for the inns and restaurants on the Maine coast that depend on students for staff. It happened that our dinner at Goose Cove coincided with the Sunday-night closing of nearby Pilgrim's Inn, and the restaurant was packed.

But although our young waiter was stretched, he'd learned his trade over the summer and could be snagged on the fly and fulfilled requests quickly.

Appetizers featured linguica and kielbasa, already familiar to us from the breakfast specials, since we were lucky enough to be staying in one of the lodge's rooms. Grilled and served with "healthy slaw and chipotle dipping sauce," the sausage starter ($6) works for someone who has spent the day kayaking. The evening's special mini-pizza also included linguica, with corn, scallions, and tomatoes ($7). Peekytoe crab cocktail with gazpacho, chilled jumbo shrimp, and tomato granite ($9), and grilled, prosciutto-wrapped peaches with a balsamic reduction and mixed greens ($7) are brilliant beginnings also on the list.

This restaurant features salads with pleasant touches, like a Caesar salad topped with crunchy oats and almonds ($5) and a spinach salad with pickled red onion, strawberries, and sunflower seeds ($6). My choice of a mixed green salad with chopped apples, feta, cucumber, tomato, and sunflower seeds ($5) appeared at the table full of impeccably fresh local greens, in a modest portion, dressed in a citrus vinaigrette that was a touch sweet. Since I had kayaked only a few hundred feet around the cove in front of the lodge, that worked.

The dining room, paneled in knotty pine and set on two levels, takes advantage of the wonderful view out into the almost mythic islands around Deer Isle, covered by the pointed firs that spread their mats of roots over the red granite bedrock and hang on for dear life. As the fog crept up over the water, the customers in the packed dining room reveled over their good bottles of wine—chosen from a list that features Portuguese reds and other finds, modest and expensive—and dug into plates of crabcakes with angelhair pasta in chorizo Bolognese ($19) or butterflied leg of lamb with Israeli couscous, cucumber, tomato, and herb mélange that was a kind of thick version of gazpacho, and kalamata olive sauce and basil oil. The intensity of the olives spiced up the bland couscous. The lamb, rare as I had requested, in a large serving, stood as the centerpiece of flavor and interest, and performed well.

Blackened swordfish, and halibut with angelhair pasta in a beurre blanc sauce, were two of the specials. Other entrées included roasted pork tenderloin in roasted shallot and grain mustard sauce with sweet potato pie ($18) and grilled flank steak in red wine sauce with Boursin mashed potatoes and wild mushroom ragout ($17). The menu stated that help would be available for vegetarian requests, although there was no vegetarian entrée. A dish of angelhair pasta with butter was served up to a finicky child, and lobsters were available to some diners, perhaps by special order.

Desserts the night of our visit were rosemary crème brûlée—an unappealing idea—chocolate trinity parfait, too creamy for a chocolate lover, and a cranberry-blueberry crisp that needed more sugar.

**Spencer Pies (207-348-9346), 151 Sunset Road (Route 15A), P.O. Box 64.** Irene Spencer sells pies she bakes fresh in her modest home alongside Sunset Road; a hand-lettered sign announces PIES when she's in the little gift shop beside her home. The blueberry pies were going for $10, and she had made cherry and lemon meringue earlier in the summer for $11. She hopes to stay open until Christmas and reopen for summer in May and would be happy to make pies to order.

**CHAPTER 7**

# Ellsworth to Hancock & Mount Desert Island

**T**HE TRADITION OF SUMMER VACATIONS HERE, the heavy traffic and the relentless crowds, make this area the site of fierce restaurant competition. Many fail, some within a single summer, like ill-fated Pagliarulo's, where I spent a happy evening eating an eggplant parmigiana that took the dish to another planet. But not enough people felt the same way. Without the customers, the expenses piled up, and the owner shut down.

Chefs seem to move around these businesses pretty regularly, too.

The hopping nighttime sidewalks of Bar Harbor are thronged with hungry people who will make someone's fortune. We can only hope the customers seek out the good things, the places like Café This Way and the Bagel Factory, and other businesses that bake and cook with integrity.

# Acadia National Park

## Jordan Pond House
**(207) 276-3316**
**Near the Bubbles**
Hospitality—College students make this place hum, with quick and intelligent service.
Open for lunch and tea 11:30–5:30 and dinner from 5:30 late June through Columbus Day
Entrées $11 to $18

☛ *The quintessence of refreshment in a national park*

Tea and popovers with strawberry jam and butter are welcome pleasures when the hikes are over and the sun has decided to shine over Jordan Pond, or you can get a table inside this often crowded building and evade the cold mist of fall.

We made a reservation an hour distant at the reservation window outside the restaurant door and walked down the trail that skirts Jordan Pond. Then we doubled back. With the low overcast that troubled our visit the hot tea and hot popovers were especially tasty.

You can eat a regular lunch in the dining room or out on the lawn, with lobster rolls, curried chicken salad, chowders, and salads to choose from. Dinners of crabcakes ($13.25), penne pasta, baked scallops, or a steamed lobster are served after 5:30.

*The Bubbles by Jordan Pond in Acadia National Park*

# Bar Harbor

## Café This Way
(207) 288-4483
14½ Mt. Desert Street
www.cafethisway.com
Hospitality—A little distracted with the relentless crowds, but otherwise fine
Open for breakfast Monday through Saturday 7–11, Sunday 8–1; for dinner
6–9, mid-April through October
Entrées $15 to $22

☞ *Sophisticated and casual, with an emphasis on pronounced flavors*

Fruit or spice or cheese or garlic often tie into the main dishes to make their tastes loud and clear. The Parmesan-crusted pork chops with chèvre butter ($16) employs two cheeses to good effect, and the sirloin with sweet onion relish and espresso barbeque sauce ($17) goes smoky and sweet a couple of ways as well.

Sesame aioli jacks up the tempo of the cashew-crusted chicken ($16), and classic fruits—apricots and blueberry chutney—bring out the savor of the East-West duck ($18). The flatbread pizza with figs, blue cheese, roasted garlic, prosciutto, and mozzarella ($7) on the appetizer list says it all.

If you can keep going for another course, there's chocolate raspberry truffle cake, or a blueberry pie from Morning Glory Bakery (see page 232).

Breakfast can be simpler. The granola with honey and cinnamon yogurt and fruit makes a delicious start ($4.75). Bagels with cream cheese, red onion, tomato, and either smoked salmon or smoked trout are another admirable classic.

But the list of omelets would satisfy the sharpest morning hunger and sustain the steepest climb on a ladder trail in Acadia.

## George's Restaurant
**(207) 288-4505**
**7 Stephens Lane**
**www.georgesbarharbor.com**
**Hospitality—Effusive, willing, and well trained**
**Open daily for dinner from Memorial Day weekend to October**
**Entrées $25; three courses—appetizer, entrée, and dessert—$37 to $40**
**Reservations likely to be necessary**

☞ *Highly civilized, with a wonderful atmosphere*

Enjoying a great meal at George's has become a Bar Harbor tradition. The place seems to have settled into a groove of summer elegance that transient waitstaff and vacationers can't disturb. On a July night the man playing the piano moved into "Bewitched, Bothered and Bewildered" and set the tone as the tables quickly filled.

Four double 12-light windows look out on trees around the end of the lower dining room, with its green-and-burgundy curtains against cream walls. A lacy hydrangea flower sat in a blue-and-white creamer on our table, and a columbine decorated the next table, avoiding even the floral clichés. Four 70-year-olds raised luminescent martinis in a toast at a table across the room.

Our Jed Steele Zinfandel ($24 for a split), proved a good choice from the wine list full of favorites found by the owner on trips out West.

We ignored the vanilla pound cake that sat in the breadbasket next to slices of dense white French bread. But as soon as the food arrived, we were inspired, because the simple salad of oak leaf lettuce held such a flavorful oil, and its sprinkling of goat cheese contrasted with the perfect note of bitterness. That portended the fanaticism in every detail that made everything far better than good—even if the pepper mill, shedding electronically milled peppercorns under its own spotlight, took us by surprise.

The porcini risotto with crisp rounds of sliced shallots, English peas, and shaved Parmigiano held al dente arborio rice in a luscious sauce, but what truly thrilled us was the taste of the fresh porcinis, sliced and brown, gushing with their own juice. The mushrooms had been flown in from the Pacific Northwest, the server found out.

Another appetizer, Spaghetti George's Way, turned out to be thin spaghetti covered in a meaty red sauce with bits of lamb and chicken, accompanied by a little dish of freshly grated Parmesan, which pleased a younger dinner guest.

Grilled lamb chops were cooked on the rare side of medium-rare, without ascertaining if I wanted them that way. Restaurant policy, no doubt, and somewhat imperious, but they were utterly to my taste, deeply flavored on the brown exterior and full of juice.

Grilled lobster tail with celery root puree, summer squash, and lemongrass lobster broth brought a new angle on the tourist favorite, raising simple lobster to eloquence. George's lobster strudel has been doing that for years, packing the tender meat in crisp, flaky phyllo and keeping the butter to a high standard. Mustard shrimp and orzo salad are another enduring favorite, which go out the kitchen faster when the summer weather heats up.

Ending our dinner with the first fresh strawberries we have seen featured on any Maine menu in the middle of strawberry season (a perpetual disappointment), we enjoyed another triumph. These were served with a champagne zabaglione that was made to give a sense of heaven on earth—or I should say, was sublime, light, rich, a fabulous flavorful cream—and the strawberries were the best we've had. Another dessert offered them in a honey-vanilla ice cream sundae with chocolate sauce. Our resident crème brûlée fanatic inevitably chose the brown sugar crème brulée and pronounced it perfect, with a crusty sugar surface and rich custard, wondering only why it was cold.

Like the piano player's "Norwegian Wood," a complicated version that seemed to strip the melody of any misogyny, George's food has been studied and arranged and understood, giving us all the benefit of masterly cooking and fine ingredients.

# Havana

(207) 288-2822
318 Main Street
www.havanamaine.com
Hospitality—Awfully good-looking servers are swift and competent.
Open for dinner daily at 5:30 in summer
Entrées $18 to $28

☛ *A fun restaurant with Latin style, serving Cuban-inspired food*

The shadows of the big dark black-eyed Susans crept up the teal and adobe red walls as the waiters swept back and forth in their indigo cotton shirts and black pants. The hair on both the men and women servers, uniformly dark on our visit, was swept back into sleek buns.

A place with Latin style is a rarity in Maine, and Havana may owe some of its reputation as "the best restaurant in Bar Harbor" to its illusion of being somewhere else. It's cool and fussy. The little piece of toast with shrimp pâté and four capers, "compliments of the chef," was pleasant. Was that peach-vanilla butter with the poppy seed–orange corn bread? The bread was almost sticky and gooey, cakelike, and not engaging. The glass of simple *vino verde* washed away the taste, and the server came by with the crumb scraper to keep us spiffy.

The halibut ($24) was fine with its dry rub and toasted pepitas crust, a mango mojo alongside a sweet pairing. The rice was a bore, but the fresh vegetables, vinegar-tinged green and red peppers, and red onion along with a roasted banana delivered some excitement.

The medium-rare pork chop with another dab of roasted banana and maple chipotle barbeque sauce ($23) was also fine. We liked the mashed potatoes enriched with olive oil.

Desserts included Havana flan flavored with Cuban coffee ($6.50), bread pudding made with tortillas and topped with a rum sauce ($6.50), and a mojito cheesecake with the flavors of that drink—rum, Key limes, and mint ($6.50).

# Maggie's Restaurant

**(207) 288-9007**
**6 Summer Street**
www.maggiesbarharbor.com
Hospitality—Accommodating and friendly service
Open for dinner 5–9:30 Monday through Saturday, June through late October
Entrées $17 to $25

☛ *With an emphasis on fresh, local seafood and produce, this place delivers delicious meals.*

The owner of this enduring establishment, its long presence in tumultuous Bar Harbor a clue to its quality, started out with a fish market, filleting fish she bought from local fishermen. The restaurant benefits from her sharp eye for freshness, and the local creatures are still the ones that are served here.

Starters feature produce from the owners' own garden in an organic greens salad with cherry tomatoes and Sunset Acres goat cheese ($7), a delightful cheese made in Brooksville. Smoked salmon with caper-mustard sauce ($7) comes from nearby, and so do the mussels steamed with herbs and wine ($7). Pizzas are offered for children who can't face the seafood ($7 for a small, $10 for a large size that feeds two).

Maine shrimp, cherrystone clams, mussels, potatoes, and chorizo in saffron-tomato sauce ($19) is a good Maine version of spicy fish stew beloved around the Mediterranean. Scallops with bacon, fresh corn, and roasted red peppers ($18) take that classic pairing of pork and shellfish in another direction with the corn's sweetness.

Everyone lauds the lobster crêpes here ($25), always on a menu that otherwise changes frequently. Chunks of lobster meat in a buttery sauce make the kind of filling crêpes were made for.

Coq au vin ($18) and a potato, eggplant, and pattypan squash napoleon with roasted tomato sauce ($170) were the only non-seafood entrées.

The pale green tablecloths with flowered undercloths, and the porch room with lace swags in the windows and little white lights, show the comfortable house, a few steps off Cottage Road, at its pristine best. With Spanish guitar music on the stereo and a dish of the zesty lemon cake ($5.50) filled with lemon curd and strewn with long strands of lemon zest, there is nothing to detract from a summer evening.

Except, perhaps, your yearning for your companion's blueberry sundae with lemon ice cream and whipped cream ($5.50). But she'll let you taste the dark sauce, like a liquid pie filling, and make the night sweet.

# McKay's Public House
(207) 288-2002
231 Main Street
Open daily for dinner 5–10 year-round, for lunch in summer
Entrées $10 to $23

🐖 *A casual restaurant that's a fine choice for quality food in a range of entrées*

"We like to get as many fresh ingredients as we can, all over the menu," said Sue Ericson, manager of McKay's. The restaurant uses local produce from several organic farms and serves beer from each of the local breweries.

The restaurant was started with the idea of serving Irish pub food, so bangers and mash ($9.95) are on the menu, and they're popular, but grade A ahi tuna ($22.95) is also listed every night, along with a crispy-rendered duck breast over bourbon sweet potatoes ($18.95). The chef has been instrumental in widening the range of food. A seafood chowder is a menu regular, and a cream of crab with shiitake mushroom bisque ($6.95) has been a featured special. The bread is baked by Agnes Smit, of the Bagel Factory (see page 232).

"We don't want to seem too pretentious or too casual," Ericson continued. The place, for one thing, has no dress code.

There are about 10 stools at the bar, and food is served there. Because McKay's is open year-round, it feeds a lot of locals. In summer an outside garden is filled with tables with umbrellas, and lanterns hang from plant stands, doubling the seating for the crowds that migrate here in good weather.

# Michelle's Fine Dining
(207) 288-2138
194 Main Street
www.michellesfinedining.com
Hospitality—A waitstaff trained to take special care of the customers
Open for dinner and breakfast May through October
Entrées $24 to $54

🐖 *Formal and traditional elegance and meals for a special occasion*

Formal and elegant, this restaurant has created a devoted following for, among other things, its lobster Thermidor ($54).

"Lobster meat is sautéed in wine, with mushrooms and shallots, returned to the shell of the 2-pound lobster, then covered with Gruyère cheese and hollandaise, heated under the broiler, and served. It's magnificent," said Judy Stanley, the owner, who named the restaurant after her daughter. Stanley bought the building and designed it as a traditional French restaurant seven years ago, completely gutting the rooms and recreating the interior of a French inn.

The rooms are filled with antiques, and a piano bar is open Thursday and Sunday night; appetizers are served, and cigars are available.

Chef William Fellner Jr., who trained in Europe, has been here for five years. He spends his summers at Michelle', and his winters as a chef at Mar-A-Lago, the resort in West Palm Beach owned by Donald Trump.

For one local businessman who dines at Michelle's as often as once a week, the filet mignon is the draw. Topped with a medallion of Roquefort, and served with a zinfandel demi-glace, the meat is aged to perfection and cooked "blue," just the way he likes it.

Another thing that makes this restaurant a favorite is the service. In fact, this man and his wife are always served by the same waiter—Shawn—who he claims is the best waiter on Mount Desert.

For dessert you can have zabaglione with berries, a crème brûlée ($10), or a dessert soufflé; there are five, from the Grand Marnier to Maine raspberry ($14).

Although I didn't eat the dinner here I did try the breakfast buffet ($12.95 per person). You can help yourself to hot-smoked salmon, mini bagels—unfortunately somewhat stale and hailing from the supermarket—and herbed cream cheese in a room with pink-lilac walls. The granola full of macadamia nuts and dried cranberries was great and looked splendid in its small, gold-rimmed bowl. Nut-crusted bacon, with a bit of sugar thrown in, was somewhere over the top for my taste, but the hot homefries actually benefited from the chafing dish.

Ornately framed, lighted artwork and bud vases with single red roses on the tables, each covered by two tablecloths, made the atmosphere tranquil. Dinner must always be a special occasion here; the setting exactly right for a big romance, or a weekly escape.

# Thrumcap Café and Wine Bar
## (207) 288-3884
## 123 Cottage Street
Hospitality—Careful, polite service, with extra care from a cordial host
Open for dinner daily except Sunday, July through October; Thursday, Friday, and Saturday, October to June.
Prix fixe $39 for a four-course meal
Reservations advised

☛ *Superb food and wonderful wines, all lined up for you with great advice*

With a "miniflight" to get the evening airborne, our meal in this elegant restaurant never faltered. The olive oil had an alluring fruitiness, the bread was crusty, and the Chartron and Trebuchet 2000 Bourgogne tasted "restrained and minerally," just as the menu advised, making an argument to drink good white wine.

The room is divided into thirds with low walls topped by handsome glass panels. Every chair is an armchair, and the tables are an assortment of ornate and simple oak. We were relaxed and happy as the first course of white bean soup arrived, accompanied by a garlicky pesto smeared on a toasted slice of baguette. Soft beans contrasted with crunchier vegetables, creating two clear textures in a modest serving of rich soup, sized just right.

The little glass of Lake Sonoma 2001 Russian River Chardonnay, sweeter and more fun than the austere French, stood up to the pesto and garlic with panache. But I preferred the French with the next course, three fried oysters. Served with an M&M-sized dollop of chipotle puree and creamed spinach, the crisp, fresh, tender oysters made my mouth water with happiness. Across from me my friend was enjoying the Cotswold cheese with its accompaniment of quince paste, *membrillo*. Her Spanish Valdeon, a blue cheese, was emphatic without malice.

Next up for my companion was ravioli, tender homemade pasta envelopes that teach everyone to adore pasta. A puree of sweet potatoes, mushrooms, and poblano chiles worked well in its miso broth.

My duck, slightly more cooked than I might have preferred, sat in its firey peach barbeque sauce and made a perfect fit with my second miniflight, two glasses of Shiraz, or syrah. The Shottesbrooke McLaren Vale 2001 Shiraz knocked me out—figuratively speaking—with its big taste. My succotash of corn and lima beans got along better with the Steele 1999 Lake County Syrah.

Rendered by now completely obedient to the menu's recommendations, there was no choice when I saw the injunction "You must have the Maury" but to order it. Host Tom Marinke came over to tell me about how this red dessert wine sits in glass demijohns and ferments in the sun before spending nine years in oak barrels. Well, it was light and still inky, potent but bright. The chocolate tart was the perfect friend to those tastes, with its dark rich chocolate, and orange zest and raspberry coulis sauce. The lemon and blueberry tart with fresh whipped cream had a perfect shortbread crust and was decorated as well with zigzags of raspberry coulis.

We couldn't have eaten and drunk as well anywhere else.

# 2 Cats
**(207) 288-2808, 1-800-355-2808**
**130 Cottage Street**
www.2catsbarharbor.com
Hospitality—Raucous and energetic, this place is hopping, but the food can be slow in coming.
Open daily for breakfast 7–1 in summer; call for winter hours
Breakfast $7 to $12 (dinner may be offered in the summer)

☛ *As long as the staff issues are ironed out, this is a fun place to eat breakfast.*

On an overcast morning the lawn at 2 Cats is swarming with customers awaiting the signal to pounce—their names will be called by the boisterous maitre d'. Meanwhile, we are all drinking coffee we poured for ourselves inside, and a fabulous fruit smoothie made up at the counter.

"Hairy kitty!" the man yells, and everyone laughs.

"It's frenetic," I say to the man at the counter, "Is it always like this?"

"Always," he confirms.

A bottle of champagne pops at a table on the porch. It's someone's birthday, and the servers deluge her with attention.

When we are led to a table on the terrace, the momentum is still with us. More coffee is poured, and a hot chocolate is sped along to take off the slight chill.

But, as it turned out, the chef had gone missing, the kitchen was understaffed, and everyone's breakfast was seriously delayed. The couple next to us got theirs half-price, because their wait exceeded an hour. Our French toast and eggs Benedict arrived in 45 minutes. The poached eggs were fabulous, the French toast was dry, but we had to get going to catch the *Island Explorer* to Northeast Harbor.

We will return, and we will try the famed omelets with smoked salmon or smoked trout, and the muffins that ran out that blue morning, and the granola sold by the pound to its dedicated customers.

Maybe we'll order champagne.

# Breakfast, Lunch, Take-Out, Coffee, and Candy

### The Bagel Factory (207-288-3903), located on Cadillac Avenue in a cul-de-sac off Cottage Street.

Open 7 AM–2 PM Tuesday through Sunday year-round. Agnes Smit, 68, makes bagels the old-fashioned way, first boiled and then baked. "It's what makes the difference in a bagel," she said. She supplies dozens each week to the Blue Hill Co-op Café and some Bar Harbor restaurants.

"People buy my bagels and bring them back to New York," she said, laughing because it seemed a little crazy.

In the late 1970s and '80s she ran the Sunflower Bakery, which delivered whole-grain bread to lots of Maine co-ops, and then ran the the Geronimo Café. She's had her hands in a lot of dough, and knows how to make the best, always a pleasure to encounter if the Maine coast has deprived you of good bread, as it can.

Her healthiest bagel might be the one made with spelt flour; the rest are sourdough. She also makes bialies on Friday and pretzels, filled with mustard and cheese, on Thursday. She makes vegetarian chili everyday, and other soups with whatever's in season. She's only allowed six chairs because her place is a take-out, but the size works for her. In nice weather you can sit in the sun outside and devour your toasted bagel in peace.

### The Morning Glory Bakery (207-288-3041), 39 Rodick Street.

Open Monday through Friday 7–4, Saturday 8–2, spring until Thanksgiving. Fresh bread is baked here, from a nutty and delicious whole wheat, to honey oatmeal, sourdough, and baguettes. Sticky buns, scones, cookies, and pies like blueberry, apple, pecan, and strawberry-rhubarb are all excellent. Sandwiches include a BLT with avocado and herb mayo ($5), and soups, quiche, and salad of the day are sold for lunch.

### J.H. Butterfield and Co. (207-288-3386), 152 Main Street, P.O. Box 181.

Sandwiches include chicken salad ($3.95), cream cheese and olive ($3.75), and egg salad ($2.95). Wine, beer, cookies, and much else.

### The Opera House Internet Café (207-288-3509), 27 Cottage Street.

Check your e-mail and enjoy a cup of coffee and a Ghirardelli chocolate brownie, bagels, and other good things on the honor system—you tell the cashier what you ate.

### Ben and Bill's Chocolate Emporium (207-288-3281), 66 Main Street.

Truffles, fudge, and many, many other sweets.

### The Bar Harbor Farmer's Market is held Sunday 10–2 in the YMCA parking lot on Main Street, Mother's Day through October.

# *Bernard*

## Thurston's Lobster Pound
**(207) 244-7600**
**Steamboat Wharf Road**
Open 11–8:30 Memorial Day through Columbus Day (closed Labor Day)
Entrées $8 to market price for lobster

☛ *The insiders' favorite lobster pound, for lobster rolls, chowder, and great lobsters*

With plastic sides available to wrap around the outside porch, this place carries on into the cooler weather and is sitting pretty on the warm days when the breeze lifts up from the waves and floats past your table. The working harbor here is a charming prospect, and the pound hasn't become overwhelmed by success. Fresh lobster, corn, and alternatives.

*There are two large decks at Thurston's Lobster Pound*

# Bucksport

**Farm stand with the pies, 227 Route 1, 1 mile north of the Bucksport Bridge and just south of the junction of Route 1 and Route 46.**

A pie here was $15 in 2004, sold by a lady sitting under a green awning. She might not tell you her name, but she'll tell you she bakes 21 pies at a time, and got up at six to do it. She's been here for 50 years. Her daughter makes jam. From June 1 to September 21 you are likely to find her near the yellow pie sign, selling strawberry, blueberry, strawberry-pineapple-rhubarb, and strawberry-rhubarb pies.

# Ellsworth

## Cleonice
**(207) 664-7554**
**112 Main Street**
www.cleonice.com
Hospitality—Intelligent and friendly
Open Monday through Saturday for lunch 11:30–2:30, tapas and desserts 2:30–5, dinner every night from 5
Entrées $19 to $24; tapas $2.50 to $7.50
Reservations recommended, especially on weekends

☛ *Real Mediterranean flair with seafood and meat dishes makes the food sing*

In a long room lined by a dark wooden bar and booths, with five ceiling fans slowly revolving, you can't help but feel ready for some noir event, some romantic entanglement, some Peter Lorre–like stranger sidling up to seek your help. The cool glass of Manzanilla, a dry sherry perfect with the tapas, assists the illusion. Downtown Ellsworth was never so exciting.

When the fellow tourists come into focus it won't matter, because you have already got your tapas, your order quickly filled from the food kept behind the bar. The little bowl of scungilli salad, made with Maine's own ubiquitous periwinkles (the temptation to scare the children with them is great), gives your mouth something to learn, the black-striped snails chewy and resilient and their salad of green olives, fennel, red onion, and peppers a bright complement.

Grilled sardines, flown in from Greece, were drizzled with balsamico, while the calamari salad was all tender small squid in lemon and olive oil with a few salty black olives for contrast. The rich spanikopita was deeply flavored with butter and lots of creamy feta.

Consultations between the brisk staff and the chef at the kitchen door brought alternate wine recommendations when the wine suggested on the menu was declined. White Rioja would work for most of us with the Turkish vegetarian Kofte ($18.50), layers of spiced bulgur and nuts, eggplant stew, and feta and kasseri cheese custard, a rich world of its own and reason enough to give up meat.

But what about the grilled Maine-raised Delmonico steak with Cabrales blue cheese butter ($20.50)? Or the *Lomo con Almejas,* Spanish-style pork tenderloin braised with chorizo, littleneck clams, tomatoes, and red wine? The glass of Borsao works there.

Cleonice uses a lot of local foods, from Frenchman's Bay mussels to Maine chickens to wild sea grass. The place is excited about its food, and so am I. I wish I lived nearby.

## Jasper's Restaurant and Motel
**(207) 667-5318**
**200 High Street (across from Wendy's in the Ellsworth Shopping Center)**
Hospitality—Grown-up female servers take good care of all their customers.
Open for lunch and dinner daily 11–9, June through mid-October, 11–8 the rest of the year
Entrées $7 to $26

☛ *Down-home meals made with Downeast harvests*

This restaurant has been around forever, serving mostly seafood, some steak, and Sunday specials like roast pork and baked stuffed chicken. George Henry, the chef, has been cooking here since 1969, feeding locals through the winter and taking care of the summer visitors and their hunger for lobster.

Henry bakes a boneless breast of chicken with a cornbread stuffing and serves it with either gravy with cranberry sauce or a cranberry cream sauce. Sunday lunches in winter brings a large church crowd and feature that chicken dish, along with another Sunday special, roast pork loin with pork gravy, served with applesauce and a choice of potato, vegetable, and salad. On the day we called Henry was fixing baked acorn squash with brown sugar and butter and steamed Swiss chard from the organic Crossroad Farm in Jonesport. Sometimes he adds a little malt vinegar to the chard. Mashed turnip sometimes makes the list as another fresh vegetable.

"I have been here for so long that I'm getting gray," Henry said. "I hear, 'Boys, you still do things the way you always did,' so I guess that must mean something." Henry certified that he uses real food, and although he does sometimes use frozen items, most of the meals come from fresh ingredients like those vegetables. It's on the strength of those vegetables that I include him here.

Four dining rooms, including one with a bar, seat about 50 a room.

## Union River Lobster Pot
**(207) 677-5077**
**8 South Street (right off Route 1, just before the Main Street bridge)**
Hospitality—Well trained, efficient, and helpful
Open for dinner daily 5–8:30, mid-June through mid-September, for lunch until Labor Day
Entrées $14 to $25

☛ *Well known for good food, from great lobster to sophisticated fish*

With outdoor cookers set up cheek by jowl to the live lobster tanks, you could count this place as one ready to appeal to tourists interested in one thing only.

*Chef/owner Brian Langley eyes the catch at Union River Lobster Pot*

But Union River pushes that envelopeand offers fresh fish served in ingenious ways. The teriyaki style makes a fine swordfish dinner, and a cilantro cream works deliciously with halibut; other fish could be given a Cajun rub and then served with a salsa full of mango, papaya, honeydew, and jalapeños. Chef-owner Brian Langley recommends the maple-mustard glaze for salmon fillets. Fish served in the St. German style gets a crown of buttered crumbs.

"We walk a fine line between casual and out of the ordinary," Langley said. Visitors often crave a lobster dinner, but locals come here for the fresh fish that Langley gets daily from Maine Shellfish, a big distributor located close by.

He's worked to oblige them all, developing those fish styles at the same time that he oversees 100 pounds of lobster meat picked every day in the busy summer, a prime ingredient in his lobster rolls, stew, and other dishes. For the roll he uses lots of lobster, a little mayo, and dares to veer from tradition with a star-cut roll—"Because it won't fit on a hot-dog roll." At $13.95, Langley called the lobster roll his loss leader, drawing in the patrons who get a glimpse of other things they come back to try.

Another tourist favorite is the Clam Slam—a lunch of clam chowder, clam cakes, and fried clams with coleslaw and french fries ($8.95).

The 72-year-old baker, who has worked for Langley for 20 years, knows exactly how to make pie.

The location makes the meal special, on the grassy banks of Union River, now healthy and clean, and every once in a while a seal swims up for a visit. It wasn't always so delightful. Langley told us that the property sold in 1859 for $4,000. A century later, in 1959, it sold for the same $4,000. The river was polluted, and the setting was not desirable.

But now it is the home of a pair of eagles, who often sit in the top of the white pines that border both the river and Langley's lawn and make some meals on the fish swimming in the clean water.

As if to corroborate his word, a bald headed eagle soared close overhead while Langley and I were talking, its white head and tail and dark wings and body so familiar, even to people with little knowledge of birds.

## The Riverside Café (207-667-7220; www.theriversidecafe.com), 151 Main Street.

Open for breakfast and lunch weekdays 6–3, Saturday 7–3, and Sunday 7–2. This bright, freshly painted space with big windows bustles in the morning. Egg sandwiches, pancakes, French toast made with homemade bread, and lots of muffins make breakfast selection difficult. For lunch you can choose from the substantial sandwiches and soups, salads, vegetarian selections, and homemade pies.

# Food Markets, Bakeries, Coffeehouses, and Ice Cream

## George's Java (207-667-2999), 4 State Street (Route 1).
Coffee and great chocolate-chip cookies.

### John Edward's Market (207-667-9377; www.johnedwardsmarket .com), 158 Main Street.

Crossroad Farm and other organic produce, organic local eggs, Equal Exchange Coffee, and a large selection of wine are all sold here.

### Larry's Pastry Shop (207-667-2557) 241 Main Street.

Open Monday through Saturday 5–5. An Ellsworth standby, this old-fashioned bakery makes donuts and delicious gingerbread. A lot of people go for the macaroon brownies; others enjoy the almond macaroons.

### Morton's Ice Cream (207-667-1146), 13 School Street.

Open in summer, Tuesday and Wednesday 11–5, Thursday through Saturday 11–8, shorter hours until Thanksgiving, special orders only in winter. This ice cream store is located in the parking lot of the Union River Gallery Frame Shop. Great ginger ice cream, and blood orange sorbet.

### Rooster Brothers (207-667-8675), 29 Main Street (Route 1).

This business roasts its own coffee beans, imbuing the atmosphere with a lovely smell. Brewed coffee can be bought in take-out cups; you can also buy freshly roasted beans, whole or ground. Upstairs is a store full of kitchen equipment.

**The Ellsworth Farmer's Market** is held Monday 2–5:30, Thursday 2–5:30, and Saturday 9:30–12:30, June through October in the parking lot of Maine Community Foundation, at 245 Main Street.

# Hancock

## Le Domaine
(207) 422-3395, 1-800-554-8498
Route 1
www.ledomaine.com
Hospitality—Highly trained, polished service
Open for dinner Tuesday through Sunday 6–9 early June through November
All entrées $29.50

☛ *A fabulous French wine cellar matched with exquisite French cuisine*

You can travel far in this dining room. Although owner and head chef Nicole Purslow is spending her summer seasons presenting a few novelties on her menu and branching out in a business next door that features Italian take-out (see page 241), her restaurant cuisine remains the epitome of Provençal cooking.

In the bright dining room, copper pots gleam around the mantel of the big fireplace, the tablecloths glow with green and yellow, and the careful, attentive service raises your awareness that things here are a little more serious than they might be elsewhere.

There's the *pâté de foie maison* ($11.50), a pâté that Purslow describes as impossible for her to improve on. You get the sense that she's tried, but can't best, perhaps with some exasperation, her mother's original creation. A warm goat-cheese tart is another appetizer, that could be well matched with a glass of the 1999 Mersault-Genevrieres Francois Jobard ($10 for a glass, or $5 for a half-glass). Three other wines are available by the glass, a lovely opportunity to get to know the rare foreigners.

Entrées, all $29.50, included grilled lamb chops with *herbs de provence,* and *escalope de veau,* thin slices of veal served with a wild mushroom cream. *Coquilles St. Jacques* sauté has been switched away from the cream mode to a ginger-cider glaze, topped with crisped ginger. And there was a filet mignon bordelaise, garnished with Roquefort butter.

The tart *au framboise,* a pastry shell filled with custard and raspberries, would make a fine end, or the bread pudding with rum-soaked currants and cream.

Purslow has one of the best reputations on the coast for the exquisite work she accomplishes here, and her magic way of taking us away from our ordinary lives for the space of a meal and setting us gently down in a rather more attentive and pleasurable place.

## Tidal Falls Lobster Restaurant

**(207) 422-6457**
**Tidal Falls Road (look for the sign 8 miles north of Ellsworth on Route 1)**
Hospitality—Come to the window and order, and the food is delivered to your table.
Open last week in June through Labor Day
Entrées $2.25 to $19
BYOB

☛ *The most fabulous view in Maine, with high-quality lobster to go along with it*

This restaurant serves steamed mussels with garlic butter and steamed lobster, for the most part. A New York strip sirloin steak, lobster salad, hamburgers, and hot dogs are also available. The lobster rolls might cost $13.95. The side of garlic bread is unique to lobster places.

Fresh-squeezed lemon juice mixed in a ratio of 3 cups of juice per gallon sweetened water make the good lemonade, served with lemon zest and mint.

"We make our own coleslaw, potato salad. We have a baked crab dip, made with cream cheese, bubbly and browned on top and baked in a 4-ounce cruet," said Karin Wilkes, the restaurant manager. Tidal Falls is now owned and operated by the Frenchman's Bay Conservancy, which protects area lands. "It's made the place more widely known, for one thing," Wilkes said.

An indoor pavilion holds 40 people, but outside is a grassy picnic area with 10 to 12 picnic tables.

Because of 2004's rainy summer, not as many people dropped in. People prefer to eat right near the water, enjoying lobsters served in a paper bag on a cardboard tray.

"People have told me that we have the best lobster around, but we don't know why," said Wilkes.

It could be because the water off Schoodic Point, where they get their lobsters, is so cold, or because the water in their holding tank is pumped from the ocean, or because the beasties don't hang out in the tank for more than four days.

But the setting and its incredible view are what distinguish this place from all others. "The tide comes into a narrow rocky inlet. When the tide reverses and the bay empties, it's just like somebody poured a pitcher of water over the rocks," Wilkes said. It's noisy, and most people sit on one side of the tables to watch. Eagles, cormorants, ospreys, and blue herons visit at low tide. Seals are more frequent at high water.

"We had a double rainbow last summer, just really intense and beautiful," Wilkes said.

You can bring your own wine or beer. The restaurant will provide complimentary wine glasses, a little elegant touch in the casual environment. A private dining area on a deck, seating four, overlooks the falls. It could be yours for a $25 reservation fee. All the profits go to the conservancy.

# Food Markets and Take-Out

### Sullivan Harbor Farm Smokehouse (207-422-3735), 1545 Route 1, Hancock Village.

Open Monday through Saturday 10–5. This growing business moved into a new building a few miles south of the old one in the winter of 2004–05; it needed larger quarters to keep up with demand for its delicious smoked salmon. The salmon is served close by at Mama's Boy Bistro; and farther away, from Boston to Florida at Legal Sea Foods restaurants; in Connecticut at the Mohegan Sun Casino; and at the Simon Pierce Restaurant in Quechee, Vermont.

In the Maine retail store, 1,000 pounds of salmon fillets, farm-raised two hours away in New Brunswick, Canada, are delivered each week. After lying embedded in coarse salt, draining water and achieving a firmer texture, the salmon is cold-smoked, packed, and ready to eat ($22 a pound).

Sullivan Harbor Farm also sells smoked scallops ($13 for a half pound), pastrami salmon ($11 for a half-pound, and roasted and smoked rainbow trout.

### Mano's Market (207-422-6500), 1519 Route 1.

Open in-season. Italian specialties, sandwiches, and more at this take-out place owned by the well-known owner of Le Domaine next door (see page 238).

# Hancock Point

## Crocker House Country Inn
### (207) 422-6806
### Point Road
www.crockerhouse.com
Open daily for dinner from May 1 to October 31
Entrées $22 to $30

☞ *High-quality dinners in a comfortable, friendly inn*

Chef-owner Rich Malaby and his wife have been here since 1980, polishing, and polishing some more, and the look of the place really shows their investment. The dining rooms are charming, comfortable, and sweetly elegant.

The meals start with some thoughtful appetizers, such as oysters on the half shell ($9.95), and oysters Rockefeller ($10.95). The warm artichoke and crab dip is one classic, and the pâté mousse is another.

Classic entrées are presented as well, with filet mignon *au poivre* ($27.95) and rack of lamb ($27.95). Roast duckling with a Grand Marnier–ginger sauce tweaks the classic enough to bring it up to date. In the Crocker House scallops ($22.95) mushrooms, scallions, garlic, and tomatoes lend their goodness to sautéed scallops, served with rice pilaf, and bring some Mediterranean flavor to the meal.

Wine and beer are served here, where the sound of a bell buoy floats into the windows from the restless sea.

*The dining room at the Crocker House Country Inn*

# Islesford

## The Islesford Dock
**(207) 244-7494**
**Little Cranberry Island, or Islesford**
Hospitality—Good in extremity, and graceful under pressure
Open daily for lunch and dinner mid-June through Labor Day, Sunday brunch
Entrées $8 to $23
Beal and Bunker (207-244-3575) runs a ferry service to Islesford from Northeast Harbor

☛ *Great meals on an island that is easily accessible*

Maybe Little Cranberry is too accessible? Perhaps that was going through the mind of one of the Islesford Dock's owners, Dan Lief, as a lunch traffic jam ensued when the second delivery of hungry tour-boat visitors appeared at his door. Customers clamored to eat, but their boat wasn't due back till 3, and he assured them there was plenty of time.

Ever so slowly the clots of customers found spots to sit down. We agreed to eat at the bar and got to sit quickly. Watching the action, rather more interesting than the lovely view, at least for a while, we enjoyed a meze plate ($12)— tiny smoked mussels and garlicky, lemony hummus on baked pita wedges accompanied by a relish made with chopped onion, carrot, cucumber, red pepper, and feta, with some fresh fruit and olives on the side. That simple plate, always on the menu and always changing, is one reason we were all here, glad to enjoy the fresh tastes that the kitchen assembles.

But Islesford Dock wouldn't be so impolitic as to neglect the typical seaside dishes. Clam chowder, steamed clams, and crabcakes are on the list, next to tuna tartar, grilled calamari, Szechuan eggplant, and grilled asparagus. There's a de rigueur steamed lobster right up alongside the Caribbean seafood stew ($20), a cinnamon and chili flavored stew of shrimp, halibut, and mussels. Pasta rustica mixes orecchiette with Parmesan, white beans, and summer vegetables. Those dishes are available if you take a dinner cruise out here, or happen to live on the island.

But the hamburgers, served with fresh-cut fries ($8), are juicy and full of flavor, and made an 11-year-old, a 15-year-old, and a 50-year-old content at the bar. Strawberry or blueberry crisp threw us for a moment, till we each ordered one and shared. Both were scrumptious with ice cream, and a quiet walk around the island afterward was all we needed to make the visit a complete pleasure.

# Manset

## Seaweed Café
**(207) 244-0572**
**146 Seawall Road**
Open daily for dinner 5:30–9 in summer, closed Sunday and Monday off-season
Entrées $17 to $23

☛ *Sushi Downeast, Asian noodles and stir fries with finesse*

This elegant restaurant has grown larger with the addition of an orange room, giving space to its happy customers who come back repeatedly to enjoy the clever entrées, like ginger lobster sauté with black Thai rice or salmon baked in parchment with curry-basil butter ($19). The *nigiri* sushi specials are reliably fresh, and all the inside-out rolls—spicy tuna, tofu, and greens—and other *maki* rolls stand out for art and inner beauty.

Sichuan shrimp and scallop stir-fry ($13 for a half-portion, $20 for a full portion) is served over brown rice and seasoned with garlic chili paste. The farthest West you can get is the crabmeat and avocado salad with a Thai basil dressing, or the roast pork loin ($18) marinated in allspice, ginger, and cider and served with a touch of bourbon.

# XYZ Restaurant
(207) 244-5221
**Bennet Lane at 80 Seawall Road**
Open for dinner at 5:30 weekends Memorial Day through June,
daily in summer through Labor Day, then weekends until Halloween
All entrées $20

☛ *The real thing in regional Mexican cuisine, with flavors from the far south*

Robert Hoyt and Janet Strong started this restaurant in 1994 and made slow progress for a while. But the word about the food got out, reached the newspapers, and began drawing crowds. X stands for Xalapa, Y for Yucatán, and Z for Zacatecas, all regions of Mexico Hoyt and Strong have traveled in and brought home the tastes of, re-creating them now in a new location up above Seawall Road. Their new space enjoys a bright red-and-white interior and vivid flower-printed tablecloths full of jaunty charm.

One appetizer mixes Maine crabmeat with onion and serrano chile ($10); another stews whole mushrooms in chipotle sauce ($6).

Mole poblano is an entrée of skinless and boneless chicken thighs sauced with four different kinds of chiles and a touch of Ibarra chocolate. *Costilla de res,* beef short ribs, are baked in adobo sauce. *Tatemado* is pork loin in the style of Colima, baked in a sauce made with guajillo and ancho chiles and shredded, then served with marinated red onions, rice, and black beans. *Chile rellenos con queso,* old friends on the list, are two ancho chilis stuffed with corn and cheese, covered with cream and baked. All the entrées include a green salad made with ingredients from nearby Folly Farm. A children's meal is suggested, helpfully—a quesadilla made with cheese, or cheese and beans ($6).

XYZ is well known for its drinks, including its own margarita, made with Sauza blanco, triple sec, and fresh lime juice ($6.50), and another margarita with 100 percent agave tequila, Cointreau, and fresh lime juice ($10). But it's the food the customers come for, said Hoyt. Since the restaurant got off to a late start at its new location in 2004, we'll be making up for it with a trip in 2005, and the business, as Hoyt pointed out, won't need to advertise to get us there.

# Mount Desert

**Beech Hill Farm (207-244-5204), 171 Beech Hill Road.**
The farm stand here is open Tuesday, Thursday, and Saturday from late June to October. This organic farm grows wonderful greens and lettuces, strawberries, raspberries, and apples, and lots of flowers.

# Northeast Harbor

## La Matta Cena
**(207) 276-3305**
**5A Old Firehouse Lane**
**Open daily in-season for lunch and dinner**
**Entrées $18 to $27**

☛ *Good-looking ingredients, and rustic, attractive quarters*

The big plates full of salad, large vessels of olive oil, and a shack with the sign FREDDO PARADISO combine to make an impression of Italy. *La matta cena* means "the crazy dinner," and refers to a spontaneous gathering in which people bring what they have and create a feast by sharing.

Lunch items seemed a little more organized, like a grilled peach salad with the fruit wrapped with prosciutto and matched with dressed greens ($9). A lobster tail club sandwich with caper Dijon mayo gave a nod to the dictates of tourism, but the grilled portobello mushrooms, layered with fresh mozzarella and tomato with pesto ($10), and the panini in a variety of flavors, kept to the ethnic theme.

Dinner pulled in the grilled peach to pair with a pork chop ($24) and also offered *pappardelle ragu,* noodles with a meat sauce ($18).

Dessert (all $7) couldn't get better than a dish of berries topped with whipped cream, except just maybe a gelato in chocolate Heath Bar crunch, blueberry, or coffee. But others may prefer the flourless chocolate torte or *baba au rhum* served with vanilla ice cream.

*Folly Farm stand, off to a good start in July*

## 121 **Main Street**

**(207) 276-9898**
**121 Main Street**
Open for dinner Tuesday through Saturday 5 to close in-season
Entrées $15 to $19

☛ *Offering small plates, salads, and thin-crust pizza,*
*with a few larger entrées*

The brick-oven pizza here, 12 inches of thin crust, can be ordered with red sauce, cheese, and pepperoni ($9) or with three cheeses—mozzarella, provolone, and Gorgonzola ($10). Larger entrées include chicken piccata with white wine, capers, and preserved lemons, and a roast turkey potpie ($15). "151 Meatloaf" is made with pork and beef and served with a wild mushroom gravy and mashed potatoes ($16).

## Breakfast, Lunch, and Take-Out

### The Full Belly Deli (207-276-4299), 5 Sea Street.
With a few tables and a big selection of sandwiches, this is a good spot to gather supplies for a picnic lunch, maybe a south of the border sandwich with turkey,

cheddar cheese, guacamole, tomato, lettuce, and sprouts ($6.69). All the classic favorites are on the menu too, from egg salad to roast beef. Baked goods for morning coffee, and desserts like brownies and cookies.

### The Colonel's Restaurant (207-276-5147), Main Street.

Open April through October for breakfast, lunch, and dinner. A full bakery means there's an array of breakfast baked goods to choose from. Breakfast is served in the space behind the storefront, with some tables outside. Pizzas, fried seafood, and burgers are available for lunch and dinner.

### Folly Farm (207-276-4224), 104 Main Street.

A lovely farm stand with strawberries in early July, and rhubarb and peonies. Come in August for the corn and tomatoes.

*Trays full of baked goods fill the bakery in the front of The Colonel's Restaurant*

**Northeast Harbor Farmer's Market** is held Thursday from 9–noon on Huntington Road across from the Kimball Terrace Inn, from the end of June to August.

# Otter Creek

## The Burning Tree
(207) 288-9331
71 Otter Creek Drive (Route 3)
Hospitality—A busy place with experienced service
Open for dinner June through Columbus Day, closed Tuesday in summer, closed Monday and Tuesday after Labor Day
Entrées $19 to $25

☞ *A premier fish and vegetarian restaurant that grows many of its ingredients*

The Burning Tree works at making vegetarian dishes really succeed, like a mint-flavored edamame wonton soup with miso broth, shiitakes, summer squash, and spicy tofu ($19.50) and a watercress cheese tart with shredded beet and dill pasta ($18.50).

But it does very well by all its meat and fish, too. Appetizers have included a squid salad with shiitakes, bamboo, ginger, and sesame seeds and a curried crab salad with mango and crispy pappadums ($9). A country pâté served with pickled grapes and toasted sourdough bread could nicely precede the prosciutto-wrapped scallops, glazed with orange-rosemary and served with arugula and Parmesan on linguini ($25).

Red meat is not served here. Instead there is a great array of finely designed fish and chicken dishes. Crabcakes and bouillabaisse with saffron aioli are old favorites, and the broiled halibut with Pernod and green peppercorn sauce ($19.25) could easily become a new one.

*The gardens at The Burning Tree grow many of the vegetables included in their fresh salads*

# Southwest Harbor

## Carlos Ristorante

**(207) 244-5227**
**386 Main Street**
www.carlos-ristorante.com
Open for dinner Monday through Saturday 5:30 to close in summer,
Friday through Sunday in winter
Entrées $13 to $15

☛ *Southern Italian, sophisticated food, and the classics that made it all popular, in a charming new place*

The friends are all here—*pasta e fagioli* (pasta and white bean soup), spaghetti marinara, and my child's favorite, *spaghetti alla carbonara* (spaghetti with egg, cheese, and pancetta).

But owner Mark Picurro is bringing back a few lesser knowns, like *coniglio all'agrodulce,* sweet-and-sour rabbit, and *pasta con le sarde,* pasta with sardines. If you can't bring yourself to try these ancient, beloved dishes, content yourself with the manicotti and ravioli, with a cannoli for dessert.

Picurro spent the first part of his working life in health care and has made a great leap of faith with this restaurant, transforming a former auto-parts store into a comfortable, warm place. His grandparents were from Asena, and cooking with his grandmother had meant so much to him that all the work here was worthwhile.

But the customers will be the ones who prove if his gamble pays off.

## The Claremont Hotel

**(207) 244-5036**
**Clark Point Road**
www.theclaremonthotel.com
Open daily for dinner 5–9 mid-June through the third week of September
Entrées $20 to $25

☛ *Elegant, Old World surroundings, with good food*

Even though this hotel no longer requires its male dinner guests to wear a jacket and tie, and has done away with the jacket collection kept handy for that purpose, you can still dress up for a dinner out here. Why not? You are not yet allowed in with jeans or shorts, or allowed in after 7 PM if you are under 12. There is a proper sense of respect for the dinner hour here; children can just eat earlier.

The dining room is as good looking as they come, with eloquent views of Somes Sound. An adjoining bar is open the same hours as the dining room, or you can enjoy a cocktail in July and August at **The Boathouse,** with its fabulous views from an open porch (open for lunch from 12 to 2).

A dinner entrée in the hotel dining room might be a grilled pork chop with spinach and pine nut stuffing ($23) or grilled salmon with a scallion pancake. Linguini with scallops, shrimp, clams, and mussels might taste good with a glass of the St. Michael Eppan Pinot Grigio ($7 a glass).

For dessert there's blueberry pie à la mode ($5.50) or a frozen vanilla Bavarian bombe ($6).

## Head of the Harbor
**(207) 244-3508**
**Main Street**
Open daily for lunch and dinner 11:30–8:30 in-season
Entrées $9 to $18

☛ *Seafood with a view, and gingerbread for dessert*

This long dining room sits on the top of a rise and overlooks the water. Inside it's hung with lobster traps and buoys, and the kitchen is serving up the standard fried seafood with a few special touches, like the fried Maine shrimp, tiny and delicate creatures that require a deft touch with the heat.

Fish chowder ($5.99) is not thickened, and tartar sauce is made here. The onion rings are freshly made, too, thin and crisp. Fried pollack and french fries ($8.99 small, $9.99 large) comes with salad, coleslaw, and the vegetable of the day. Some of the people in your group might be grateful for the chicken parmigiana, or the seafood salad plates. Desserts are plain, simple, and appealing, like the gingerbread with whipped cream ($3.50) and the root beer float. The very limited wine and ale list has drinkable Blackstone Merlot and a couple of Casco Bay microbrews.

## Red Sky
**(207) 244-0476**
**14 Clark Point Road**
www.redskyrestaurant.com
Open daily for dinner 5:30–10 in summer, closing more frequently off-season
Entrées $17 to $28

☛ *The latest up-to-date addition in the upscale food world of Mount Desert Island*

Patrons of this cool bistro praise the leek and tomato tart and the lobster risotto with porcinis. Owners Elizabeth and James Lindquist and chef Adam Bishop seek out the best local produce suppliers to make it all happen. An aged New York strip sirloin is always on the menu, along with varying homemade pastas. Elizabeth's favorite duck dish, a roast breast with a raspberry demi-glace ($24), is sometimes offered.

The wine list carries about 50 bottles, averaging $30, and 10 wines are available by the glass. House-made crusty bread rounds out the meals along with organic greens from Vernal Acres Farm in Surry.

Desserts are made here and range from a fallen chocolate soufflé cake ($7) to gingerbread with fresh ginger juice with caramel sauce and cream cheese whipped cream to a peach tart.

# Lunch, Breakfast, Take-Out, Wine And Cheese, and Ice Cream

### The Quiet Side Café and Ice Cream Shop (207-244-9444; www.quietsidecafe.com), 360 Main Street.
Open in-season for lunch and dinner. Fish and clam chowder, sandwiches, and salads, along with fried fish and hot subs are all on the menu. Ice cream is available in 20 flavors; surely one will go with homemade blueberry pie.

### Jumpin' Java Coffee Shop (207-244-7491), 350 Main Street.
Open year-round Sunday through Friday 7–4, Saturday 7–2. Smoothies as well as espresso and cappuccino. No credit cards.

### Eat-A-Pita (207-244-4344), 326 Main Street.
Open daily for breakfast 8–12, and lunch 8–4 in-season. Call in an order for one of the salads or a stuffed pita sandwich, like curry chicken with carrots, celery, and onion ($6.95), or Greek salad, olives, and feta stuffed ($5.95). Soups and a crabcake sandwich on a bulky roll ($9) are also featured. Dinner is served in **Café 2,** all in the same colorful green space with old wood tables; seafood, meat, and vegetarian entrées are served Tuesday through Sunday from 5 to 9.

## Little Notch Bread and Café (207-244-3357), 340 Main Street.

Open Monday through Saturday 7–7, Sunday 8–6 in summer; Monday through Saturday 8–6, Sunday 9–5 in the off-season. The local source for good bread, with loaves of sourdough, whole wheat brown rice, honey wheat walnut, and more. Sandwiches, simple pasta dishes, and pizzas. Also cookies, brownies, scones, and sticky buns.

## Sawyer's Market (207-244-3315), Main Street.

The smell of ham floats across the worn wood floors of this grocery store; and across Main Street, **Sawyer's Specialties (207-244-3317)** carries an excellent wine selection, over 1,000 varieties, and a cheese case with finds. Both can supply you with whatever provisions you need.

# Trenton

## Trenton Bridge Lobster Pound
**(207) 667-2977**
**Route 3**
www.trentonbridgelobster.com
Hospitality—You pick the lobster, and hand it off to be cooked
Open for lunch and dinner Monday through Saturday, Memorial Day through Columbus Day
Entrées vary with lobster market price

☛ *A classic place to rip open a crustacean and enjoy*

The wood fires under the big cookers here pull the passing cars over all summer long, and boiling seawater cooks the lobsters with the touch of salt that makes the flavor laugh out loud. The menu sticks to what is good with lobster—steamed clams, coleslaw, potato salad, and butter. You can also order a few other lobster or shellfish dishes, including a lobster roll, lobster stew, clam chowder, and lobster or crab cocktail. But mostly you are here for the essence of Vacationland—the salty, buttery, tender, sweet meat of lobster.

## CHAPTER 8

# Schoodic and North

**T**HIS FAR EAST END OF MAINE, and of the United States, has always been renowned for its dramatic landscape, fringed with boreal forests and combed by winds rushing off the sea. Here you can stand on promontories overlooking the Atlantic and ride out over the water to an island to approach the puffins, both the birds and their admirers enjoying a lonely emptiness no other part of the Lower 48 coastline has. You can hike down a half mile of bog bridge on the Bold Coast Trail, or around a boardwalk on a bog in Lubec, and encounter ravens and eagles.

You can see and smell and breathe a vigorous world kept, for the most part, clear of people.

For the same reason, however, it hasn't been all that easy to find a great meal here.

The places people have liked and crowded into, like Helen's Restaurant in Machias, might just never have been as good as people claim. And right now some of them aren't good at all. Some try to feed people with processed and frozen foods that may keep prices low and require less work in the kitchen, but the meals leave customers hungry, however high the plate is filled. Their stomachs might feel full, but their souls are starved.

You can always ask for what is fresh. I've tried, and if people are being straight, the places listed here use as much fresh fish as they can. I've listed those that use fresh food, including fresh fish and fresh vegetables, when they can get them.

But sometimes red tide arrives on the Maine coast in summer and shuts down all the clam flats, keeping the local clammers from making any money, and forcing the local fried-fish places to use frozen or canned clams for their clamoring customers.

That might be a great time to choose a different kind of shellfish.

Lobsters, thank goodness, are always fresh in Maine, however much companies finagle with freezing methods designed to get them to Japan. But a clam shack could use frozen lobster meat for its lobster rolls. They might save money that way, or time, but it won't taste as good. Ask if the lobster rolls are made with fresh-cooked lobster that's been shelled by the restaurant.

Scallops are in-season between September and mid-April. Picked by divers starting in December, scallops are a good choice if your visit comes later in the off-season.

Rising to the challenge of finding great ingredients, more and more people in Downeast Maine are finding ways to make a living making dinner. The Artist's Café in Machias blazed a path eight years ago, and more places have opened, giving more choices to diners eager to find good cooking.

Winter Harbor and nearby Birch Harbor are enjoying a big summer business that extends into the fall, now that Mama's Boy Bistro rose up on the lot that used to hold Winter Harbor's original small café. Competition is filling restaurant tables there and across the street and down the road, as curious people who have heard the buzz come looking for something new.

Farther Downeast in East Machias and Cutler, newcomers are at work building up business for elaborate meals, enticing locals who might have grown indifferent to a night out to make another attempt and adopt the practice as a regular pleasure.

But in Calais, and elsewhere, keeping things the same has proven exactly the best approach. The same bread pudding that might have pleased your grandparents on their visit is ready for your own meal, when you want to order it, at the Chandler House.

A few other places sustain the oldest, simplest traditions, like using fresh berries for pie. If the newest places think they are starting that practice for the first time, let them.

Let the old places that have stayed good, and the new places that have started good, feed us all.

# Birch Harbor

## Bunkers Wharf
**(207) 963-2244**
**260 East Schoodic Drive**
Hospitality—Fabulous. This place is run with an emphasis on welcoming people and taking care of them.
Open for lunch and dinner from before noon–10 PM May through October
Entrées $17 to $26
Reservations appreciated

☛ *A fun, friendly, and sophisticated place with delicious seafood and meat*

We like this restaurant a lot. The big dining room with tall ceiling and knotty pine paneling overlooks Bunkers Harbor, a tranquil working cove full of lobster boats at their moorings. A tall stone chimney holds a fireplace to warm up the early spring and late fall nights, and an outdoor patio welcomes customers in the warm weather. For dinner the tables are covered with white tablecloths, and customers in summer fill the space with happy conversation. Bunkers Wharf is immediately recognizable as a neighborhood restaurant, frequented by people who know where to go for good food.

On our visit a 2 Brothers Big Tatoo red from Spain ($5.25 a glass, $18.95 a bottle) started things out right with its big taste. Whites available by the glass included a Chateau Ragotiere Muscadet ($5.95 a glass, $19.95 a bottle), and a St. Michael Eppan Pinot Grigio from Italy ($6.95 a glass, $22.95 a bottle). Wines here start at low prices, a friendly gesture from a management that likes to see people enjoying themselves. A dish of prosciutto oil—"Good stuff," Bill Osgood, the owner, told us—did make a fine dip for the tender focaccia. The baked haddock with stuffing, and green beans and spinach in a thyme sauce ($18.95), though slightly dry around the edges, had a tender center and a lovely flavor. The stuffing was buttery manna, straight out of Thanksgivings past.

Chicken and sausage farfalle with a Parmesan cream sauce ($17.95) was the goal of one of us from the moment her eyes lighted on it on the menu; rich and strongly flavored, it made a pleasurable meal, though the portion was enough for an Olympic athlete.

*An array of desserts at Bunker's Wharf*

Other entrées included a lobster dinner with roasted cornbread pudding ($25.95), grilled tuna with a chili-garlic sauce ($24.95), and grilled rack of lamb with whipped red potatoes ($23.95).

We chose a simple maple crème caramel for dessert, and the tender custard set on rays of chocolate sauce, with an orchid in a pile of whipped cream, was a good finish to the intense flavors of the main course. The evening's four desserts (all $5.95) were presented on a silver tray festooned with scrolls and spirals of various colored sauces. Along with the custard that night, you could have chosen a brownie with mocha-rum sauce, a flourless chocolate cake, or a piece of cheesecake.

The lunch menu lists hamburgers, a haddock sandwich, a lobster roll, and fish-and-chips, as well as a couple of salads. And appetizers looked tempting, with Gorgonzola, chèvre, and mozzarella pizza and lobster stew.

This is the place to go when you're exploring Acadia National Park's Schoodic Peninsula, as lovely as its more famous setting on Mount Desert Island.

# Calais

## The Chandler House
**(207) 454-7922**
**20 Chandler Street**
Hospitality—An experienced staff takes care of the customers
Open for lunch 11–2, for dinner 3:30–9 daily Memorial Day
through Labor Day; closed Monday off-season
Entrées $13 to $29

☛ *An old-fashioned restaurant that serves inexpensive, good food*

The average dinner usually runs $20 here, including drinks—lunch amounts to $10.

For 25 years the Chandler House has been serving good meals at modest prices, and William Condon, who has been there 13 years, just wants to "keep doing what we've been doing." His father started the business in this old house, and the rooms that seat 40 still have tables covered with tablecloths and lighted by candles.

"Everything is like you would make at home," Condon told me; all the soups are homemade, the chicken dishes are fresh. The chicken salad is made from poached chicken that is pulled apart in the kitchen, not with canned or frozen chicken.

Fresh seafood comes locally from Canada, and a local clammer, William Mitchell, brings fresh clams once a week. Chandler House chefs shuck them to make chowders and fried clams.

"It's old-school kind of techniques," Condon continued. The restaurant often serves two vegetables a night, and zucchini, summer squash, and fresh carrots were on the menu at the end of summer.

The restaurant's signature dish, prime rib roasted on the bone, is served every night with Yorkshire pudding ($16.95, $18.95 for extra large). The dinner rolls are made in the kitchen too.

Desserts are homemade. Blueberry pie is $3 with ice cream, or you could try strawberry shortcake, walnut cake, or a hot fudge sundae. Condon's grandmother devised the recipe for the bread pudding ($3 with whipped cream) that is still served, made with milk, bread, coconut, raisins, cinnamon, eggs, and sugar.

Chandler House is located behind McDonald's, and not so easy to find. But, "When people find us, they usually come back," Condon said.

# Cherryfield

### Spring Brook Gardens (207-546-2936) Route 1.

Open Tuesday through Saturday 9–5:30 in-season. This new organic farm, certified in summer 2004, offers its abundant harvest alongside Route 1. Fresh-picked bouquets make the stand charming.

# Columbia

## Judy Ann's Restaurant
### (207) 483-2045
### Route 1 (a half-mile south of the four-corner shopping center)
Open daily for three meals 5:30 AM–8 PM, 9 PM on the weekend
Entrées $6 to $19

☛ *The Maine coast standards, many made with local seafood*

Much of the seafood here is fresh. The clams are bought in Steuben, except when the noxious red tide shuts down the coastal clamming business. The scallops and

*Spring Brook Gardens' farm stand in Cherryfield is full of charming flowers and delicious-looking vegetables*

shrimp are caught by Cutler fishermen, but the haddock is frozen. The seafood platter, with fried haddock, clams, scallops, and shrimp, sells for $18.99. Judy Ann's makes homemade chowders, and desserts from peanut butter pie to coconut cream pie. Chococo pie, a combination of chocolate and coconut, "was a mistake that turned out to be something that's selling quite well," according to the owner.

## Farm Stands

### Anthony's Farm (207-483-2260), Main Street (just off Route 1).
Open May through October. This farm stand sells strawberries, blueberries, and vegetables in-season.

### Blue Barrens Farm (207-483-4196), 88 Pea Ridge Road.
Open Wednesday through Sunday noon–5, late June through September. Preserves are available over the phone, and you can pick your own crops at the farm, or buy them picked for you at the farm stand.

*Wild Blueberry Land is a startling feature alongside Route 1*

# Columbia Falls

**Wild Blueberry Land (207-483-2583; www.wildblueberryland.com), Route 1.**

You cannot fail to see this great big blue geodesic dome on the ocean side of Route 1 when you drive this way. There are blueberries inside, pies are being baked, and jars of blueberry jam and syrup and dried blueberries are for sale. A whole geodesic dome full of stuff awaits you. The store will overnight ship frozen blueberries anywhere you like. A 10-pint box costs $20 (plus shipping). Blueberry gingerbread can be found on the Web site's recipe page.

**County Road Cranberry Bog (207-483-4055), 1256 Route 1, 1 mile past Route 187 toward Machias.**

This shop is open in October and November; products are available for shipping year-round. Judy Farnsworth makes cranberry vinegar, cranberry jam, blueberry syrup, cranberry syrup, cranberry-pineapple and cranberry-orange jams, and hot pepper jelly. Fresh cranberries are sold when they're ripe, usually the first week of October. Frozen berries are available in winter. The bog is visible from Route 1, and visitors love to go check it out.

**Molly's Orchard (207-483-4178), Point Street, which runs out from the village, a turnoff from Route 1.**

Open in early summer for pick-your-own strawberries and in the fall for pick-your-own apples, this farm is run by Rick and Jolene Farnsworth.

# Cutler

## Tide Run Harborside Inn & Café
**(207) 259-3800**
**Destiny Bay Road**
www.tiderun.com
Hospitality—A ride from your boat to the café is on offer.
Open for lunch 11:30–2, dinner 5–8 by reservation only, Tuesday through
Saturday; closed in late winter
Entrées $10 to $20

☛ *A rarity so far Downeast, serving some ambitious entrées, upscale*
*appetizers and desserts, and no fried food*

Linda and Richard Houghton opened their first restaurant in 2004 with three
full-time chefs and seven servers.

"My husband just fell in love with Cutler," explained Linda. She and her husband originally bought the house they turned into an inn and café to use as a
second home, but they ended up selling their house in Florida and moving to
Cutler year-round.

"The people here are just the salt of the earth," she said.

Houghton is a vegetarian, and has made sure the café emphasizes vegetarian
dishes, keeping a sweet-and-sour tofu and pepper entrée ($10) on the menu.

But the crowd pleasers are the haddock with crabmeat in champagne cream
sauce ($20) and a Provençal seafood stew with saffron, leeks, tomatoes, and
potatoes.

The 30-label wine list focuses on bottles from California and France that work
with the café's French bistro–style cooking.

Visitors drive in from St. John, New Brunswick; Calais; and Ellsworth, and
yachters tie up at a friend's wharf. Call ahead for arrangements that include "Linda's
taxi service" from that nearby dock.

The menu changes almost daily. Young's, in Belfast, delivers fresh seafood,
and although some entrées feature big pieces of lobster, and a lobster roll is on
the lunch menu, the restaurant does not serve whole lobster. "There are all kinds
of places to eat lobsters on the Maine coast," Houghton said. She's interested in
serving meals that are more ambitious.

Four hundred residents live in Cutler year-round, so the café is dependent
on visitors for its business. Hiking trails have been a big draw, including the West-

ern Head Trail that leads to a cliff on the Atlantic overlooking Grand Manan. Another Cutler resident, Andy Patterson, takes visitors in his boat to see the puffin colony on Machias Island. People can walk there in designated areas, the better to keep the puffins undisturbed by human visitors. Those trips are another reason people come to Cutler and find themselves eating dinner at Tide Run.

Houghton said she hopes to be able to stay open until Christmas, or later, and close only briefly before opening up again in early spring. But it's best to give her a call before planning a trip.

# East Machias

## The Riverside Inn
**(207) 255-4134**
**Route 1**
www.riversideinn-maine.com
Hospitality—Two summer servers, working weekends off-season, care for up to 20 guests.
Open for dinner 5–8 Tuesday through Sunday late May through mid-September, Thursday through Sunday the rest of the year; open for Sunday brunch year-round, except closed in January
Entrées $18 to $23

☛ *An ambitious restaurant that has grown its business mostly by word of mouth*

The Culinary Institute in Albuquerque, New Mexico, gave Rocky Rakoczy, 54, a degree in advanced culinary studies in April 2003, at the same time that he and his wife, Ellen McLaughlin, 48, bought the Riverside Inn.

"We were planning on having an inn with a small restaurant in a small dining room," he said. They found this one along the tidal Machias River.

With a nearby university, a hospital, and Washington Academy, a prep school started in 1865 that brings people to the area from all over the world, Rocky and Ellen decided East Machias was the place for them. It didn't hurt that there wasn't a lot of competition.

Retired from American Airlines after 35 years as an operations crew chief, Rocky is enjoying his new life as a restaurant chef.

"It's been fun. It's been busier every month," Rocky said. "People know we're here now." Dinner meetings for the hospital doctors, guest speakers at the university, and staff parties for nearby schools fill tables on off-season nights, and regular summer visitors return with high expectations.

"We serve a variety of menus, different kinds of lamb, a London broil, pork medallions, Jamaican baby back ribs, butterflied pork chops," Rocky began. He listed weekly specials and five different kinds of fish, including a lobster dish served over pasta with capers and cream.

The inn's salmon ($17.95), stuffed with crab, scallions, shallots, and mushroom combined with paprika, lemon pepper, and mayonnaise, surrounded by broiled salmon strips and served with a turmeric-dill sauce, is the most popular dish. Rocky calls it "the pride of the Riverside."

Coming in second is Lambs Shezaseis, a boneless leg of lamb butterflied and stuffed with red pepper, feta, and spinach laced with garlic. Rolled and seared, then baked to order in individual servings, this is usually served with sweet potatoes a l'orange, made with sweet potatoes, Yukon Gold potatoes, carrots, parsnips, pineapple, and pearl onions, all baked in orange juice with nutmeg and ginger, and asparagus or a sautéed vegetable ($19.95).

The inn grows many of its own vegetables, from squash, tomatoes, and peppers to all the herbs the kitchen needs. They also use Tide Mill Farms organic lettuce. Thirty wines, with 7 available by glass, 23 beers, and a basic full bar satisfy the customers, who like to make reservations for the holiday menus that are served on Valentine's Day, Christmas Eve, and New Year's Eve.

# Eastport

## Raye's Mustard Mill (207-853-4451, 1-800-853-1903; www.rayesmustard.com), Route 190. P.O. Box 2.

The center of all things mustard. Tours of the mill, which has been making mustard since 1903, and its old stone grindstones are given at 10 and 3 weekdays and some Saturdays, if mill operations allow it. The retail store sells good mustard varieties along with other things from this region at the farthest eastern tip of the United States, including Mainely Smoked Seafood.

# Gouldsboro

## The Old Post Office
(207) 963-7280
679 South Gouldsboro Road (Route 186)
Hospitality—This place is on a small scale, with seven tables and a lone employee when we arrived. He took care of us, waited on another table, and cooked their meal with no trouble.
Open April through November, daily 11–8 in summer, closed Tuesday off-season

☛ *Pizza, subs, and dinners, in a little room for modest prices*

When the old post office shut down in South Gouldsboro and the residents had to go to Gouldsboro's post office to mail their packages, it didn't take long for someone to see a fine tiny little restaurant in the old building. Open in summer 2003, this place fits seven tables with red-and-white checked oilcloths. You can get a ham dinner with cranberry sauce, mashed potatoes, a vegetable, and a roll ($7.95).

The "huge haddock dinner" with fries, coleslaw, and roll will set you back a mere $9.95.

A gas stove keeps the small room warm in fall and spring, when a piece of pie would taste great. The blueberry ($2.25) is homemade. You can order ahead to get sandwiches packed to go for trips to Schoodic Point or to have the pizza ready when you get there.

## Farm Stand and Winery

**Darthia Farm (207-963-2770, 1-800-285-6234; www.darthiafarm .com), 51 Darthia Farm Road.**
Open Monday through Friday 8–6, Saturday 8–12, May through October. Run by Bill and Cynthia Thayer, assisted by Jake and Erin Bent, this organic farm made a covenant with the future to remain intact and organic. The Thayers plow and haul wood out of the forest with the strength of three purebred Haflinger draft horses—Gus, Teddy, and Stefan. Cynthia writes novels that paint her land and fictional neighbors in lucid, fascinating colors, and spins and knits sweaters and other garments with the wool of her farm's sheep. You can buy both the novels, published by St. Martin's Press, and the handmade garments in the farm store. You could also buy raspberries, raspberry jam, winter squash, tender lettuce, or whatever is in-season. The blueberry-rhubarb jam tastes great on toast.

*Darthia Farm produce is overflowing with produce on August days*

A tour of the farm if offered in the summer at 2 on Tuesday and Thursday, and the opportunity to learn how to farm here may be available for those looking to apprentice in return for room, board, and a small stipend.

### Bartlett Maine Estate Winery (207-546-2408; www.bartlett winery.com), P.O. Box 275 (a half mile south of Route 1, 23 miles east of Ellsworth; watch for signs).

Open 10–5 Monday through Saturday. One of the most pleasant hours you can spend lies at the end of a short wooded path in the tasting room of the Bartlett Maine Estate Winery. Your well-spoken host will pour tastes of about eight different wines made here, describing each one with well-wrought phrases. There is no obligation to buy, and the tasting is free.

*A wine tasting at Bartlett Maine Estate Winery*

I went home with a bottle of Winemaker's Reserve 1999 Pear Wine, aged in French oak barrels for at least 12 months; the bottle was signed by vintner Robert Bartlett. It was one of the winery's more expensive bottles, at $25; I drank it with a roasted venison tenderloin, and thoroughly enjoyed its clear, dry flavor.

Bartlett wines are growing in fame, winning awards and diverting grape wine lovers to an occasional glass of fruit wine, a far different creature from the horrible apple wine you might be ashamed to have loved when you were underage. These wines, from the modestly priced Coastal Red, made with blueberries and apples, and Coastal White, pear and apple, to the pricier bottles of reserve and dessert wine are sophisticated, delicate, and good with a wide variety of meals. We drank the Coastal Red at a Maine bar to accompany Thai mussels; the glass of wine, with a fruitiness that worked well with Thai curry sauce, was great.

The winery buys its fruit and blends it to achieve its different wines. Mead, made with Maine wild blossom honey and spring water, is a strange creature, but it made sense in those woods, as it does in the Tolkien woods, and perhaps I should make a better acquaintance. That was the driest at my tasting. The sweetest was a blackberry wine it would be possible to drink with dessert, but that really explains the existence of thimble-size cordial glasses. I still don't know if I would recommend the semi-dry blueberry wine to go with smoked seafood, as the wine host did, but I'm a convert to these wines with spicy meals and roasted meat, and grateful for these new pleasures.

# Harrington

## The Mexican Restaurant
**(207) 483-2002, (207) 598-7297**
**Timkin Pike Plaza**
Hospitality—A little Spanish helps, but you'll be well taken
care of without any at all
Open daily
Entrées $5 to $9

☛ *Run by Central American immigrants; this is delicious, authentic Mexican, Guatemalan, and El Salvadoran food, served in plain quarters.*

The restaurant shares space with a store that sells foodstuffs to the area's growing Latino population; restaurant and retail are divided only by a line of bead curtains. Clear plastic sheets cover the plastic laminate tables, and the brown-plastic bench seats are attached to the table. That utter informality makes it comfortable to browse around the store shelves while you wait for your order, examining the matte-brown seed pods of tamarind, for example, in a crate on the floor.

The shop and restaurant owner's mother, Rubenia Ayala, took good care of us without speaking a lot of English. We worked it out with our own rudiments of Spanish, confined to words like *enchilada verde* and *burrito.* I ordered the *tamarindo* to drink, and was served a tall cup of icy, very sweet tamarind-flavored water that slowly turned delicious as I drank it and grew accustomed to the new flavor.

The menu provides the plain English for all the items it lists. A tostado, for instance, is one crisp corn tortilla topped with, among several choices, a ceviche made with cooked shrimp marinated in lime juice with tomatoes, onions, cilantro, and fresh avocado ($2.99). The quesadilla was a 13-inch flour tortilla folded and grilled, with sour cream, cheese, *carne asada,* and guacamole ($2.99). We could have tried a burrito with beef tongue, mole, onions, cilantro, and green sauce ($2.99), or with fried catfish, tartar sauce, and chopped tomato salsa ($3.99).

But the chicken, cheese, and avocado burrito ($2.99) was perfect for a young friend. It was stuffed and very fresh, the flavors were pleasant, and the meat was tender as butter.

Another selection, two enchiladas verdes stuffed with chicken and topped with green sauce, Monterey Jack cheese, and sour cream, proved extraordinary after a long fishy haul up the Maine coast. The soft, fresh tortillas were lit up by that hot green sauce, which set the stewed, melting chicken on fire. The sprinkle of Jack cheese proved mild and sweet, a small quantity fresh of cheese curds, not a molten lead blanket you might have assumed was standard south of the border.

*Rubenia Ayala (left), mother of Mexican Restaurant owner Doris Ayala, is a server, and Tereza Fidelina of El Salvador (right) is the chef.*

You wouldn't necessarily know any better, if you ate most of what passes for Mexican in Maine (but see XYZ in Manset, page 244, for another exception).

Inside the kitchen Tereza Fidelina, from El Salvador, was stirring a huge pot of pork ribs in a spicy red sauce. Anyone who lives nearby has a God-given opportunity to eat the wonderful food she devises, and the hotter Mexican dishes that Juan Perez, the owner's husband, grew up eating when his family moved from Guatemala to Mexico, before they found their way to Downeast Maine.

Latino immigrants pick Maine's blueberries and apples and pack Maine's sardines, and some of them have started to settle here. About 100 live in nearby Milbridge, and people from all over Central and South America depend on Doris Ayala's place to find the supplies for their meals, or to eat them already prepared. Doris, who is from Honduras, started the store in 2001, the restaurant in 2002. She serves Venezuelans, Cubans, and Puerto Ricans, to mention just a few, along with the Mainers and visitors who make their way here. I heard of a couple from Oklahoma who were grateful to get here now and then and eat real Mexican food, instead of the bastardized versions served elsewhere, where the flavors are toned down to a faint echo, or a defeated whimper, and the plates are paved with cheese.

### Dallas' Lobstah (207-483-2227), Route 1.

Open Tuesday through Sunday11–8 in summer, Thursday through Sunday 12–7 in early fall. This new spot has an outdoor lobster cooker for lobster lovers, and uses local clams for its fried dishes. A few tables outside make a nice spot for the classic Maine summer meal. Clean and simple.

*The outdoor cooker at Dallas' Lobstah steams all day long*

# Jonesport

## Tall Barney's Restaurant

**(207) 497-2403**
**Main Street**

Hospitality—Intense ribbing from the fishermen if you are a "flatlander" translates as endearment (really)—but ignore them and enjoy the quick assistance of the servers.

Open 4 AM–8 PM year-round

Entrées $7 to $23

☛ *Pleasant, renovated rooms full of conversation among the tables, and great, simple food*

*Tall Barney's owner John Lapinski*

A newcomer might want to be warned about the Liars' Table, a long table angled down the dining room, aslant just like the claims made by its occupants, fishermen and locals who find anyone amusing, especially each other, and still would be likely to try to save their life in a crisis. Irritating men you wouldn't want to miss meeting, or live without.

When John Lapinski heard a description of this place and that table on NPR in 2002, he called up the restaurant and asked if it was for sale. In three weeks he bought it. He sold his insurance business in New Jersey, and then he moved to Jonesport with his wife, Linda, to join the Liars' Table, or at least listen to it.

Linda makes fabulous pies, like one we enjoyed made with blueberries from Sanford Kelly's fields overlooking the bay. The thin crust holds a warm ample treasure of the dark blue fruit that loves to grow in Maine, not too sweet ($3.25). Her lemon meringue ($3.25) features a high meringue and sweet lemon filling. You might also find blueberry pound cake or apple crisp on the dessert table.

But the owner doesn't fancy sweets. Lapinski said he came here to change his life and did. He lost 90 pounds and stopped needing medication for his type 2 diabetes. How? He became more active, he said, spending three days a week as a stern-man on a lobster boat in the summer and fall. But mostly he slowed down when he ate.

"I don't sit down and wolf a meal any more," he said, "I sit down and enjoy it." That means he pushes a plate of food away when he's finished—he doesn't let it finish him.

He also managed to renovate the restaurant, installing a new kitchen and fixing up the dining room, while never closing for the first year and a half he owned it.

Sneaking onto the menu are a few innovations, like calamari, veggie burgers, and a guacamole omelet. But the standard Maine fare of chowders, fried seafood, and meat is what the menu is all about. Lapinski is not interested in changing the kind of restaurant this is. He has, however, hiked up the quality, using the best vegetable oil for the frying, and getting scallops from a local boat when it's scallop season on the Maine coast. The clams are also local.

The haddock burger ($4.75) is popular, and the seafood platter ($22.95) impresses his customers with its gargantuan size. "You eat a seafood platter here and you'll have a bellyful," said one man in a booth behind us.

"If you finish it, I'll buy you dessert," Lapinski said, laughing. The offer is good for anyone who wants to attempt it. But the platter includes fried scallops, shrimp, clams, and haddock, a vegetable, a choice of homemade roasted-garlic mashed potatoes or (packaged) french fries, and a roll. Only one customer has managed to get that free dessert.

Sometimes Lapinski barbecues beef on a grill outside, cooking steaks and chops. His customers enjoy that, and so does he.

The only thing he misses about New Jersey is the produce; he gave us a New Jersey tomato to show off the taste. He canned pickles with his grandmother when he was a kid, and his grandfather was a butcher, so he feels at home in his restaurant, even though it's his first. He said the biggest challenge was learning how to stock enough food for his hungry customers.

## Emporium Natural Foods
**(207) 497-5634**
**56 Sawyer Square**
Hospitality—This tiny place will cater to special diets and requests.
Open for take-out (or eat in at two tables) Monday through Tuesday 11–2, Wednesday through Saturday 11–3
Lunch items $3 to $7

☛ *A health-food store with a take-out kitchen that uses all natural meats and organic vegetables*

Anyone with special needs, like gluten-free bread or vegan meals, can find what she or he is looking for here, something that could be hard to come by so far Downeast. But of course you'll also be looking for good food, and the chowders here, made with organic cream, butter, and milk—seafood chowder is always available in the fall—won't disappoint. For meat lovers, the BLT ($4.25) is made with Applegate Sunday pork bacon, free of nitrites, in a wrap with mayonnaise and would make a delicious lunch.

There is always an organic soup of the day, and in the summer a crab roll ($6.95) stays on the menu board. Chef salad ($5.95), with romaine, turkey, chicken, ham, and boiled egg, or Caesar salad ($3.95) could contain produce from Crossroad Farm, a big organic farm just up the road that supplies both the café and the natural food store.

Lunch can be delivered to you during lunch hour on Wednesday, Thursday, and Friday. Store hours are Monday through Wednesday 10–5, Thursday and Friday 10–6, and Saturday 10–4.

# Farms and Bakeries

### Crossroads Farm (207-497-2641), 314 Crossroad.

Mr. and Mrs. A. Pearlman run a huge organic farm here, growing 30 varieties of lettuce alone, but they no longer operate a farm stand. Instead, you can get produce by calling ahead, asking for it, and arranging a time to pick it up. Crossroad Farm supplies produce to many of the best area restaurants; stocks John Edwards, a store in Ellsworth, and the Emporium in Jonesport; and makes regular trips south with the harvests. On our visit we met up with Linda Lapinski, who was picking up some broccoli for Tall Barney's, the restaurant she runs with her husband (see page 269). That was lucky, because otherwise we might not have met the farmers—they were out in the fields, hard at work.

### The Mason Bay Berry and Egg Farm, home of the Farm Bakery, with a produce stand (207-497-5949), 1561 Mason Bay Road (3 miles from Route 1 on Route 187).

Open 10–4, July, August, and some of September. Special orders taken all year. Lois Hubbard is known for her gingersnaps and English toffee cookies, as well as blueberry and raspberry pies. Honey whole wheat and cinnamon-raisin bread are favorites. Fudge is another big seller; flavors include peanut butter and chocolate raspberry.

**The Jonesport Area Farmer's Market** is held Tuesday and Friday 9–1:30 from the end of May to the end of September, in downtown Jonesport across from Church's Hardware Store. **Fitch Farm and Gardens** sells their perennial and herb plants there, including rugosa roses.

# Lubec

## Phinney's Seaview Restaurant
**(207) 733-4844**
**Route 189, P.O. Box 110**
Open daily for lunch and dinner 11–9, April through mid-October
Entrées $8 to $18

☛ *Good-quality fried seafood and other Maine dinners*

Roast turkey, grilled steak, and lobster dinners are offered in this place set on a hill, with a view of the water on three sides—one side overlooks Johnson's Bay, the others Lubec Channel and Grand Manan. Casual dining, "homespun Downeast seafood," with seafood baked or fried are the features. The fish is fresh, never frozen, according to restaurant owner Sandra Phinney, who described the fish as coated with a light batter, and fried crispy and golden. "I have the best food in town without a doubt," Phinney said. She has owned and run this restaurant for 13 years; the 20 years prior had been spent owning a restaurant in Campobello. When she sold the first she realized she didn't like retirement and took up the second.

# Machias

## The Artist's Café
**(207) 255-8900**
**3 Hill Street**
Open for lunch Monday through Friday 11–2, dinner Monday through Saturday 5–8 early spring through mid-October
Entrées $20 to $30

☛ *Unpretentious but full of goodness, this place feeds the heart and soul.*

The artist Susan Ferro is taking winter off this year, 2004–05, to paint. She looks forward to getting her hands messy with something other than chopped garlic and anadama bread dough.

But with eight years in the restaurant she started in the midst of culinary wilderness, the cooking habit is well formed. Her customers will be grateful when the doors reopen in the spring. She makes what they love.

"I thought I was going to shape the food I served," she said with a laugh. "My customers have shaped my business." She serves up some entrées, for instance, with a cream sauce people dote on.

Her paintings are part of the décor in the pretty, small rooms of her building on a hill on the way into Machias, and the artfully arranged meals could put you in mind of their colors and design. But if that doesn't, the sandwich menu served at lunch will, with its choice of the Impressionist (sliced chicken with pesto mayonnaise on a baguette, $6.50) or the Surrealist (grilled and undoubtedly dripping Swiss cheese, with fresh garlic and dill butter on two slices of the anadama).

You could order a lemon square ($1.50) or an oatmeal chocolate-chip cookie for dessert, likely portraits of what the regular lunch crowd rightfully admires from the kitchen.

Ferro gets her bread shipped up from Boston but makes a few special loaves herself. The likely problem of her baker's business being bought and the bread losing its quality troubles her as she strives to serve the best quality food she can both afford and find. She gets her haddock from Campobello, serving it one week sautéed with bread crumbs and a mix of summer squashes, red peppers, and shallots, along with a tomato salad and homemade tartar sauce.

Her roast turkey dinner comes with a piece of homemade sausage made by Joe Parisi (see page 275), one of the many people she has found to work with, a local version of the slow food movement that's improving the dining Downeast. Farms provide some vegetables, like those in the caponata, made with eggplant, tomato, onions, and olives, that accompanies her thin breaded veal chop ($24).

She and her customers have long agreed about the gingerbread, with its sliding topping of really fresh whipped cream ($4). The tiramisu, chocolate gâteau, and cheesecake (all $5) are sometimes part of the dessert menu. And the coffee is just as strong as she likes it, even if that's something some customers might object to.

# Joyce's Lobster House
**(207) 255-0719**
**Route 1 (just at the north Machias line)**
Open for lunch and dinner 11:30–8 or 9, June through August
Entrées $7 to $17
BYOB

☞ *Dine on Italian classics or a fresh lobster roll and listen to Dean Martin sing.*

The lobster rolls, served in a hot dog roll toasted on the grill, use fresh lobster meat mixed with mayonnaise. Lobster is shelled for sautéed lobster and lobster stews, too. Since 1968, when this place was started by Debbie Farrar's mother, Joyce O'Riley, this has been a popular place for seafood.

"We have everything from sautéed lobster to a peanut butter and jelly sandwich," Peter Rossi, Farrar's partner and companion, said.

But Italian food is another draw, like veal Parmesan ($10.95), shrimp Alfredo ($11.95), and crabmeat Alfredo ($14.50). The antipasto plate ($7.95) is a garden salad with cheese, salami, and peppers. Rossi brought these dishes into the menu. He makes his own marinara with tomatoes, but wouldn't specify more than that, refusing to reveal his special recipe.

"It's a basic marinara sauce. It just happens to be popular," he said cagily.

You can bring in your own bottle of wine, and the restaurant will provide glasses and a corkscrew—no fee. "The only thing is we ask is that they buy a meal," Rossi joked.

Right across the street stands a variety store that sells wine and beer.

Farrar makes blueberry and raspberry cream pies, employing the native berries—these pies aren't made when the berries aren't in-season. A chocolate peanut-butter mousse pie ($3.95) is quite popular and very filling, Rossi said. "It's like a great big huge peanut-butter cup."

"We hear an awful lot of compliments about our music," Rossi said. They play music by singers like Dean Martin, Frank Sinatra, Tony Bennett, and Bobby Vinton, "All those crooners, Las Vegas types, I guess you'd call them." Rossi said it's good music to eat by, and something people don't often hear when they go out.

# Markets and Festivals

**Joe's Sausages (207-255-0054), 14 West Street.**
Open Monday through Friday and most Saturdays 8–5. Joe Parisi, whose parents immigrated to the United States from Sicily, makes sausage and grows a huge vegetable and fruit garden. His peers in the food business extol his sausage, made fresh with no preservatives from pork deliveries that come twice a week. One neighbor called him, "An Italian sweetheart from the old country." The usual hot-spicy and mild-sweet varieties are embellished with the addition of wine, or Romano cheese, garlic, and parsley. Call ahead to place an order for seasoned pork roasts, or to check on weekend hours. Starting in mid-May, his 4,000 asparagus plants start their two months of production. By July 1 the strawberries are ripe for about three weeks, and you can pick your own. In late summer the eggplant and peppers, along with essential flat-leafed parsley, are among the produce he sells. He also maintains the farthest Downeast outpost of Micucci's, a Portland wholesale business, with Asiago, fontina, fresh mozzarella and Parmigiano-Reggiano available for purchase. He sells Cinqueterre Farm bread (see page 276).

There's a picture of a painted pig on his lawn, which is on the first street south of the post office.

**The Machias Farmer's Market** starts in early May and goes through October, located on Route 1 across from Helen's Restaurant, Saturday 8–noon. There are often farmers selling produce in this location other days of the week as well.

**The Machias Maine Wild Blueberry Festival (Machias Chamber of Commerce, 207-255-4402; www.machiasblueberry.com)** rolls around the third weekend of August, and in 2005 the annual event will turn 30. The blueberry is central, and stars in the blueberry pancake breakfast early on Saturday in Machias's Centre Street Congregational Church. Blueberries blaze out in all kinds of desserts in the church vestry all day long; you are sure to find pie and muffins and much else.

But in between meals with blueberries, the festival presents a Friday night fish-fry, and on Saturday volunteers serve lunches that feature chowder and lobster, crabmeat, and chicken rolls.

The wild blueberry pie–eating contest might be doable next year, if we practice hard enough.

# Milbridge

**The Milbridge Farmer's Market** runs from the end of May through October, Saturday 9–noon, in the Milbridge Market parking lot. Mandala Farms, one of several present, sells their organic produce, from arugula to melons to sweet corn. They also raise cashmere goats, so you might be able to buy some of the nicest yarn around.

*Joshy's Place is a roadside refuge*

### Joshy's Place (207-546-2265), High Street.

Open Monday through Saturday 11–9 in summer. A hot dog is $1.35 at Joshy's, and a double-bacon cheeseburger, at the apex of the burger menu, is $4.10. We're sure the woman in the counter window here isn't always so surly, but maybe you should try to catch her earlier in the day, or earlier in the summer.

She wasn't keeping folks away, however, from this crowded Route 1 pit stop with a $6.50 lobster roll and a haddock burger for $3.75. Ice cream comes in four sizes, a really nice feature for the littlest customers and people who opted for that double-bacon cheeseburger. A baby soft-serve cone is 75¢, hard ice cream cone $1. You can also go for a milkshake and a banana split.

### Tibbets Seafood Market (207-546-3435), 13 Main Street.

Open 9–5:30, daily in summer, Tuesday through Saturday in winter. Haddock, hake, tuna, sole, swordfish, lobsters, crabmeat—the full array of fish, with local clams and everything from Maine unless it's not in-season or doesn't swim by.

# Pembroke

### Cinqueterre Farm and Bakery (207-726-4766), Ox Cove Road.

Open Memorial Day through Labor Day, but call first, as this small operation could be on the verge of retirement. This farm down a road off Route 1 does a big business in the summer selling fresh baked goods. Baguettes, raisin bread, multigrain bread with ground flaxseed, and French country bread are among the loaves baked here. With so few good bakeries in the area, some residents invest in a freezer's worth from Cinqueterre to get through the winter. Pies can be ordered or bought if you're lucky, and jams are made throughout the summer. The bread is for sale in Machias at Joe's Sausages (see page 275).

### Yellow Birch Farm (207-726-5807), 272 Young's Cove Road.

Call for hours. Organic vegetables and chicken, pork, and lamb, along with balsam Christmas wreathes available by mail.

# Perry

## The Friendly Restaurant
### (207) 853-6610
### 1014 Route 1 (just north of Route 190)
Open for lunch and dinner 11–8 in summer, closes earlier off-season
Entrées $6 to $12
Reservations recommended on weekends

☛ *Good cheap food and drink*

This popular local restaurant was owned by Sheldon and Priscilla Patterson, who bought it 17 years ago. After Sheldon died and Priscilla retired, their son Robert and his wife, Jennifer, took over. Jennifer has been working here since 1990, after she married into the family.

Lobster rolls and seafood are the main draws. Asked what she thinks makes the place special, Jennifer said, "I think our portions. We give a good portion."

A lobster roll, something neighbors praise as big, is $10.35 with fries and coleslaw, $9.35 without.

Daily specials are offered all day, from corn chowder with grilled cheese ($4.79) to a Reuben sandwich ($4.09) to Caesar salad with chicken ($5.79). Jennifer makes lemon meringue pies, and blueberry pies when the blueberries are in-season. She also makes a chocolate raspberry pie—a layer of raspberry, a layer of cream cheese, and whipped cream covered by a layer of melted semi-sweet chocolate. All pies cost $2.45 a slice.

Weekend nights are really busy, with Friday-night reservations a must. Three or four tables are filled with patrons who come every Friday and keep a standing Friday night reservation.

Cheap wine, either Almaden Chablis or Mountain Burgundy ($1.50 a glass), beer, and mixed drinks make the dinners taste even better.

"Everybody knows everybody around here. . . . Usually you'll see people hopping from table to table," Jennifer said. With her kids in a school of only 118 students, Jennifer is glad to stay right where she is, where the traffic doesn't amount to much and the person in the passing car is very likely to wave hello.

## Smoked Salmon

**Mainely Smoked Salmon (207-853-4794; www.mainelysmoked salmon.com), South Meadow Road.**

John Constant, who has worked in the salmon business for 13 years, sells hot- and cold-smoked salmon that has been farm-raised in nearby Passamaquoddy Bay and farther north. It can be ordered through the Web site, and shipped overnight.

"We got lucky and had a good product," Constant said. True North, owned by Cook's Aquaculture, was providing the salmon fillets to Mainely Smoked Salmon in 2004. The fish are grown on farms both sides of the border, from New Brunswick to Jonesport. He said the fillets are the best-looking fish he's seen in 13 years.

Constant won't use wild fish, because they can be caught at the wrong time in their life-cycle and make a poor-quality smoked fish. The fish Constant is buying are prepared for harvest with special diets and precise culture.

He builds houses for a living. "I pound nails when I'm not doing this," he said. But he's hoping to go to the state fairs with his product in the future.

Raye's Mustard Mill sells Constant's fish (see page 263). But most of the business is on the Internet. Constant said he has some of the lowest prices in the smoked salmon industry, and he's using that feature to attract wholesale business.

# Prospect Harbor

## West Bay Lobsters in the Rough
(207) 963-7021
Route 186, (3 miles from Route 1)
Hospitality—Simple, friendly assistance in a plain setting
Open for dinner 5–8, May through October
Hard-shell lobsters were $10.95 a pound cooked, shedders $8.95 in 2004.

☛ *A place to concentrate on eating lobster, with great fixings and no distractions*

With four picnic tables and two linoleum tables set in a plain interior, this place is exactly what's in its name: rough. Since that is also exactly how lobsters are best enjoyed, many of us interested in a lobster dinner will opt to come here. The plastic tablecloth with the big bowl set in the middle are familiar from family clambakes, where informality is the rule and the pleasures of the table reside in the taste of the food. You can choose your own lobsters out of the tank and wait for them to be cooked on the outdoor stove.

A menu on a board lists the simple offerings, starting with hard-shell and shedder lobsters—people often prefer the hard-shell because their meat fills the shell. However, while a shedder will drain a lot of water, its soft shell is awfully easy to get inside of. The lobsters that have most recently shed can be torn apart with your hands. Some of the older hard-shells can require a hammer blow, or a rock, to smash through that dark red carapace, convenient when you are right on Maine's rocky shore but perhaps less fun elsewhere.

Take a break from the labor, if you bought a big old hard-shell, with an ear of corn ($1), coleslaw ($1.75), or a dish of baked beans that are cooked daily from either soldier beans, the northerners' preference, or pea beans, favored by Bostonians. According to Gina Clark's research, northerners acquired their preference for soldier beans when they found that those beans stayed soft after being frozen and reheated, as when they were hauled from lumberjacks' camps to the day's work in winter woods in a lunch pail. Pea beans became hard.

When the time comes for dessert, there is pie and ice cream.

# Take-Out and Fish Markets

### Down East Deli (207-963-2700), junction of Routes 186 and 195, P.O. Box 230.

Open 10–8 Sunday through Thursday, until 9 Friday and Saturday, closed Sunday and at 7:30 PM in the off-season

Using bread shipped from Boston bakeries, this deli's Philly cheesesteak sandwiches contain sliced Delmonico steak, cheese, mushrooms, green peppers, and onions. Leon Harrington, the owner, said he's had customers from Philadelphia who tell him his Philly cheesesteak is as good if not better than ones at home. The Italian hoagie includes Italian capicola (a spicy ham), salami, pepperoni, and Virginia ham, with a choice of vegetables and a homemade Italian dressing made of oil and vinegar with herbs.

A lot of people in Maine call an Italian anything on a hoagie roll, Harrington said, but an Italian made south of Maine always contains that variety of meats, and other people expect them when they ask for an Italian.

The previous owner had an excellent menu, Harrington said, that he has not changed so much as built on since he reopened the business in October 2003, after it was shut for a year and a half.

Pizza ranges through 30 or more toppings, made with New York dough, then hand stretched. Harrington said owners of competing pizza places come to his place to eat pizza, a claim I cannot prove.

### Prospect Harbor Trading Company (207-963-7956), 178 Main Street (Route 186).

Come between 11 and 3; closed Sunday in June, July, and August. Lobsters are available here throughout the year, though they're scarcer in the winter. By 3 PM lobster boats are arriving and it's impossible to serve retail customers. As many as 20 lobster boats deliver to this company, which ships out most of the shellfish to Inland Seafood the same day.

When she was going bed one night in October 2003, manager Sylvia Smith saw two Gouldsboro residents in a boat, towing the company's lobster crates full of lobsters away from the dock. She trained a light on them and called 911, telling the operator not to put the alert on the scanner. "Otherwise you'd get everyone showing up down here," she said. She told the 911 operator to call an officer on the patrol-car phone. The thieves were caught at a different dock. "Good thing I didn't go to bed 15 minutes earlier," she said.

### Stinson Seafood Company (207-963-7331), Prospect Harbor.

This is a subsidiary of Bumblebee Tuna, and the phone number given takes consumers to operators in San Diego. Beech Cliff Sardines, the kind packed at this plant, cannot be bought at the plant, but they are for sale at Hannaford and Shaw's supermarkets and local stores. On a coast that once had many fish-packing plants, only this sardine plant and one in Bath remain. Some of this area's growing Latino population—which supports the wonderful Mexican restaurant in Harrington (see page 266)—work at the Prospect Harbor plant.

# Robbinston

## Katies on the Cove (207-454-3297; www.katiesonthecove.com), 9 Katie Lane.

Open June 15 through September 15, 10–5:30 Tuesday, Thursday, and Friday, 10–5 Wednesday; 10–3 Saturday. This little store sells handmade chocolates that are easy to love. Between the end of October and March, they can ship the candies, but have stopped shipping during warm weather, when costs have proved too high.

Maine potato candies, otherwise known as Needhams, chocolate-covered coconut creams, are made here, along with old-fashioned mint patties and chocolate-covered dried blueberries and cranberries. The Web site is a lot easier to get to than the store, if you aren't driving north from Eastport to Calais. But if you are, look for the yellow house covered with flowers, and consider buying the coffee creams. You can buy the candies farther south at Maine's Own Treats, on Route 3 in Trenton on the way to Mount Desert, or at Raye's Mustard Mill in Eastport (see page 263).

# Steuben

## Country Charm Restaurant
### (207) 546-3763
### 326 Pigeon Hill Road
Hospitality—Efficient, country service
Open 5 AM–8 PM in summer, Sunday breakfast buffet, closed Monday off-season
Entrées $5 to $15

☞ *Simple surroundings and simple food*

In these plain rooms with simple pine benches and paper placemats, an antique woodstove sitting by the front door keeps things extra comfortable in winter. You can enjoy a plate of liver and onions ($7.95), or a seafood platter ($14.95)—the most expensive thing on the menu aside from the market-price lobsters—with its fried haddock, Maine shrimp, scallops, and clams.

A little buzzer goes off when you come in, go out, stand by the stove, or slide into the seat of the booth by the door, so don't let it startle you. And you must take time to admire the miniature tractor trailers lined up outside the door that

belong to the restaurant owner, Bob Crabtree, a member of the Anah Temple of the Shriners, and a participant in a group called the Wheelers, who take their miniature trucks to parades around the country. He

*Country Charm Restaurant shows off miniature local trucks in its parking lot*

and the Wheelers participated in the Bar Harbor Parade in 2004, a swarm of 10 to 12 little trucks, and goes all over the place for parades. In his workshop off the far dining room he was working on a miniature lobster boat, which will be driven on a tractor-trailer bed in a future parade.

## Portside Snack Bar
**(207) 546-7676**
**522 Route 1**
Open 10–8 daily in summer, three or four days a week in the off-season
Entrées $4 to $9

☛ *Sandwiches and burgers and ice cream*

A Steuben mother and her three daughters own and operate this seafood and pizza place that opened in February 2004. One of the daughters, Nadine Barnes, said the business was becoming well known and drawing in lots of local customers for sandwiches and other recipes she'd grown up eating in the house next door. Homemade meatballs and homemade fish chowder are standbys.

The Dagwood sandwich (bologna, cheese, veggies, and Miracle Whip, $3.95), a hot ham and cheese grinder ($4.25), and a taco salad ($6.25) are some of the popular items on the menu. "We're really known for our haddock burger," Nadine said. Once you order at the counter, the staff brings the food to you either inside at one of eight booths, at the large table for big families and groups, or outside at a few picnic tables on the porch. Giffords ice cream, including its popular flavor Maine Black Bear, with streaks of black raspberry in a vanilla base, is available for dessert.

# Fish Market

## Bushey Enterprises (207-546-2804), Route 1.

Open 8–5 Monday through Friday; December 1 through April 15 for fresh scallops; live lobsters available year-round. They will ship fish through the continental United States. Maine shrimp (fresh in January and February) can be bought frozen, whole or peeled; and frozen haddock, flounder, and scallops are available year-round. Ask to be called when fresh fish is delivered; it goes into the freezer after one day.

# Sullivan

## Chester Pike's Galley
### (207) 422-8200
### 2336 Route 1
Open daily 6–2, except Sunday 7–2; Friday night fish-fry; call for winter hours
Lunch $5 to $5.50

☛ *Plain food made with care, from real cream to homemade bread*

Opened June 18, 2004. The first summer was busy from the get-go. Breakfast and lunch feature home cooking, with homemade breads and hamburger and hot dog buns, and homemade blueberry jam.

"The Chester fries are getting pretty popular," part-owner and baker Amy McGarr said, who listed the ingredients as homefries with green pepper, onions, ham, and cheddar cheese. Blueberry pancakes ($4.25), with homemade blueberry topping and fresh whipped cream, not out of a can, McGarr insisted, and with fresh-picked blueberries during the blueberry season, are another favorite.

Apple pancake and Belgian waffle sales don't keep up with sausage gravy over a biscuit ($2.50). It sounds bad, McGarr admitted, but people like it.

Lunches include club sandwiches on homemade bread—a turkey club is $5 and so is a Reuben. The Downeaster haddock sandwich goes for $5.50.

Jane Fogg, McGarr's business partner, makes a great seafood chowder, McGarr said, and it's not too thick.

McGarr and her partner worked years ago at the Everglades Club in Palm Beach, Florida, but both are originally from Bar Harbor. McGarr returned in 1994; Fogg came back more recently, decided to buy a restaurant, and enlisted McGarr's help.

The place seats 50, with a separate barroom, but though they do serve wine and beer there is not a big bar scene, because it wasn't something McGarr and Fogg wanted.

A Sorrento women's group comes in every Tuesday morning, putting two tables together. It's the perfect kind of breakfast scene for them.

## Tracey's Seafood
**(207) 422-9072**
**Route 1 (next to the Grange Hall)**
Hospitality—Helpful and friendly
Open for lunch and dinner 11–7 daily in summer, closed Monday through Wednesday off-season; closed early October through February
Entrées $9 to $14

☛ *A family business with counter service and an indoor area to eat boiled lobsters*

This place has a wood-fired lobster and clam cooker outside, just like its more famous southern competitor by the Trenton Bridge. The Friday night fish-fry, serving up fried haddock with salad or coleslaw and french fries or onion rings ($8.95), keeps business busy until 8 that weekend night. Polly Tracey and her husband, Levon, a lobsterman, make sure their supplies are the freshest. The clams come straight from a nearby processing plant where they are dipped in hot then cold water, shucked, and then "capped"—cut away from the siphon. They are delivered every morning to Tracey's to be fried. A clam dinner goes for $12.95, and a large order of onion rings is $2.50. For dessert, a three-scoop cone of hard ice cream runs $3.40, and one scoop $1.40. Fried foods are served through the ordering window, as are ice cream cones and sundaes.

# Whitneyville

## First Frost Farm (207-255-4773), 172 South Main Street.
Jon Robichard sells produce at the Machias Farmer's Market, delivers to seniors in the senior farm share program, and sells vegetables from the farm itself. He grows 60 varieties of vegetables and herbs, along with some blueberries and melons. Potatoes, like the Russian Banana, French fingerling, and All Blue, and lots of basil, from Sweet Genevieve to Purple, are some of the many fruits of his labors.

# Winter Harbor

## Chase's Restaurant

(207) 963-7171
193 Main Street
Hospitality—Helpful and fast
Open 6 AM–9 PM in summer, 6 AM–8
PM or earlier off-season; closed
Monday
Entrées under $10

*Beth Gilman, friendly waitress at
Chase's Restaurant*

☛ *A plain restaurant with inexpensive food and friendly manners*

This country restaurant feeds its local customers simple, popular favorites like a fried haddock sandwich or fish-and-chips ($8.95). The breakfast mainstay is the small special—two eggs as you like them with a choice of sausage, bacon, or ham and toast and coffee ($3.95). The pies are reliable. We asked the friendly waitress, Beth Gilman, what was homemade and she brought out a slice of coconut cream pie. Under clouds of stiff whipped cream the coconut filling was sweet as sin, just the right consolation for pulling into town when Gerrish's, the ice cream and sandwich place, had closed at 3, and dinner places were not yet open.

Chase's has been around forever. The last time we visited, three years earlier, it was filled with tobacco smoke; the atmosphere is clear now, obedient to the state law banning cigarette smoking in restaurants.

"Most people are glad there's no smoke," Beth said.

## Mama's Boy Bistro

(207) 963-2365
Newman and Main streets
www.mamasboybistro,cim
Hospitality—The bartender was delightful when we couldn't get a table after arriving without a reservation
Open for dinner Tuesday through Sunday 5–9 Memorial Day weekend through Columbus Day, brunch Saturday and Sunday in summer
Entrées $20 to $28
Reservations recommended

☛ *High-flying style—but the food may need to catch up to the architecture*

In 2002, Mama's Boy was a bakery and café in a little red house. The locals speak only praise for those days. The scones and bread made a mark, fed a hunger, and gave a lot of satisfaction.

But owner Lucas St. Clair, who happens to be the son of Roxanne Quimby, owner of the company that makes Burt's Bees products, has—or has recourse to—what another restaurant owner calls "deep pockets." Still a different restaurateur said simply, "He has a different business model."

In other words, Mama's Boy Bistro, with its disarming name, doesn't need to make immediate profits—or at least that's what everyone thinks. There was funding for an elaborate building that replaced the little red house, and a simple café was transformed into a restaurant shooting for the moon, or at least New York City. A farmer we met up with called it a "New York–style restaurant" with a tone of wonder. Winter Harbor, across Frenchman's Bay from Bar Harbor, is a very small town, even though it enjoys its own small colony of wealthy summer folks.

The present big building, which can seat 90, opened in June 2003, and the café fledged into a bistro. The space is magnificent, the details opulent, the surfaces lustrous, and the lighting sophisticated.

*The elegant bar at Mama's Boy Bistro*

The wines are expensive, certainly. Renwood Viognier from the Sierra foothills was $10 a glass, an Argentine Salentien Merlot $9. The bottles ran clear around the world in a long list that included a big bunch of Italian wines, most over $64. A bottle of Hahn Merlot went for $19. That and a $23 bottle of Ponzi Tavola Pinot Noir were lonely cheapies.

Owner Lucas St. Claire will be adding a wine cellar in the winter of 2004–05, he said over the phone a few weeks later. It will have enough room for 5,000 bottles. He stocked about 1,500 before that, with 270 labels on the list.

The exterior of Mama's Boy Bistro

Appetizers offer up Sullivan Harbor smoked salmon, a local brand made with farmed Canadian salmon, served with greens and green beans in a dill vinaigrette ($9), and local Jonah crab with Asian cucumbers, radishes, chive oil, and home-made garlic crackers ($12). One entrée that was eaten with pleasure the night of our visit was "Mandala's Farm half-roasted chicken" (probably a roasted half chicken) with garlic, parsley, and lemon and roasted Darthia Farm organic new potatoes ($25). You could also have ordered a farmer's market organic veggie plate with a seared Jasmine rice cake and a chilled spiced carrot salad ($20). Other entrées included beef tenderloin with a Gruyère and onion tart ($28) and hal-ibut from EcoFish. According to the EcoFish Web site, EcoFish halibut is caught on long lines in Alaska, a fishing practice that it has judged won't dam-age the population or habitat.

For dessert there was, among others, vanilla crème brulée ($6), a lemon curd tart with lemon and blueberry cream ($7), and a goat-cheese cheesecake with candied pistachios, Maine honey, and organic basil syrup ($8).

The menu touts its suppliers, many of them long-standing residents of Downeast's lonely reaches who were making a living before Mama's Boy put on its long pants. They must be glad for their big new customer, but I could hear distant teeth grinding as I was told the restaurant had started a new "movement" of organic farming that included a farmer's market in the parking lot.

Yet none of this matters—the big money, the big building, the big talk—if the restaurant can pull off the feat of making great food worth the prices it gets. I'm looking forward to seeing how it does.

# Fisherman's Inn Restaurant

(207) 963-5585
7 Newman Street (at the flagpole)
Hospitality—They go out of their way to make sure you get what you'd like.
Open for lunch 11:30–3, dinner 4:30–9 mid-May through mid-October or
later depending on business
Entrées $14 to $23

☛ *The motto is "Real food, done well," and the casual atmosphere,
home baking, and personal attention make it a standout for Maine
seafood.*

The owner of this restaurant, Karl Johnson, also owns the Grindstone Neck of
Maine smokehouse just up Route 186 (see next page), so working with seafood,
finding great sources, and knowing his suppliers is an old habit. That makes the
Grindstone Neck appetizer a good choice. For $8.95 you can taste smoked
salmon, mussels, scallops, and shrimp, with a relish of capers.

The restaurant's clam chowder has won in local competitions. The lobster
bisque ($5.95 a cup, $10.95 for a bowl) is made with homemade stock and a
little sherry, and is well provided with lobster meat.

Over a hundred pounds of lobsters are cooked here every day, for bisque, lobster pie, and lobster salad, among other delicious things.

Knocking out a wall has created a water view, giving the dining room a
panorama of Winter Harbor. Right across the road is Mama's Boy Bistro.
Although the Fisherman's Inn lost business in 2003, Mama's Boy Bistro's first
year, 2004's business was off the charts, Johnson said. The restaurant plans to be
open till Christmas in 2004, and could continue to open late in fall if there are
customers to warrant it. He attributes his good fortune to competition.

Mussels from Hancock, like most of the Fisherman's Inn seafood caught or
grown within a 15-miles radius, can be ordered either steamed with white wine
or cooked in a spicy Thai sauce. Johnson and his son go to Thailand every year
for formal training in Thai cooking, and that has also resulted in the menu's crispy
Thai-style salmon, made with fresh lemongrass, *galangal* and other Thai ingredients, like Kafir lime leaves. A dozen plants provide the last for Johnson, but
he has to import the rest.

The short wine list, with most wines available by the glass, include Pepper-
wood Grove Pinot Noir from California ($6.95 a glass or $28 a bottle), Dr.
Weins-Prum Riesling from Germany ($6.50 a glass, $26 a bottle), and Las
Brisas Sauvignon Blanc from Spain ($4.95 a glass, $20 a bottle). "We serve under-

exploited, reasonably priced wines," Johnson said.

The most popular item, the seafood mixed grill, includes steamed lobster tail, broiled fresh haddock, and scallops wrapped in bacon, all served with a pot of native shrimp and crabmeat in drawn butter.

Pat Weaver, in his 50s, has been baking delicious pies and making all the desserts since 2000. Blueberry pie is very good, and the most popular, but it would be hard to forgo the chocolate espresso tart or fresh strawberry shortcake (in-season).

And you will want to make the acquaintance of whatever odd-colored lobster is hanging out in the tank by the front door. The blue lobster of 2004 will undoubtedly be gone, but local lobstermen will keep the place supplied. Some of them have been taking the strange-colored ones and throwing them back in one place along the coast, a waitress told us, so the next one here could be white, yellow, or even bicolored.

# Casual Eating, Take-Out, and Food Markets

### The Barnacle (207-963-7733), 159 Main Street.
Seasonal take-out owned by Gail Nelson, who works at the Winter Harbor Post Office.

### J.M. Gerrish Provisions (207-963-2727), 352 Main Street.
Open 8–3 Tuesday through Saturday, closed Sunday and Monday. This old-fashioned soda fountain was bought by the owners of Mama's Boy Bistro and has gone upscale with espresso and machiato. The old stools, with brass footrests shaped like a flat stirrup, are still planted on the checkerboard tile floor next to the counter, where you can order ice cream ($2 for a small cone) in flavors from vanilla to peanut butter. Or you could opt for a fruit smoothie ($4.25). Sandwiches, salads, and soups can be enjoyed here or to go. Wine, cheese, fancy mustards, and other supplies fill the shelves.

### Grindstone Neck of Maine (207-963-7347, 1-866-831-8734; www.grindstoneneck.com), 311 Newman Street (Route 186).
Open daily 9–5. On the day we dropped in, some other visitors from away instigated a tasting, and we had a chance to compare the farm-raised Atlantic salmon ($6.50 for 4 ounces), the organic, farm-raised Scottish salmon ($8.95 for 4 ounces), and the wild salmon ($9.50 for 4 ounces), all cold-smoked on the premises. The high fat content of the Scottish fish made it more "buttery," and

that and the Atlantic were both delicious; but the taste of the wild salmon, with its intense, near-scarlet deep orange, rang like a bell in our mouths. It has a lower fat content and a more intense clean flavor. It's also more expensive. Grindstone Neck buys truckloads of it from Alaska to smoke and pack during its three-week season, but it travels far to get to our wild-salmon-less East Coast.

Grindstone Neck also makes smoke-roasted salmon, maple-cured trout, and smoked haddock, scallops, and mussels. Oysters are smoked when available ($13.95 for 6 ounces at the store, $14.25 on the Internet) and would be well worth a try.

**The Winter Harbor Farmer's Market** is held in the parking lot of Mama's Boy Bistro 9–noon Tuesday and goes from June to September.

# Index